Synbio and Human Health

Iñigo de Miguel Beriain
Carlos María Romeo Casabona
Editors

Synbio and Human Health

A Challenge to the Current IP Framework?

Springer

Editors
Iñigo de Miguel Beriain
University of the Basque
Country UPV/EHU
Bilbao
Spain

Carlos María Romeo Casabona
University of the Basque
Country UPV/EHU
Bilbao
Spain

ISBN 978-94-024-0341-1 ISBN 978-94-017-9196-0 (eBook)
DOI 10.1007/978-94-017-9196-0
Springer Dordrecht Heidelberg New York London

Printed on acid-free paper

Springer is part of Springer Science+Business Media (www.springer.com)

Foreword

Synthetic biology is a relatively new field of scientific endeavour, emerging over the past 10 years. Rather than seeking to understand living organisms, researchers in synthetic biology aim to design and build entirely new living systems at the molecular, cellular, tissue and organism level. Synthetic biology utilises tools and mechanisms from many scientific disciplines, notably engineering, genetics and biochemistry, but also nanotechnology, physics and computational modelling. A key attribute is the use of principles of engineering with components from the life sciences to build or exploit living organisms rather than machines. Synthetic biology encompasses the intentional and rational design of artificial biological systems, using either naturally occurring or entirely synthetic components or parts. The emphasis is on *creating* these systems from scratch, as opposed to seeking to understand naturally occurring systems. Applications of synthetic biology research include environmental and health benefits, for example bio-fuels, biosensors and new therapeutics.

It is obvious that a new approach in biotechnology like synthetic biology raises a lot of ethical and legal questions. For example, what are the ethical and philosophical implications of creating new lifeforms and artificial analogues to existing lifeforms? Does synthetic biology raise new ethical challenges and to which extent can they be dealt with in current ethical and philosophical frameworks? How should we deal with the legal issues that can be connected with synthetic biology like for example commercialisation of human body parts and intellectual property aspects? The SYBHEL Project[1] was set up in 2009 to investigate the ethical, legal and policy issues that might be raised by synthetic biology in respect to human health and wellbeing. The project (www.sybhel.org) was funded by the European Commission in the Science in Society Program[2] and consisted of four partners: The University of Zurich, The University of Deusto, The Rathenau Institute in the

[1] SYBHEL is an acronym for the full title of the project: Synthetic Biology for Human Health: Ethical and Legal Issues.

[2] Funding Scheme SiS-2008-1.1.2.1: Ethics and new and emerging fields of science and technology Grant Agreement Number: 230401.

Hague, and the Centre for Ethics in Medicine at the University of Bristol (Co-ordinator of the Project).

The chapters in this volume were presented in two workshops organised in the Workpackage titled 'Regulation and Commercialisation of Synthetic Biology for Human Health' led by Dr. Inigo de Miguel Berain and Prof. Carlos Romeo Casabona of the Interuniversity Chair in Law and the Human Genome. The chapters give excellent insight not just in the legal aspects of patenting 'SynBio' products, but also in philosophical perspectives on commercialisation of the human body, patenting and patent rights regarding these products, and European and global developments in respect to patenting 'SynBio' products. The authors of the chapters are all highly distinguished experts in the field of law, health law, patent law, philosophy of law and biomedical ethics.

I am very grateful to Prof. Romeo Casabona and Dr. Miguel de Berain, not only for their excellent leadership in co-ordinating the SYBHEL workpackage on the legal issues of synthetic biology, but also for their efforts in editing this book which is the first Academic Volume on the legal and philosophical issues of the use of synthetic biology for human health.

Bristol, UK
March 2013

Prof Ruud ter Meulen
Co-ordinator of the SYBHEL Project

Acknowledgements

We would like to thank Prof. Ruud ter Meulen and Dr. Ainsley Newson for their invitation to be part of the SYBHEL Project. It was our great pleasure to work with them and all the partners involved.

We would especially thank Alex Calladine for his patience, kindness and efficiency during this long process.

We would also like to thank the EU for supporting the SYBHEL Project and the Basque country (Grant S-PEIZUNOB, SAIOTEK 2012). Without their generous grant, this would have never been possible.

Contents

1 **Synthetic Biology in Health and Disease** 1
Mark W.J. van Passel, Carolyn M.C. Lam,
Vítor A.P. Martins dos Santos, and María Suárez-Diez

2 **Synthetic Biology: Solving the Pharmaceutical Industry's Innovation Problems?** 11
Joachim Henkel and Robert Lüttke

3 **Synthetic Biology and Global Health in the Age of Intellectual Property** 19
Henk van den Belt

4 **Synthetic Biology and IP: How Do Definitions of "Products of Nature" Affect their Implications for Health?** 45
David Koepsell

5 **Synthetic Biology, Biotechnology Patents and the Protection of Human Health. A Consideration of the Principals at Stake** 55
Anna Falcone

6 **Patents and Living Matter: The Construction of a Patent System Attractive to Biotechnology** 77
Ana Paula Myszczuk and Jussara Maria Leal De Meirelles

7 **Patents Originating in Human Tissue and Data: Questions on Benefit Creating and Benefit Sharing, on Morality and Property** 87
David Townend

8 **Patenting SynBio in Anglo-America and Europe: Chaos or Opportunity** 101
Amina Agovic

9 Synthetic Biology: Challenges and Legal Questions 123
Jürgen Robienski and Jürgen Simon

10 Exclusions and Exceptions to Patent Eligibility Revisited: Examining the Political Functions of the "Discovery" and "Ordre Public" Clauses in the European Patent Convention and the Arenas of Negotiation 145
Ingrid Schneider

11 Patentability, Synthetic Biology and Human Genome 175
Carlos María Romeo Casabona

12 Patentability of Synthetic Biology Under the European Patent Convention (EPC) 187
Francisco J. Fernandez y Brañas

13 Synthetic Biology and IP Rights: In Defence of the Patent System 201
Iñigo de Miguel Beriain

14 Stepping Stones: Extending the Open Source Idea to Synthetic Biology 211
Stephen M. Maurer

Index 225

Chapter 1
Synthetic Biology in Health and Disease

Mark W.J. van Passel, Carolyn M.C. Lam, Vítor A.P. Martins dos Santos, and María Suárez-Diez

Abstract Synthetic biology draws on the understanding from genetics, biology, chemistry, physics, engineering, and computational sciences to (re-)design and (re-) engineer biological functions. Here we address how synthetic biology can be possibly deployed to promote health and tackle disease. We discuss how drugs can be produced in more affordable ways, how new medicines can be developed, how the re-design of cellular pathways can correct endogenous malfunctioning in a series of diseases, how bacteria can be engineered to kill tumors, and how bacterial communities in the intestine can be modulated to restore gut homeostasis and prevent metabolic diseases. We indicate how new biomedical materials can be synthetized to replace tissues, how new biosensors can assist in diagnosis and prognosis, and how synthetic biology can help preventing the onset of disease in those cases in which until now only diagnosis was possible. On the basis of this, we discuss towards what directions synthetic biology in health and disease may develop in the future.

Keywords Synthetic biology • Microbial biosynthesis • Biosensors • Biohybrid materials • Gene therapy • Signal engineering • Genetic circuits • Quorum sensing

M.W.J. van Passel • M. Suárez-Diez (✉)
Laboratory of Systems and Synthetic Biology, Wageningen University,
Dreijenplein 10, Building number 316, 6703 HB Wageningen, The Netherlands
e-mail: maria.suarezdiez@wur.nl

C.M.C. Lam • V.A.P. Martins dos Santos
Laboratory of Systems and Synthetic Biology, Wageningen University,
Dreijenplein 10, Building number 316, 6703 HB Wageningen, The Netherlands

LifeGlimmer GmbH, Markelstraße 38, 12163 Berlin, Germany

I. de Miguel Beriain and C.M. Romeo Casabona (eds.), *Synbio and Human Health: A Challenge to the Current IP Framework?*, DOI 10.1007/978-94-017-9196-0_1,

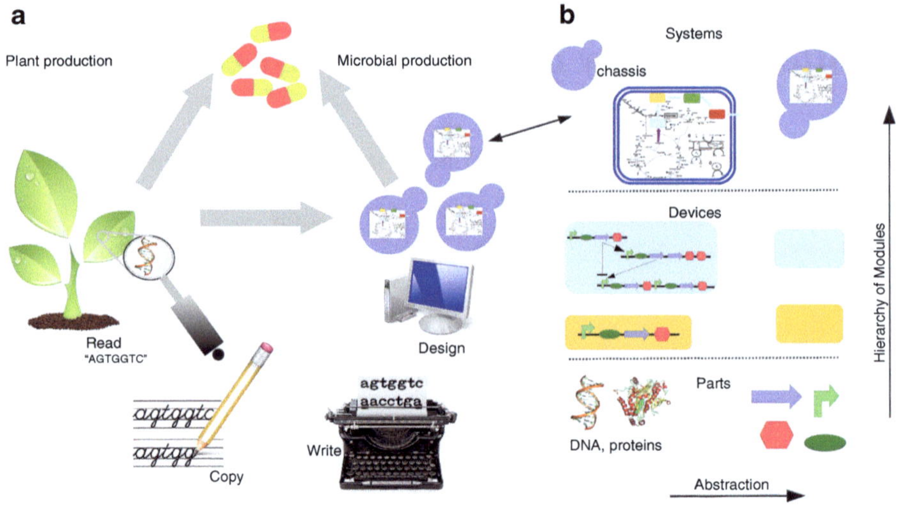

Fig. 1.1 Traditional production of drugs versus synthetic biology approach of new production methods and novel drugs design. (**a**) Instead of extracting compounds from the natural host, the relevant genes are read, copied, written in different ways to explore their properties, and eventually new pathways are designed and assembled into new or existing hosts using tools in synthetic biology. (**b**) Details of abstraction levels in synthetic biology, such as biological parts made from DNA/proteins, devices, and chassis in increasing order of hierarchical modularity

1.1 Introduction

Humans have been trying to grasp life as long as they exist. Understanding how organisms function warrants identifying and characterizing the fundamental building blocks of biological cells and the mesh of underlying interactions. Similarly to learning a new language – which involves reading alphabets, learning definitions of words and grammatical rules, and subsequently composing new texts – a foundation of knowledge about functions and properties of genes, proteins, metabolites, and other biological molecules is a pre-requisite for mastering the design of novel biological units and functions. Synthetic biology distills the understanding from genetics, biology, chemistry, physics, engineering, and computational science to transform biological systems with an a priori knowledge of how to achieve new target features. It goes beyond the discovery aspect in systems biology or the modification approach in genetic or metabolic engineering, for synthetic biology aims at a creative writing and design dimension (Fig. 1.1). As an example, all living organisms, with only a few exceptions, use the same basic building blocks in the form of DNA to store genetic information in gene sequences, and each gene codes for a protein with specific functions. However, different organisms use the code in a slightly different way, known as codon bias, similar to geographical variation of the preferred choice of words for the same meaning in the same language. This codon bias leads to non-optimal protein expression when a gene from one species is expressed in another host, but it can be overcome by rational design of genes in synthetic biology to enable ideal protein production according to the codon bias favored by the host cell. The concept of designing biological units from scratch in synthetic biology has popularized construction of gene functions which are built to be reusable in various cell hosts, a feature known as modularity, and has increased the accessibility of tailor-made biological properties in terms of standardized gene circuits to a wide range of users. The number of potential species usable as candidates for synthetic biology is vast, but due to the need of detailed characterization before a cell host is suitable for expressing synthesized gene functions, it is favorable to use one or a handful of well-characterized cell hosts, including streamlined genomes (Leprince et al. 2012), to act as "chassis" (platform) for different gene expression requirements. Such expansion of tools essential for designing new DNAs in synthetic biology is capable of influencing many aspects of our daily life. Here we focus on the health-associated potential of synthetic biology to explore how it can be utilized to promote the wellness of humanity and towards what directions it may develop in the future.

1.2 Applications to Human Health

1.2.1 Microbial Production of Drugs

Throughout the history of mankind, the battle against illnesses generally depended on medications or the defense mechanisms of our immune system. Initially, most medicines came from natural sources. When chemical structures of effective medical compounds became well-understood, chemical synthesis and development of new drugs took over as an important method for producing pharmaceutical products. Our gradually maturing knowledge of biological systems has so far enabled us to use different species to produce drug compounds and to create synthetic genetic circuits to detect or modify biological functions. Biological production has the potential to deliver compounds that are currently obtained through chemical synthesis or from non-renewable sources. The short generation times of bacteria and their metabolic versatility, i.e. their ability to produce a broad range of compounds, makes them a preferred host for biosynthesis as compared to either plants or animals (Lam et al. 2012). Current challenges are to increase the yields and to find ways to produce compounds for which no microbial pathways are available.

The first efforts to transfer drug production capabilities from animals to microbes date back to the early 1980s. Until the beginning of the 1980s, insulin obtained from the pancreas of slaughtered farm animals was the only treatment to alleviate the symptoms of diabetes. DNA recombination by restriction enzymes, discovered in 1968 by P. Berg, was used by H.W. Boyer and N. Cohen to introduce the human gene responsible for insulin production in the laboratory organism *Escherichia coli*, which allowed these bacteria to produce insulin that was chemically indistinguishable from the one produced by humans and therefore had its same therapeutic effects.

As previously stated, synthetic biology has been made possible by the enlargement of the toolbox to write, and therefore modify DNA. We are now able to construct full pathways leading to the production of the desired compound by combining elements from different organisms. Perhaps the best-known example is the production of the antimalarial drug precursor artemisinic acid by Ro et al. (2006). Artemisinin is the antimalarial treatment recommended by the World Health Organization (WHO) and it is a natural extract from the plant *Artemisia annua*. Although two pharmaceutical companies (Novartis and Sanofi-Aventis) have agreed with the WHO to produce the drug on a non-profit basis, still the average cost of the treatment, 4 ~ 10$, is too high for the populations most vulnerable to malaria. Synthetic biology has succeeded in developing new methods for microbial biosynthesis of artemisinic acid, which can be purified and converted into artemisinin by a relatively inexpensive process, leading to a reduction of the production cost. To engineer this metabolic pathway, ten genes from three different organisms: bacteria, yeast, and plant were combined in a single chassis (yeast). The chosen genes encode enzymes able to turn a key metabolite naturally produced in microbial cells (acetyl coenzyme A) into artemisinic acid. Additional effort was devoted to the regulation of each step of the pathway to avoid the accumulation of toxic or deleterious compounds for the cell. The final outcome was transgenic yeast able to produce artemisinic acid at a similar biomass fraction as the plant; however the main difference in the productivity is due to the much shorter time, 4–5 days compared to about 8 months. Currently, agreements have been reached with the pharmaceutical company Sanofi-Aventis to optimise the scale-up to an industrial process and bring down the cost of synthesis, with the goal of market availability by 2013.

When comparing both examples, insulin and artemisinic acid production, similarities arise: in both cases genes were inserted into a microbe to produce the desired compound. It would seem that the main difference is due to the "scale" of the problem: 1 versus 10 genes. However, in the artemisinin case the regulation of the pathway and of each step was one of the key elements to obtain high yields: this required to consider the interactions among each individual element of the pathway and also the interactions among each element and the host cell.

1.2.2 Fighting Infections

The human microbiome are human-associated bacterial communities such as the gut microbiota. These commensal microorganisms are naturally adapted to the host environment and they can be engineered to carrying synthetic circuits that provide prophylaxis against infection (Goh et al. 2012). Quorum sensing mechanisms are cardinal elements to modulate the social interactions among bacteria and offer ample opportunities to engineer the behaviour of the community. Duan and March (2010) altered these mechanisms to obtain protection from cholera infection. *Vibrio cholera* is only able to secrete virulence factors at low population densities and the population density is sensed by the concentration of the CAI-1 protein, so that only in low concentrations of CAI-1 is cholera disease produced. Duan and March engineered *E. coli* to produce CAI-1, effectively driving *V. cholera* harmless. It is counter intuitive that incorporating genes from a pathogenic bacteria into a harmless one would lead to a health benefit, but the key is that the main effect of these genes is not linked to pathogenesis but only to the disruption of signaling pathways within the pathogenic bacteria: the engineered bacteria fed to infant mice prior to infection by *V. cholera* lead to a reduction of the mice's mortality rate.

Malfunction of the regulatory systems leading to homeostasis leads to disease; however constructs can be designed to be integrated with the endogenous malfunctioning network and drive the systems back to the homeostatic behaviour (Karlsson and Weber 2012). For example, too high uric acid concentrations (hyperuricemia) might lead to diseases such as gout. Kemmer et al. (2010) engineered a cellular sensor to detect conditions with disrupted homeostatic behaviour: high concentrations of uric acid. The sensor responded by the *in situ* production and delivery of a therapeutic molecule (ureate oxidase) to eliminate uric acid and to correct imbalances. In transgenic lab mice with acute hyperuricemia the engineered system was able to restore uric acid homeostasis. In this case codon bias optimization was required for the optimal expression of the ureate oxidase of fungal origin.

1.2.3 Treatment of Genetic Disorders

Furthermore, synthetic biology can provide means to avoid the onset of disease in those cases which until now only diagnosis was possible, such as Huntington disease (HD). There exists a precise genetic test that can predict the disease years before the first symptoms of HD appear. However, only palliative treatments are available. HD is caused by a mutation in one of the two copies of the human *HTT* gene and the therapeutic goal is to reduce the expression of the mutant huntingtin protein while leaving the expression of the non-mutated one unaffected. Garriga-Canut et al. (2012) designed a new, non-natural protein that is able to accomplish this goal. Furthermore they successfully delivered these proteins to the brain of mice with HD and reduce huntingtin expression by up to 60 %. In this case, the researchers used the accumulated knowledge on protein structure and function to design a new biological part (a protein) with a targeted functionality and able to accomplish its function even when embedded within a complex system.

1.2.4 Sensing Environmental Pollutants

Environmental factors are, in many cases, determinants of disease, and exposures to pollutants remain a major public health issue. Therefore the development of efficient and low cost biosensors of contaminants can greatly improve the health and living conditions of the populations, especially in developing countries that tend to have high pollution levels. Over billions of years, life has penetrated all biological niches on earth, and correspondingly adapted to examine its environment for a large range of signals. Such signals communicate either beneficial or detrimental conditions, to which an organism can then trigger appropriate responses. Since numerous signals reach an organism simultaneously, it is no small feat that life has adapted so well in responding to so many conditions. And it seems that none has adapted to a wider range of conditions than microbes, most notably extreme temperatures, extreme pHs, confined in cells of other organisms, and even in the low water activities of an asphalt lake (Schulze-Makuch et al. 2011). For the engineering discipline of synthetic biology, such potential of microbial signal perception, processing and response modules constitute a nearly limitless supply of genetic components with which to devise biosensors. Still, few such sensors have been tested outside the lab in 'real-world' conditions.

In 1990, King et al. (1990) presented a bioluminescence-based bioreporter for a single compound, the polycyclic aromatic hydrocarbon naphthalene (or its metabolite salicylate), which resulted in a rapid, sensitive and robust detection assay. This was achieved by transcriptionally fusing bacterial luciferase gene cluster (known as the *lux*-operon), which enable light emission, with the catabolic genes involved in the naphthalene degradation pathway in *Pseudomonas fluorescens*. This bacterial bioreporter was tested on contaminated soils, and the authors suggested that bioluminescent reporter technology could represent a useful tool to detect a range of chemical agents. As expected, a large number of chemicals of environmental concern is now detectable by biosensors, and are based on a diverse transcriptional activators that detect these compounds (Van der Meer and Belkin 2010).

Another famous example for biosensors is based on heavy metal detection systems in bacteria. Again, combining the luminescent *lux*-operon with a set of genes related to mercury resistance, semiquantitative biosensors were developed already in 1993, which were found to detect minute amounts of the toxic mercury in contaminated habitats including both (diluted) salt and fresh water (Selifonova et al. 1993). However, in many other cases, metal-responsive sensor proteins display an extended affinity for different metal-ions, reducing the specificity and thereby their potential applicability. For example Tauriainen and co-workers developed recombinant luminescent bacteria that could detect simultaneously arsenite, antimonite and cadmium (Tauriainen et al. 1997), which surpassed the sensitivity of earlier detection systems (Corbisier et al. 1993). Interestingly however, Hakkila and co-workers succeeded in establishing increased cadmium-specific sensory proteins (Hakkila et al. 2011). They showed the potential of shifting the specificity, in this case via a combination of mutagenesis and selection steps. This suggests that other relatively unspecific biosensors could similarly be re-directed to specifically detect novel compounds.

The previous examples utilized visually detectable outputs using fluorescent or luminescent systems. However, a new design in generating biosensors was proposed by Gu et al. (2010), which is based on a microbial fuel cell that transforms the biological input to a measurable electrical output signal. This initiative stemmed from the international genetically engineered machine (iGEM) competition, where undergraduate students spend a summer on a synthetic biology project of their own making (www.igem.org). Many teams focus on biosensors, and the winning team of 2012 in fact designed a system that detects meat spoilage (http://2012.igem.org/Team:Groningen). Other projects have included the detection of volatile compounds (http://2012.igem.org/Team:TU-Delft), or substances found in cigarette smoke (http://2011.igem.org/Team:ETH_Zurich). In addition, the occasional team has designed generating microscopic flow devices that could be used in the context of biosensing (Hesselman et al. 2012).

1.2.5 Detection of Infections

Besides designing sensing systems and designated detectable outputs, biosensors can also be applied in more radical ploys. In 2011, Saeidi and co-workers (Saeidi et al. 2011) engineered the bacterium *E. coli* to sense and kill the pathogenic *Pseudomonas aeruginosa*. This represented a new direction in applying synthetic biology in tackling infectious diseases. Basically, the engineered *E. coli* behaves as a biosensor, detecting specific molecules from *P. aeruginosa*. Next, it produces several 'outputs'; the toxic pyocin, but also a lysis protein so that the device self-destructs and releases the 'reporter', killing the pathogen. This approach is still far away from being tested in humans (or animals) but initial laboratory tests show the high success of the method. Since antibiotic resistance in pathogens is becoming a serious health issue, alternative approaches for challenging infectious diseases are of great importance. Also, since the genetic design of the search and destroy system has been arranged according to an assembly standard, it is relatively straightforward to re-engineer this system to aim for other human pathogens.

1.2.6 Combating Cancer

Cancer cells induce dramatic changes in their environment; tumors have different oxygen, pH, and metabolite levels, among others, than those present in healthy tissues. Biosensors can be engineered to identify these different micro-environments and attack cancer cells. For example, *E. coli* show a natural affinity towards tumor tissue, and upon ingestion they tend to accumulate in the vicinity of tumors. The natural ability of some bacteria to target tumor makes them ideal candidates to build tumor targeting factories, that upon colonization of tumor cells are able to produce anticancer compounds to fight disease. In an early example, Anderson and colleagues (2006) introduced in *E. coli* the *inv* gene from *Yersinia pseudotuberculosis* that selectively allows *E. coli* to invade (and damage) cancer cells. Expression of *inv* was under the control of the quorum sensing mechanism of these bacteria, so that *inv* was only expressed upon high bacterial densities and a hypoxic environment (such as is found in tumors). Bacterial anticancer therapies have successfully been tested in mice and nowadays human trials have started to show the potential of these techniques to combat melanomas and carcinomas among others (see Forbes (2010) and references therein).

1.2.7 Biohybrid Materials

Throughout the years research in biology has accumulated knowledge on how organic materials (proteins and DNA) interact with small molecules, this knowledge can be used within the field of synthetic biology to produce synthetic materials (e.g. hydrogel) that would dissolve and release drugs upon the addition of specific compounds (Weber and Fussenegger 2011). Furthermore, the combination with other disciplines, aimed at developing new materials will lead to the creation of new biohybrid materials that can be used as drug vehicles (Jakobus et al. 2012). Kemmer et al (2011) implemented a cow insemination device that released microcapsules, encapsulating the sperm, that were only degraded upon estrus, therefore synchronizing sperm administration and ovulation.

1.3 Future Perspectives

Most of the discussed examples are still in their early developmental stages, however the development of tools to synthesise longer and longer DNA molecules have made it possible to build a full genome: in 2010, Gibson and co-workers were able to write a series of letters that represented the genome of a bacterium, synthesise a DNA molecule with this code and replace the DNA of a different bacteria with the synthetic one. The new cells were controlled by the chemically synthesised genome and were capable of continuous replication. So, indeed synthetic biology has succeeded in creating new living entities.

Drug administration is generally a non-targeted process with the drug distributed over the whole body. In addition, the relationship between drug concentration at the site of action and the resulting effect might show huge variations during the time course therefore causing alterations in the intensity of therapeutic and adverse effects (pharmacodynamics properties). Synthetic, tissue specific, and autonomous delivery systems might be able to overcome some of the limitations of drug administration and their side effects.

Synthetic biology is expected to enable further improvement in prevention, detection, and treatment of diseases through application and evolvement of those existing tools. As the field continues to mature, more challenges await us ahead, as well as deeper insights into the fundamentals of biology and the capabilities of synthetic biology for improving the quality of life.

References

Anderson JC, Clarke EJ, Arkin AP, Voigt CA (2006) Environmentally controlled invasion of cancer cells by engineered bacteria. J Mol Biol 355(4):619–627. doi:10.1016/j.jmb.2005.10.076

Corbisier P, Ji G, Nuyts G, Mergeay M, Silver S (1993) LuxAB gene fusions with the arsenic and cadmium resistance operons of *Staphylococcus aureus* plasmid pI258. FEMS Microbiol Lett 110(2):231–238. doi:10.1111/j.1574-6968.1993.tb06325.x

Duan F, March JC (2010) Engineered bacterial communication prevents *Vibrio cholerae* virulence in an infant mouse model. Proc Natl Acad Sci 107(25):11260–11264. doi:10.1073/pnas.1001294107

Forbes NS (2010) Engineering the perfect (bacterial) cancer therapy. Nat Rev Cancer 10(11):785–794. doi:10.1038/nrc2934

Garriga-Canut M, Agustín-Pavón C, Herrmann F, Sánchez A, Dierssen M, Fillat C, Isalan M (2012) Synthetic zinc finger repressors reduce mutant huntingtin expression in the brain of R6/2 mice. Proc Natl Acad Sci. doi:10.1073/pnas.1206506109

Gibson DG, Glass JI, Lartigue C, Noskov VN, Chuang R-Y, Algire MA, Benders GA et al (2010) Creation of a bacterial cell controlled by a chemically synthesized genome. Science 329(5987):52–56. doi:10.1126/science.1190719

Goh Y-L, He H, March JC (2012) Engineering commensal bacteria for prophylaxis against infection. Curr Opin Biotechnol 23(6):924–930. doi:10.1016/j.copbio.2012.03.004

Gu X, Trybiło M, Ramsay S, Jensen M, Fulton R, Rosser S, Gilbert D (2010) Engineering a novel self-powering electrochemical biosensor. Syst Synth Biol 4(3):203–214. doi:10.1007/s11693-010-9063-2

Hakkila KM, Nikander PA, Junttila SM, Lamminmäki UJ, Virta MP (2011) Cd-specific mutants of mercury-sensing regulatory protein MerR, generated by directed evolution. Appl Environ Microbiol 77(17):6215–6224. doi:10.1128/aem.00662-11

Hesselman MC, Odoni DI, Ryback BM, de Groot S, van Heck RGA, Keijsers J, Kolkman P, Nieuwenhuijse D, van Nuland YM, Sebus E, Spee R, de Vries H, Wapenaar MT, Ingham CJ, Schroën K, Martins dos Santos VAP, Spaans SK, Hugenholtz F, van Passel MWJ (2012) A multi-platform flow device for microbial (Co-) cultivation and microscopic analysis. PLoS One 7(5):e36982

Jakobus K, Wend S, Weber W (2012) Synthetic mammalian gene networks as a blueprint for the design of interactive biohybrid materials. Chem Soc Rev 41(3):1000–1018. doi:10.1039/c1cs15176b

Karlsson M, Weber W (2012) Therapeutic synthetic gene networks. Curr Opin Biotechnol 23(5):703–711. doi:10.1016/j.copbio.2012.01.003

Kemmer C, Gitzinger M, Daoud-El Baba M, Djonov V, Stelling J, Fussenegger M (2010) Self-sufficient control of urate homeostasis in mice by a synthetic circuit. Nat Biotechnol 28(4):355–360. doi:10.1038/nbt.1617

Kemmer C, Fluri DA, Witschi U, Passeraub A, Gutzwiller A, Fussenegger M (2011) A designer network coordinating bovine artificial insemination by ovulation-triggered release of implanted sperms. J Control Release 150(1):23–29. doi:10.1016/j.jconrel.2010.11.016

King JM, Digrazia PM, Applegate B, Burlage R, Sanseverino J, Dunbar P, Larimer F, Sayler GS (1990) Rapid, sensitive bioluminescent reporter technology for naphthalene exposure and biodegradation. Science 249(4970):778–781. doi:10.1126/science.249.4970.778

Lam CMC, Suárez Diez M, Godinho M, Martins dos Santos VAP (2012) Programmable bacterial catalysis – designing cells for biosynthesis of value-added compounds. FEBS Lett 586(15):2184–2190. doi:10.1016/j.febslet.2012.02.030

Leprince A, Van Passel MWJ, Martins dos Santos VAP (2012) Streamlining genomes: toward the generation of simplified and stabilized microbial systems. Curr Opin Biotechnol 23(5):651–658. http://dx.doi.org/10.1016/j.copbio.2012.05.001.

Ro D-K, Paradise EM, Ouellet M, Fisher KJ, Newman KL, Ndungu JM, Ho KA et al (2006) Production of the antimalarial drug precursor artemisinic acid in engineered yeast. Nature 440(7086):940–943. doi:10.1038/nature04640

Saeidi N, Wong CK, Lo TM, Nguyen HX, Ling H, Leong SSY, Poh CL, Chang MW (2011) Engineering microbes to sense and eradicate *Pseudomonas aeruginosa*, a human pathogen. Mol Syst Biol 7:521. doi:10.1038/msb.2011.55

Schulze-Makuch D, Haque S, DE Sousa Antonio MR, Ali D, Hosein R, Song YC, Yang J, Zaikova E, Beckles DM, Guinan E, Lehto HJ, Hallam SJ (2011) Microbial life in a liquid asphalt desert. Astrobiology 11(3):241–258. doi:10.1089/ast.2010.0488

Selifonova O, Burlage R, Barkay T (1993) Bioluminescent sensors for detection of bioavailable Hg(II) in the environment. Appl Environ Microbiol 59(9):3083–3090

Tauriainen S, Karp M, Chang W, Virta M (1997) Recombinant luminescent bacteria for measuring bioavailable arsenite and antimonite. Appl Environ Microbiol 63(11):4456–4461

van der Meer JR, Belkin S (2010) Where microbiology meets microengineering: design and applications of reporter bacteria. Nat Rev Microbiol 8(7):511–522. doi:10.1038/nrmicro2392(52)

Weber W, Fussenegger M (2011) Emerging biomedical applications of synthetic biology. Nat Rev Genet 13(1):21–35. doi:10.1038/nrg3094

Chapter 2
Synthetic Biology: Solving the Pharmaceutical Industry's Innovation Problems?

Joachim Henkel and Robert Lüttke

Abstract Synthetic biology holds great promise for a number of application areas, and in particular for human health care. It may help to address the challenge of ever increasing innovation cost that the pharmaceutical industry is currently facing, with the number of new drugs approved per billion US dollar spent on research and development halved every 9 years since 1950. In this book chapter we review the challenges that the pharmaceutical industry is confronted with, present and analyze examples of applications of synthetic biology in this field, and discuss potential changes to the industry's intellectual property management that the advent of synthetic biology might bring about.

Keywords Synthetic biology • Applications • Human health • Pharmaceutical industry • Innovation • Patents

2.1 Introduction

Health care industries, and the pharmaceutical industry in particular, have been using biotechnology tools and methods for many years. Accordingly, the emerging field of synthetic biology is seen to have great potential for pharmaceutical research, development, and production. Some of this potential has already been realized, with synthetic biology increasingly moving toward applications (see Erickson et al. 2011 and, for medicine in particular, Folcher and Fussenegger 2012; Weber and

---

J. Henkel (✉) • R. Lüttke
TUM School of Management, Technische Universität München, Munich, Germany
e-mail: henkel@wi.tum.de; luettke@wi.tum.de

I. de Miguel Beriain and C.M. Romeo Casabona (eds.), *Synbio and Human Health: A Challenge to the Current IP Framework?*, DOI 10.1007/978-94-017-9196-0_2,

Fussenegger 2009, 2011).[1] We review in this book chapter three cases of synthetic biology applications where known drugs are produced more efficiently using synthetic biology methods. All three recently entered or soon will enter the health care market. We also sketch some less mature applications related to drug discovery and therapies (Weber and Fussenegger 2009, 2011), and discuss if these cases could serve as a model for how synthetic biology will affect human health care and the pharmaceutical industry in particular. We finally speculate about how a widening use of synthetic biology in pharmaceuticals may affect the management of intellectual property in this industry.

These are obviously difficult questions, since synthetic biology as an emerging research area is confronted with huge uncertainties and significant challenges on its path toward biomedical applications (Cheng and Lu 2012). Yet with, as of 2012, more than 50 companies and 100 universities and research institutions examining issues surrounding synthetic biology in the U.S. (5 and 40 respectively in Europe) (Synthetic Biology Project Maps Inventory 2012), the global synthetic biology market is estimated to grow fast (BCC Research 2011; Transparencymarketresearch.com 2012).

In the following, we sketch the human health care industry and its innovation problems, present in detail the three existing applications mentioned above, and discuss synthetic biology's potential for contributing to the solution of the pharmaceutical industry's innovation problems and for altering its intellectual property *management.*

2.2 Human Healthcare Today

2.2.1 Potential for Improving Human Health

Health as defined by the World Health Organization (WHO) is "a state of complete physical, mental and social well-being and not merely the absence of disease or infirmity" (WHO 1946). Medical progress has led to considerable improvements in human well-being.[2] Yet, a huge potential for further improvements remains. We support this claim in the following using statistics on disability-adjusted-life-years, costs to society, and comparisons of funding between diseases.

Disability-adjusted-life-years, short DALY, measure the years of life lost due to premature mortality plus the weighted number of years lived with disability or reduced well-being (where the weighting factors depend on the severity of the

[1] Note that we use the term "synthetic biology" in the broader sense of "the design and fabrication of biological components and systems that do not already exist in the natural world" (http://syntheticbiology.org/FAQ.html). In the narrower sense, synthetic biology means to employ, in such design and construction, a standardized set of parts.

[2] For example, live expectancies in the U.S. rose 1948–2008 from 64.6 (69.6) to 75.6 (80.6) years for male (female) newborns United Nations (1997, 2011).

condition) (Murray et al. 2006). The worldwide DALY for the year 2004 was calculated as 1.52 bn (WHO 2008), amounting (with a global population of 6.44 bn) to an average of 0.24 years per person. Estimated with simple assumptions[3] this number amounts to an average loss of 16 healthy years during a lifetime due to disabling diseases or premature death. Thus, from the perspective of individuals there is definitely a huge potential for improving human health further.

Also with respect to the cost that diseases cause to society considerable gains would result from such improvement. The most costly ones in the U.S. (2009) in terms of total (direct plus indirect) cost are heart and cardiovascular diseases (USD 475 bn), alcohol abuse and dependence (USD 301 bn), digestive diseases (USD 260 bn), cancer (USD 240 bn), and mental diseases (USD 217 bn) (Kockaya 2010). The top four categories of disease alone thus account for more than USD 1.275 trillion per year.

Finally, comparing data on spending between categories of diseases suggests that some might have been, relatively speaking, neglected compared to others, and so for these in particular there should be a considerable potential for improving human health. Some researchers criticize that decisions on disease funding have long been based mainly on mortality (Zoler 2011). However, many diseases commonly treated with pharmaceuticals are less mortal. For neuropsychiatric diseases in particular a stark contrast is perceived between the burden of disease and funding (Zoler 2011).

2.2.2 *Challenges for Innovation in the Pharmaceutical Industry*

The pharmaceutical industry's potential for improving human health is contrasted by a twofold challenge with respect to innovation, namely, increasing cost and reduced returns. We address both in turn.

In the past 60 years the pharmaceutical industry has seen major scientific and technological advances with direct impact on drug research and development. Still, this industry is faced with "Eroom's law," which states that the number of new drugs approved per billion US dollar halved every 9 years since 1950 (Scannell et al. 2012). Eroom's law corresponds to an average annual cost increase of 8 %. DiMasi (DiMasi et al. 2003) reports similar results, concluding that "total capitalized costs were shown to have increased at an annual rate of 7.4 % above general price inflation." Other estimates even yield compound annual growth rates of more than 13 % (Munos 2009). Whatever the precise rate, though, all estimates reveal a dramatic increase over the last decades in the cost of innovation per new drug. This increase will partly be due to the fact that the low hanging fruits in drug discovery have all been harvested, but is to a large extent also driven by the tightening of regulations. As Dickson and Gagnon (2004) state: "Since the mid-1960s, the process of drug

[3] Assuming an average life expectancy of 68 years WHO (2009) and constant DALY numbers throughout life.

approval has been modified to significantly improve the safety and efficacy of drugs for use by the general public. A consequence of these scientific and regulatory changes has been an increase in the time taken and cost of bringing a new drug to market." Furthermore, in order to avoid intense product-market competition firms tend to direct their R&D [research and development] investments toward new therapeutic targets characterized by high uncertainty (Pammolli et al. 2011). Pammolli and coauthors conclude that "this reorienting of investments accounts for most of the recent decline in productivity in pharmaceutical R&D."

The increase in the time to market mentioned above directly affects the second challenge, reduced returns to innovation. Patent protection for pharmaceuticals lasts a maximum of 25 years. On average, about half of this time will be over when the new drug finally hits the market (e.g., DiMasi et al. 2003). The time window for generating revenues under patent protection, before generics exert price pressure and reduce the original drug's market share, is thus limited and shrinking. And even under patent protection, innovative drugs aiming at established markets may be subject to reference pricing schemes and so are often "reimbursed at the same level as older drugs" (Pammolli et al. 2011). Corporations anticipate this squeeze and, as explained above, direct their R&D investments toward new therapeutic targets.

2.3 Synthetic Biology in Healthcare: Examples

We have shown that a huge potential exists for improving human health further, but also that the pharmaceutical industry is facing the double challenge of reduced R&D productivity and pressure on its revenues. To assess if and how synthetic biology might help to address this challenge in the future we analyze three already existing applications in the field of pharmaceuticals: Sitagliptin, Cephalexin, and artemisinin (Synthetic Biology Project 2012). We also sketch several more novel applications related to drug discovery and therapies.

Sitagliptin (a dipeptidyl peptidase-4 inhibitor) is a drug against type II diabetes, marketed by Merck and Co., Inc., under the name of Januvia (Singh 2011a). While Sitagliptin had been produced by Merck before, Codexis, Inc. developed in collaboration with Merck an improved manufacturing route. This achievement earned the innovators the 2010 Presidential Green Chemistry Challenge Award: "This collaboration has led to an enzymatic process that reduces waste, improves yield and safety, and eliminates the need for a metal catalyst" (U.S. Environmental Protection Agency). The scientific base was published in Science (Savile et al. 2010).

DSM's application of synthetic biology methods to the production of Cephalexin is quite similar to our first example. As Singh (Singh 2011a) describes, by using these methods DSM "dramatically improv[ed] an existing process for commercial production of Cephalexin, a synthetic antibiotic. Starting with a penicillin-producing microbial strain, DSM introduced and optimized two heterologous genes encoding acyl transferase and expandase respectively for a one-step direct fermentation of adipoyl-7-ADCA. This product was then converted into Cephalexin via two enzymatic steps, replacing a process requiring 13 chemical steps." The improved process is reported to save 65 % of energy and materials and to cut the cost by 50 % (Singh 2011b).

Also our third example is about the production of an existing drug with improved processes based on synthetic biology methods. Amyris Biotechnologies was able to engineer yeast to produce artemisinic acid, a precursor to the key ingredient, artemisinin, to the most effective drugs against malaria.[4] The established production process for artemisinin, starting from plant leaves, was expensive and lengthy, and so a more efficient manufacturing route was more than welcome. Sanofi, the pharmaceutical company, licensed the yeast in 2008 to produce artemisinin on an industrial scale, and reported to have produced 39 tonnes in early 2013.[5]

While the examples above relate to improved production processes of known drugs, Weber and Fussenegger (2009, 2011) review a number of more novel applications of synthetic biology to the study of disease mechanisms, disease prevention, drug discovery and production, and new approaches to infection and cancer therapies (see also Ruder et al. 2011 and Medema et al. 2011). They report, among other things, how synthetic biology methods have helped to understand the emergence of the severe acute respiratory syndrome (SARS) pandemic of 2002 and 2003, to pioneer a live vaccine against the poliovirus, and to construct "screening devices for the class-specific discovery of new drug candidates" (see p. 25).

2.4 Synthetic Biology's Contribution to Solving the Pharmaceutical Industry's Innovation Problems

Juxtaposing the innovation challenges that the pharmaceutical industry is facing with the range of existing and prospective applications of synthetic biology in this field clearly confirms the huge potential attributed to synthetic biology. Still, a closer look is warranted.

The first main problem is the exponential increase in development cost per new drug. Several emergent applications of synthetic biology promise to address this issue, in particular its use in understanding disease mechanisms, in drug discovery, for the construction of screening devices, and for novel therapeutic solutions. Notably, however, the most mature applications of synthetic biology in the field of health care relate to improved production processes of existing drugs. While the resulting cost savings are welcome to industry and society alike, they do not address the fundamental issue of exploding R&D cost. To be fair, though, the introduction of new drugs identified using synthetic biology methods is obviously a lengthier and more difficult process than the establishment of a new production process, and so more time will be required to observe the impact of synthetic biology on R&D cost.

---

[4] The facts about Amyris are based on "Amyris Biotechnologies," Stanford Graduate School of Business, Case E331, 2009.

[5] See http://www.nature.com/news/malaria-drug-made-in-yeast-causes-market-ferment-1.12417.

This is particularly true for applications in mammalian systems to develop entirely new therapeutic solutions, an effort that Khalil and Collins (2010) have called for.

The second main problem is the squeeze on revenues that the pharmaceutical industry is facing. Also for this challenge synthetic biology holds considerable promise. With new methods of drug discovery and the potential for entirely new therapeutic approaches, odds are that solutions can be developed that differ radically from existing treatments. Innovators would thus have a greater chance of avoiding reference pricing schemes, and might also be more successful at keeping generics manufacturers at bay. As for solutions to the problem of R&D cost, however, such relief will require more time.

An important moderating factor in the present context is the patent system and its interaction with the technology at hand. The pharmaceutical industry has traditionally been based on a "discrete" technology, which means that each product is based on very few individual and individually patentable inventions (Cohen et al. 2000). To the extent that synthetic pathways employ increasing numbers of genes, synthetic biology morphs into a "complex" technology (Henkel and Maurer 2007, 2009). If patents cover these genes and are enforced—which will likely happen as soon as sizable revenues are realized—then cross-licensing, patent pools, or clearing houses (Van Zimmeren 2009; Verbeure 2009) become the order of the day, but likely also patent infringement and litigation. Overall, IP management in pharmaceuticals may come to resemble that in information and communications technology. Barring patent pools and other cooperative solutions, the tragedy of the anticommons (Heller and Eisenberg 1998) may become more aggravated, and research progress might be hampered through "a patent system that was developed for a discrete model of innovation and an essentially linear relationship between knowledge elements" (Allarakhia and Wensley 2005, see also Rai and Boyle 2007). It will depend on the intellectual property management of the relevant actors in the industry as well as the patent authorities how these potential impediments play out.

2.5 Conclusions

The pharmaceutical industry is facing the double challenge of exponentially increasing cost per new drug and pressure on its revenues. Synthetic biology may offer relief, promising to boost pharmaceutical innovation in several ways: through an improved understanding of disease mechanisms, disease prevention, drug discovery and production, and new approaches to infection and cancer therapies (Weber and Fussenegger 2009, 2011; Medema et al. 2011; Ruder et al. 2011). Yet, the most mature applications of synthetic biology in this field relate to improved production processes of known drugs, not to newly discovered drugs or even entirely new therapeutic solutions. More time will be required to observe the impact of synthetic biology on the cost of pharmaceutical R&D. These issues will be compounded by the increasing complexity of engineered genetic systems and concomitant changes to the management of intellectual property in this field (Henkel and Maurer 2009). These uncertainties notwithstanding, synthetic biology clearly offers a considerable potential to address the pharmaceutical industry's main challenges.

References

Allarakhia M, Wensley A (2005) Innovation and intellectual property rights in systems biology. Nat Biotechnol 23(12):1485–1488. doi:10.1038/nbt1205-1485

Allen AC, Timothy KL (2012) Synthetic biology: an emerging engineering discipline. Ann Rev Biomed Eng 14:155–178

Cohen WM, Nelson RR, Walsh JP (2000) Protecting their intellectual assets: appropriability conditions and why U.S. manufacturing firms patent (or not). Working Paper 7552 NATIONAL BUREAU OF ECONOMIC RESEARCH, Cambridge, MA 02138, http://www.nber.org/papers/w7552

Dickson M, Gagnon JP (2004) Key factors in the rising cost of new drug discovery and development. Nat Rev Drug Discov 3(5):417–429. doi:10.1038/nrd1382

Dimasi JA, Hansen RW, Grabowski HG (2003) The price of innovation: new estimates of drug development costs. J Health Econ 22(2):151–185. doi:10.1016/S0167-6296(02)00126-1

Erickson B, Singh R, Winters P (2011) Synthetic biology: regulating industry uses of new biotechnologies. Science 333(6047):1254–1256. doi:10.1126/science.1211066

Folcher M, Fussenegger M (2012) Synthetic biology advancing clinical applications. Curr Opin Chem Biol 16:1–10

Heller MA, Eisenberg RS (1998) Can patents deter innovation? The anticommons in biomedical research. Science 280:698–701

Henkel J, Maurer SM (2007) The economics of synthetic biology. Mol Syst Biol 3:117:1–4

Henkel J, Maurer SM (2009) Parts, property and sharing. Nat Biotechnol 27(12):1095–1098

Khalil AS, Collins JJ (2010) Synthetic biology: applications come of age. Nat Rev Genet 11(5):367–379. doi:10.1038/nrg2775

Kockaya G (2010) What are the Top most costly diseases for USA? The alignment of burden of illness with prevention and screening expenditures. Health 02(10):1174–1178. doi:10.4236/health.2010.210172

Medema MH, Breitling R, Bovenberg R, Takano E (2011) Exploiting plug-and-play synthetic biology for drug discovery and production in microorganisms. Nat Rev Micro 9(2):131–137. doi:10.1038/nrmicro2478

Munos B (2009) Lessons from 60 years of pharmaceutical innovation. Nat Rev Drug Discov 8(12):959–968. doi:10.1038/nrd2961

Murray CJL, Lopez AD, Mathers CD, Ezzati M, Jamison DT (2006) Measuring the global burden of disease and risk factors, 1990–2001. In: Lopez AD, Mathers CD, Ezzati M, et al., editors. Global Burden of Disease and Risk Factors. Washington (DC): World Bank; 2006. Chapter 1. Available from: http://www.ncbi.nlm.nih.gov/books/NBK11817/

Pammolli F, Magazzini L, Riccaboni M (2011) The productivity crisis in pharmaceutical R&D. Nat Rev Drug Discov 10(6):428–438. doi:10.1038/nrd3405

Rai A, Boyle J (2007) Synthetic biology: caught between property rights, the public domain, and the commons. PLoS Biol 5(3):e58. doi:10.1371/journal.pbio.0050058

BCC Research (2011) Synthetic biology: emerging global markets. http://www.bccresearch.com/market-research/biotechnology/global-synthetic-biology-markets-bio066b.html

Ruder WC, Lu T, Collins JJ (2011) Synthetic biology moving into the clinic. Science 333(6047):1248–1252. doi:10.1126/science.1206843

Savile CK, Janey JM, Mundorff EC, Moore JC, Tam S, Jarvis WR, Colbeck JC, Krebber A, Fleitz FJ, Brands J, Devine PN, Huisman GW, Hughes GJ (2010) Biocatalytic asymmetric synthesis of chiral amines from ketones applied to sitagliptin manufacture. Science 329(5989):305–309. doi:10.1126/science.1188934

Scannell JW, Blanckley A, Boldon H, Warrington B (2012) Diagnosing the decline in pharmaceutical R&D efficiency. Nat Rev Drug Discov 11:191–200

Singh R (2011a) Facts, growth, and opportunities in industrial biotechnology. Org Process Res Dev 15(1):175–179. doi:10.1021/op100312a

Singh R (2011b) Better living through science: biotech, food and the future. http://www.germaninnovation.org/shared/content/documents/Presentation_Singh.pdf

Synthetic Biology Project (2012) Inventory of synthetic biology products – existing and possible. Draft. http://www.synbioproject.org/process/assets/files/6631/_draft/synbio_applications_wwics.pdf. Accessed 01 Jan 2013

Synthetic Biology Project Maps Inventory (2012) Mapping the emerging synthetic biology landscape. http://www.synbioproject.org/library/inventories/map/. Accessed 01 Jan 2013

Transparency Market Research.com (2012) Synthetic biology market. Global industry analysis, size, growth, share and forecast, 2012–2018. http://www.transparencymarketresearch.com/synthetic-biology-market.html

United Nations (1997) Demographic yearbook – historical supplement. Expectation of life at specified ages for each sex: 1948–1997 (Table 9b), United Nations DYB-CD, Sales No.: E/F.99.XIII.12, United Nations Publications New York, Geneva http://unstats.un.org/unsd/demographic/products/dyb/dybhist.htm. Accessed 01 Jan 2013

United Nations (2012) 2011 Demographic yearbook. Department of Economic and Social Affairs, United Nations, New York. https://unstats.un.org/unsd/demographic/products/dyb/dybsets/2011.pdf. Accessed 01 Jan 2013

U.S. Environmental Protection Agency (2010) Greener reaction conditions award. http://www.epa.gov/greenchemistry/pubs/pgcc/winners/grca10.html. Accessed 01 Jan 2013

Van Zimmeren E (2009) Clearinghouse mechanisms in genetic diagnostics: conceptual framework. In: Van Overwalle G (ed) Gene patents and collaborative licensing models. Cambridge University Press, Cambridge, pp 63–119

Verbeure B (2009) Patent pooling for gene-based diagnostic testing: conceptual framework. In: Van Overwalle G (ed) Gene patents and collaborative licensing models. Cambridge University Press, Cambridge, pp 3–32

Weber W, Fussenegger M (2009) The impact of synthetic biology on drug discovery. Drug Discov Today 14(19–20):956–963. doi:10.1016/j.drudis.2009.06.010

Weber W, Fussenegger M (2011) Emerging biomedical applications of synthetic biology. Nat Rev Genet. doi:10.1038/nrg3094

WHO (1946) Preamble to the Constitution of the World Health Organization as adopted by the International Health Conference, p. 16. Official Records of the World Health Organization No. 2, Summary Report on Proceedings Minutes and Final Acts of the International Health Conference held in New York from 19 June to 22 July 1946. http://whqlibdoc.who.int/hist/official_records/2e.pdf. Accessed 16 Jun 2014

WHO (2008) The global burden of disease: 2004 update. GBD 2004 summary tables. http://www.who.int/healthinfo/global_burden_disease/DALY10%25202004.xls. Accessed 02 Jan 2013

WHO (2009) Global health observatory. Life expectancy at birth. http://www.who.int/gho/mortality_burden_disease/life_tables/situation_trends_text/en/index.html

Zoler ML (2011) Neuropsychiatric disorders dominate disease burden in Europe. From the annual congress of the European College of Neuropsycho-Pharmacology. http://www.internalmedicinenews.com/specialty-focus/mental-health/single-article-page/neuropsychiatric-disorders-dominate-disease-burden-in-europe.html. Accessed 31 Dec 2012

Chapter 3
Synthetic Biology and Global Health in the Age of Intellectual Property

Henk van den Belt

Abstract Although synthetic biology (SB) conjures up a future cornucopia of new medicines and other health applications, the antimalarial drug artemisinin is still one of the few concrete illustrations to substantiate this promise. As SB's favorite poster child, it is atypical because it exemplifies a rather unusual mixture of lavish philanthropy and ad hoc institutional arrangements. A more probing analysis of the moral issues that SB and its medical applications are likely to raise, especially from the angle of global justice, has to look beyond the special circumstances of this particular case. The current international situation is characterized by a confrontation between a still dominant trend to strengthen and expand patents and other intellectual property rights (the IP frame) and an emerging movement to ensure access to knowledge and information (the A2K frame). The contrasting approaches of Craig Venter's model of proprietary science and the 'open-source' model of the BioBricks school show that SB is located right at heart of this major contest. The eventual outcome of this legal, political and scientific contest will also be decisive for whether or not developing countries and the world's poor are to remain at the receiving end of decisions taken by western companies and philanthropists or can rely more on their own initiatives to improve their health situation.

Keywords Artemisinin • Gene patents • Co-evolution • Open source • Commodification • Access to knowledge • Global justice

H. van den Belt
Department of Social Sciences, Wageningen University,
Hollandseweg 1, Wageningen, 6706 KN, The Netherlands
e-mail: henk.vandenbelt@wur.nl

I. de Miguel Beriain and C.M. Romeo Casabona (eds.), *Synbio and Human Health: A Challenge to the Current IP Framework?*, DOI 10.1007/978-94-017-9196-0_3,

3.1 Introduction: Some Awkward Questions Raised By a Poster Child

The antimalarial drug artemisinin is the showpiece most often cited to prove the great potential of synthetic biology (SB), illustrating the enticing prospect of new medicines, biofuels and a plethora of other useful products that this revolutionary undertaking "to make biology easy to engineer" holds out to humankind. The ETC Group, a well-known technology watchdog, called it the "poster child" of the new field and compared it with Golden Rice in agricultural biotechnology (ETC Group 2007, 52). The "Artemisinin Project", as the main protagonists themselves declared, "hopes to show that the power of biotechnology can be harnessed to provide solutions to global health problems" (Hale et al. 2007, 198). "By leveraging the promise of synthetic biology" the partners involved in this project "seek to dramatically reduce the cost of antimalarials for the people who most need them" (Institute for One World Health, press release April 12, 2006). A poster child application will of course not be representative of the regular accomplishments that an emerging technological field can be expected to offer, precisely because it is strategically used to raise money and recruit social and political support for the new domain of investment. Still it might be worthwhile to delve more deeply into the details of this particular case to learn some general lessons about the ethical issues that are likely to be raised by the medical and pharmaceutical applications of SB with regard to patenting and property. Even if the example may be atypical in several respects, artemisinin is one of the few concrete instances to which SB can point until now to substantiate its promise of success.

It all started around 2000 with the research of Jay Keasling and his team at the University of California at Berkeley. They were looking for ways to reengineer microbes into tiny cell factories for the synthetic production of organic compounds belonging to the class of isoprenoids, which includes many vegetable scents and flavors. Artemisinin only became the target for the research effort after a graduate student found out by chance that amorphadiene (a chemical precursor of artemisinin) also belongs to the isoprenoids. As the point of the research was simply to provide "proof of principle" for the efficacy of the new techniques of metabolic engineering, Keasling and his co-workers decided they could just as well focus their efforts on this particular substance of medical importance (Specter 2009). At the time artemisinin, the main ingredient of combination therapies against malaria, could only be obtained from sweet wormwood (*Artemisia annua*), a plant grown by farmers in Asia and Africa. Its supply, however, fell far short of what was required to meet world demand at prices that would be affordable to the hundreds of millions of poor people who needed the antimalarial treatments. A new source of supply from microbial cell factories, so it was thought, could overcome these problems and make the medicine accessible to the world's poor.

In 2003 Keasling and his team reached a first milestone in their project when they succeeded in building entirely new metabolic pathways for the production of amorphadiene and other isoprenoids into *E. coli* bacteria. The group later switched to strains of yeast (*S. cerevisiae*), which could be better reengineered for higher yields. With his first successes in hand, Keasling looked for financial support from the business world to further develop his artemisinin project. When he could not find a corporate sponsor, he turned to the Bill and Melinda Gates Foundation, a philanthropic organization that was active in the field of global health and had a special interest in malaria (Hamm 2009).

The Gates Foundation was willing to fund what was to be called the Artemisinin Project and made arrangements among various parties to expedite its progress. In 2004 the Foundation provided a grant of US$42.6 million to the San Francisco-based Institute of One World Health (IOWH), the first non-profit pharmaceutical company in the USA, and established a three-way partnership that also included UC Berkeley and Amyris Biotechnologies, a spin-off biotech startup founded by Keasling and his co-workers. UC Berkeley would issue a royalty-free license to both the IOWH and Amyris to develop the technology (a patent on the biosynthesis of amorphadiene, US7192751, was issued on 20 March 2007 and assigned to the Regents of the University of California). In exchange, Amyris would produce the drugs at cost, while IOWH would clear regulatory hurdles and oversee commercial development (IOWH press release, December 14, 2004). At the end of 2005 Keasling and his team met the next technical milestone by proving that the biosynthetic method of producing amorphadiene in reengineered yeast strains can be achieved at the laboratory scale; the task remaining was largely for Amyris to increase yields several hundred fold and scale up the process to an industrial level. In 2008 IOWH decided to team up with the French pharmaceutical company Sanofi-aventis for the commercial development of artemisinin. Market introduction is expected to occur in 2013.

This public-private partnership of the Artimisinin Project appears to be a perfect example of what Bill Gates called "creative capitalism" in his famous speech at the World Economic Forum held in January 2008 in Davos, Switzerland. On that occasion he recognized that "capitalism harnesses self-interest in a helpful and sustainable way, *but only on behalf of those who can pay*" (Gates 2008; my italics). The challenge was to design a system where market incentives would drive companies and scientists to do more for the poor: "I like to call this idea creative capitalism, an approach where governments, businesses, and nonprofits work together to stretch the reach of market forces so that more people can make a profit, or gain recognition, doing work that eases the world's inequities" (*ibid.*). Gates was however well aware that the global economic system did not usually work out particularly well for the least advantaged: "The great advances in the world have often aggravated the inequities in the world. The least needy see the most improvement, and the most needy get the least – in particular the billion people who live on less than a dollar a day" (*ibid.*). In this connection Gates also alluded to the egregiously skewed distribution of research effort in global pharmaceutical innovation: "Diseases like malaria that kill over a million people a year get far less attention than drugs to help with baldness" (*ibid.*).

If the dice are loaded so heavily against the world's poor, one might obviously wonder whether the kind of philanthropic interventions initiated by the Gates Foundation are even remotely sufficient to rebalance the system. Granted that companies like Sanofi will probably gain valuable "recognition" through the PR value of the project, would that in itself establish a viable business model that is capable of more widespread use? At the launch of the Artimisinin Project, Keasling opined that "the nonprofit nature of this partnership could be a model for attacking neglected diseases in the developing world" (IOWH press release, December 14, 2004), and in 2007 several participants reiterated that "the partnership is a paradigm of how groups with critical knowledge and skills can pool talents to address a major global health problem" (Hale et al. 2007, 198). Alas, this does not mean that Keasling and Amyris Biotechnologies have themselves embraced this model or paradigm and will now move on to attack the next neglected disease in the developing world. Instead, they will go after much bigger game such as highly lucrative next-generation biofuels in which major corporations have expressed an interest. As journalist Steve Hamm remarks, Amyris will not make a profit on the Artimisinin Project, but nonetheless it has given the company revenue, technology and "a launchpad for a different project – the startup has raised $120 million in venture capital" (Hamm 2009). It is thus returning to business as usual, in which, as Gates so keenly observed, "the least needy see the most improvement, and the most needy get the least". So, it seems, any repetition of the philanthropic model to deal with other neglected diseases would require a generous injection of fresh money from a major charity.

In his Davos speech, Gates was remarkably silent about one essential element linking the innovative efforts of companies to the needs of wealthy markets: patents. These are actually a strategic part of the incentives that help contemporary capitalism harness self-interest for attaining the purposes of "those who can pay" (Gates can hardly be suspected of being oblivious to the role of patents, as his company Microsoft has gained notoriety for its aggressive patenting policy). In the current Age of Intellectual Property, the institutional reach of patents has become extremely broad. Since the US Bayh-Dole Act of 1980, it has also become customary for universities and public sector institutions to take out patents on the results of publicly funded research projects. Patents are often useful in forging strategic partnerships with existing business firms or in founding new spin-off companies by university staff themselves. It may have been somewhat unusual for UC Berkeley to provide a royalty-free license on university intellectual property (Hamm 2009), though in this case the decision has probably been eased by the generosity of the Gates Foundation and the reputational rewards of a poster child application of SB. In general, however, it would be wishful thinking to presume that IP held by universities or university staff is automatically available for grand global health projects.

The Artemisinin Project has come in for some harsh criticism from the ETC Group. This civil-society organization has expressed concern about the livelihoods of the thousands of Asian and African growers of the sweet wormwood plant who might be displaced by the biosynthetic production of (a precursor of) artemisinin in fermentation vats in California (ETC Group 2007). The ETC Group also denied that the shortfall of natural artemisinin production to meet world demand was inevitable and permanent; following an analysis by the Royal Tropical Institute of the Netherlands, they pointed out that the cultivated area could be easily extended to allow production to match demand. However, they warned that the prospect of synthetic artemisinin could itself become a destabilizing factor in the world market. Developments since 2007 have partially born out these assessments (ETC Group 2012). That there is no absolute shortage was clearly brought home by the fact that the year 2007 showed a huge overproduction, resulting in dramatic price drops and lots of farmers abandoning wormwood growing (Van Noorden 2010). Rather than being limited by natural constraints, the supply of plant-derived artemisinin is characterized by severe boom-and-bust cycles. This situation has led to a subtle reformulation of the official goals of the Artemisinin Project. Originally conceived as "a high-technology solution to bring down the cost of treatment to well under a dollar" (IOWH press release, December 14, 2004), the synthetic version of the substance has meanwhile been redefined as "a *complementary*, high-quality source of non-seasonal and affordable artemisinin" (IOWH press release, July 7, 2010; italics mine). As Richard Van Noorden writes, "Although it began as a way to make the drug more cheaply, the mass-produced semi-synthetic will be no cheaper than the plant-derived version – partly because Sanofi-aventis does not want to undercut farmers. Instead, it will be used to smooth out the cycle of boom and bust in crop-based artemisinin supply" (Van Noorden 2010, 673). Whether it will live up to these expectations, only the future can tell.

We can leave the question undecided whether the poor in the developing world will benefit considerably from the future availability of synthetic artemisinin in its newly defined role (I would at least grant it some benefit of the doubt). What the SB poster child so glaringly illustrates by completely ignoring the interests of third-world wormwood farmers, however, is that people in developing countries usually figure merely as passive objects of western charity and philanthropy. Too often they find themselves at the receiving end of decisions taken by companies and agencies headquartered in first-world countries. To escape from this predicament, developing countries arguably need to build some autonomous research capacity of their own. It remains to be seen to what extent the global IP regime allows them to build such capacity, especially in newly emerging technologies like SB.

3.1.1 Imagining an Uncertain Future

The examination of SB's famous poster child in the preceding section has already brought home the lesson that the future is radically uncertain. The focus of Keasling's team on artemisinin was itself more or less the result of chance. We have seen that in the course of just a few years the official goal of the Artemisinin Project had to be redefined as the initial expectations about the potential supply of the plant-derived drug turned out to be erroneous. It is also hard to say whether currently held assumptions about the stabilizing role of synthetic artemisinin and its projected contribution to global health will prove valid. In more narrow technical terms the project has moved ahead very smoothly as crucial milestones were duly met in time, but this amount of success could neither have been securely predicted from the outset. Nor is it a foregone conclusion that the patents that are applied for will actually be granted. It is also not possible to foresee whether the cooperative partnership model adopted in this case will be emulated for other neglected diseases. In similar cases universities or university staff might not be willing to provide royalty-free licenses for the use of their patents. The degree of uncertainty will increase even further if we do not confine ourselves to the examination of a particular case but set out to anticipate the medical applications of SB in general and the IP strategies with which they will be accompanied.

Forecasting then is a rather hazardous exercise, especially if the aim is to predict the future. Any sketch of the likely development of SB in the near and more remote future is speculative, as would be an outline of expected trends in patent law. So an exercise in which these two forecasts or explorations are to be combined, would be doubly speculative. Proponents of SB sometimes admit that the field is still in its infancy and has yet to overcome some major technological challenges. These include the need to improve and accelerate the design cycle and to move beyond microbial systems (on which current work in SB is still mainly focused) towards mammalian systems, especially when the aim is to develop therapeutic applications for human health (Khalil and Collins 2010). But often this sense of appropriate modesty is overridden by more overweening attitudes. Following Craig Venter's rather hubristic statement in 2010 that "we are entering an era limited only by our imagination", SB enthusiasts repeatedly claim that the potential of the new field is limited "only by the imagination of researchers and the number of societal problems and the applications that synthetic biology can resolve" (Khalil and Collins 2010, 377). If this is true, one immediately wonders who will set the research agenda for the field. Why not focus, for example, on medical and pharmaceutical applications that will benefit the poorest two billion of the planet? However, the odds are that the imagination of synthetic biologists will be more selectively determined by the prospect of applications that promise to offer, through patents, the highest payoffs.

International patent law is at present also very much in flux. There are ongoing debates on what types of discoveries or inventions in the life sciences actually are (or should be) patentable and the economic and political pressures on companies and research institutes to either adopt vigorous patenting strategies or alternative, more 'open' policies are shifting.

What then would be the best approach, in the light of the difficulties and pitfalls sketched above, to tackle the legal and moral issues raised by SB and its medical applications with regard to property and patenting? My preferred strategy would be a two-pronged approach.

On the one hand I would like to put contemporary developments in a historical perspective. This provides some immunity against the hypes and exaggerated expectations that inevitably surround a new field like SB. The rise of SB can be seen as a continuation, and provisional culmination, of some longer-term trends that are characteristic of major strands in western science and technology, e.g. the "informatisation" of life since the beginnings of molecular biology or the attempted implementation of the Kant-Vico-Feynman principle "What I cannot create I do not understand", which has previously been followed in organic chemistry (Van den Belt 2009). Another recognized source of inspiration is electrical engineering, from which the key concept of "circuits" has been adopted (Trafton 2011). SB is also a continuation and radicalization of genetic engineering or biotechnology. Thus there is historical continuity as well as discontinuity. That also applies to the development of patent law (or more broadly intellectual property law). It is very important to realize that "the history of intellectual property rights is a history of contestation" (May and Sell 2006), so as to avoid the widely held misconception that IP issues have become controversial only recently.

The other prong of my two-pronged approach would be to give free rein to the moral imagination by proliferating possible scenarios for the future of IP and SB (as was done in a major study commissioned by the European Patent Office, see EPO 2007) and by elaborating institutional re-designs explicitly aimed at the normative goal of global justice (as is done, for example, by Thomas Pogge and other advocates of the Health Impact Fund). In a sense, this is making a virtue out of necessity, as it is openly acknowledged that the future is radically uncertain.

The two prongs of my approach are held together by an historically informed interpretation of the current international situation in IP law as representing a major political contest between two frames, namely the "IP frame" and the "A2K frame" (access-to-knowledge frame) (Kapczynski 2008; Shaver 2009; Krikorian and Kapczynski 2010). The first frame holds that intellectual property rights like patents, copyright and plant breeders' rights are a just reward for those who have expended creative effort in realizing inventions, artistic works and other innovative products and that the prospect of such exclusive rights constitutes an indispensable incentive for future innovative activities. The adherents of this frame also assume that you cannot have too much of a good thing too readily, so that if intellectual property is good, *more* intellectual property is even better. The second frame questions the assumption that exclusive rights are always indispensable for invention and innovation by referring to the contrary experience with free and open-source software in recent decades. It also points to the importance of access to existing knowledge and information as essential inputs for further innovation. Its adherents finally hold that human rights (like the right to health, to adequate food, to education and to participation in cultural life and scientific advancement) should never be subordinated to the protection of IP rights. The first frame has dominated the past three decades, but the second frame is in the ascendant. Within SB, the IP frame is represented by Craig Venter's "chassis school", while the "BioBricks school" exhibits more affinity for the A2K frame.

3.2 Technology-Neutrality of Patents Versus "Co-construction"

The debate on SB and patents is often framed by the prior assumption that the patent system is, or should be, "neutral" with regard to the kind of technologies for which legal protection is being sought. This neutrality is even enshrined in the TRIPS agreement. Article 27.1 states that "… patents shall be available for any inventions, whether products or processes, in all fields of technology, provided that they are new, involve an inventive step and are capable of industrial application". Thus in a recent article on SB and patents, EPO official Berthold Rutz remarked: "One of the reasons for the long-lasting success of the patent system is its *non-discriminatory character*. The same basic patentability criteria apply to all fields of technology: novelty, inventive step and industrial application" (Rutz 2009, S14).

I think the technology-neutrality of the patent system is a myth. There has never been a patent system that is completely or even approximately "technology-neutral", nor can there be such a system. The myth presumes that the three basic requirements can be applied to any newly emerging field of technology in a straightforward and "mechanical" way, without needing much additional interpretation. It also passes over the problem of patentable subject matter.

Article 27.1 of the TRIPS agreement unjustifiably grants the moral high ground to pharmaceutical companies opposing provisions in national patent laws that exclude product patents for drugs, as if "Thou shalt not discriminate!" were the first of the Ten Commandments in patent legislation. In the past, however, many countries (e.g. Germany, Italy, India) have excluded medicines from patenting on the legitimate and respectful grounds that this would serve public health best. What deserves ethical censure is rather that such provisions have been outlawed by the TRIPS agreement. At any rate, patents in the area of health have always been a sensitive issue. Medical doctors usually considered it contrary to their honor and dignity to apply for patents on new therapies and medicines. An editorial comment in the *American Journal of Public Health* stated in 1926: "One of the glories of the medical profession has been that discoveries for the betterment of mankind and the relief of suffering have always been given freely to the public… Patent and proprietary medicines have been and are a stench in the nostrils of the profession" (Editorial 1926). Thus Howard Florey and his team at Oxford University did not file patents on penicillin in 1940–1941 "because patenting was then against ethical medical principles" (Macfarlane 1980, 369). The earlier example of insulin (1920–1921) is only an apparent exception: "… medical men, such as Macleod and Banting, were bound by their profession's code to make all advances in health care freely available to humanity… [I]t would violate a physician's Hippocratic oath to engage in the profiting from a discovery that patenting normally implied" (Bliss 1988, 133). When the University of Toronto nonetheless decided to patent the insulin extract it was only as a purely defensive measure that would stop nobody from making the extract: "In fact the point was to stop anyone from ever being in a position to stop anyone else" (*ibid.*). In others words, the university made an attempt at "copylefting" the patent system. Finally, when Jonas Salk was asked in the 1950s why he hadn't patented his polio vaccine, he is famously reported to have answered: "Can you patent the sun?". (However, his legacy does not prevent the Jonas Salk Foundation today from aggressively patenting as much of their research outcomes as they can, including new vaccines).

If technology-neutrality were really a sacrosanct principle of patent law, it would hardly be defensible and in fact downright inconsistent for the TRIPS agreement to allow Members to exclude diagnostic, therapeutic and surgical methods (Art. 27.3.a) or plants and animals from patentability (Art. 27.3.b) (For plants, Members must provide either protection by patents or an effective *sui generis* system of plant variety protection or any combination thereof.) However, the proponents of plant and animal biotechnology have no reason to complain about "discrimination", as the North American and European patent authorities have granted very special concessions to the holders of patents in this area by allowing them to also claim the transgenic offspring of genetically modified organisms and to extend the protection of patented genes to every organism in which such genes may be found, thus turning "natural" processes of reproduction and multiplication potentially into acts of infringement (as is illustrated by the notorious case of Monsanto versus Percy Schmeiser). Around 1900 the influential German jurist Josef Kohler argued that patents on living, self-reproducing organisms would be absurd because "patent law can govern only human action, it cannot constrain nature in those cases in which nature causes everything or at least the main part" (see the discussion of his views in Van den Belt 2009, 1322–1326). Patent law in western countries has moved a long way from Kohler's common sense.

Against the myth of technology-neutrality we can put the idea of the "co-construction" or "co-evolution" of technology and patent law. In science and technology studies (STS) it is indeed not unusual to conceive of the relationship between science/technology and society (or the social, legal and political order) as one of mutual shaping, thus avoiding the extremes of scientific/technological determinism and social determinism. When a new field of technology emerges, patent law does not provide a list of ready-made criteria by which the technical accomplishments in the new field can be judged as patentable inventions. Instead, the conditions of patentability have first to be worked out and elaborated vis-à-vis the new technology, if only because the notion of "invention" is not strictly and universally defined but open to historically variable interpretation. Thus with the rise of synthetic dye chemistry in the second half of the nineteenth century decisions had to be made about the precise meaning and scope of "a *particular* process" to which the German Patent Act of 1877 had limited the patentability of chemical inventions; or on how high (or rather low) the bar for inventiveness had to be put to allow the patenting of "inventions" routinely produced on a large scale by the new R&D laboratories of the chemical industry (Van den Belt and Rip 1987). As a major stakeholder, the German chemical industry often lobbied vigorously to influence the shaping of patent law (see also Dutfield 2009).

The development of patent law and biotechnology provides another clear example of "co-construction" or "co-evolution". The first question to be answered was if this part of law applied at all to this new area of technology. In the landmark case of *Diamond v. Chakrabarty* a 5-to-4 majority of the US Supreme Court held in 1980 that anything new under the sun that is made by man, whether living or non-living, can in principle be patented. Chief Justice Burger argued on behalf of the majority: "[T]he patentee has produced a new bacterium with markedly different characteristics from any found in nature and one having the potential for significant utility. His discovery is not nature's handiwork, but his own; accordingly it is patentable subject matter under § 101." This verdict occasioned a huge capital influx into the emerging biotech industry in the following years. Together with the Bayh-Dole Act of 1980, which allowed universities to take out patents on the results of federally funded research, it also led to a rapid commercialization of molecular biology. During the 1980s the patentability of living organisms was further extended from bacteria to multi-cellular organisms and to higher plants and animals (cf. the "oncomouse" patent of 1988). Equally important for the biotech industry was that patents on isolated and purified genes and DNA sequences have also been recognized as legally valid. The reasoning behind this view was that a gene is just a chemical compound and that the isolation and purification of a particular DNA sequence from the body turns it in something radically different from its natural state and thus into an invention eligible for patenting.[1] This doctrine would seem to be a rather thin justification – the Australian jurist Luigi Palombi disparagingly calls it the "isolation contrivance" (Palombi 2009, 205–225) – but nonetheless it has provided the legal underpinning for the practice of granting gene patents by the US, European and Japanese patent office for more than two decades (see also Calvert and Joly 2011 for a critical history of gene patenting).[2] By 2005, it was found that some 20 % or one-fifth of human genes had already been captured by US patents (Jensen and Murray 2005). One can therefore imagine that the decision by Judge Robert Sweet on May 29, 2010, in the high-profile case against the patents of Myriad Genetics on the BRCA1 and BRCA2 genes related to breast and ovarian cancer, must have sent shock waves through the entire biotech industry. Judge Sweet dismissed the isolation doctrine as a "lawyer's trick" and declared that human genes constitute unpatentable subject matter (Schwartz and Pollack 2010). The US biotech industry was understandably relieved when a higher court (the Court of Appeals for the Federal Circuit, a specialized patent court that is well-known for its pro-patent stance) reversed this decision in late July 2011, but then the plaintiffs appealed to the Supreme Court. On March 26, 2012, the latter sent the case back to the appeals court for reconsideration, which on August 6, 2012 reaffirmed Myriad's right to patent the "isolated" genes (Reuters 2012). This will probably not be the end of the saga.

From about 1980, modern biotechnology has "co-evolved" not just with patent law, but also with other parts of the social and political order. Indeed, the extension

---

[1] This view is often presented as if it were a logical consequence of the Chakrabarty decision, but Palombi argues that the case for patents on isolated and purified genes would not pass the US Supreme Court's criteria, as such genes do *not* have "markedly different" characteristics from their natural counterparts (Palombi 2009).

[2] In 1988 the European Patent Office, the US Patent and Trademark Office and the Japanese Patent Office issued the following joint statement: "Purified natural products are not regarded under any of the three laws [US; EU; Japan] as products of nature or discoveries because they do not in fact exist in nature in an isolated form. Rather, they are regarded for patent purposes as biologically active substances or chemical compounds and eligible for patenting on the same basis as other chemical compounds" (quoted in Palombi 2009, 179). It may be noted that in Europe the patentability of genes and DNA sequences was only officially established with the passing of the European Directive for the Protection of Biotechnological Inventions in 1998 (European Directive 98/44/EC), so the EPO already ran ahead of the political decision.

of patentable subject matter to include genes and DNA sequences, cultivated cells and tissues and transgenic organisms was itself part of a wider movement of strengthening and extending intellectual property rights (not just patents, but also copyrights and breeders' rights) on national, regional and worldwide scales that fitted well with a neoliberal agenda of privatization, globalization and the reduction of the public sector.[3] In recent years, however, this dominant "IP frame" is increasingly challenged by the "A2K frame" or "access-to-knowledge frame" (Kapczynski 2008).

An interesting corollary of "co-construction" or "co-evolution" between technology and patent law is that it could lead to *path effects* that may in turn give rise to *mismatches* between subsequent technologies and intellectual property regulation. Thus the proliferation of patents covering hundreds of thousands of genes or DNA sequences on the human genome and the genomes of other organisms, a direct outcome of the prior "co-evolution" of classical biotechnology and patent law, might constitute an obstacle for the development and application of new technologies like DNA-microarrays ("gene chips") and whole-genome sequencing. At present the legal situation is still highly uncertain: "Promising new methods for full-genome analysis might or might not face patent infringement liability" (Cook-Deegan 2011, 874; for a more skeptical assessment, see Holman 2012). SB will also have to confront the legal legacy of the biotech gold rush.

3.3 The Contest Within Synthetic Biology: The A2K Frame Versus the IP Frame

3.3.1 The BioBricks Approach: An Ethos of Sharing

It is not difficult to understand why patents could be a major threat to the realization of that particular strand of SB that aims at the construction of complex biological systems on the basis of well-defined standard parts, i.e. genetic sequences with known functions that can be used as building blocks in biological syntheses. Construction of one biological system may easily require hundreds or even more than 1,000 different components. If only a small percentage of the needed parts were encumbered with patents (or other IP constraints), it could become prohibitively costly to obtain "freedom to operate" to assemble the entire system. A patent thicket would doom the prospects of this strand of SB: "One roadblock to synbio's

[3] Amy Kapczynski cites William Landes and Richard Posner, who point to the "free-market ideology" that came to prominence in the late 1970s and argue that "it was natural for free-market ideologists to favor an expansion of intellectual property rights" (Landes and Posner, quoted in Kapczynski 2008, 842). However, a longer historical perspective should warn us against the "naturalness" of a close relation between economic liberalism and a pro-IP stance. In the mid-nineteenth century the adherents of Free Trade in Europe were generally *against* patents, which they saw as obsolete "privileges" of the *Ancien Régime* and as impediments of free competition.

future is the messed-up patent environment in biotech, where every tiny protein pathway and gene sequence has an owner wanting to get paid … [U]nless basic components are made freely available it will be too expensive to make anything useful or complex" (Herper 2006).

Deeply concerned that their fledgling field could be smothered already in its cradle, several SB enthusiasts from MIT, Harvard and the University of California have set up the BioBricks Foundation, which administers the Registry of Standard Biological Parts, a steadily growing online collection of parts on which SB practitioners (including the undergraduate students participating in the immensely popular annual iGEM [international Genetically Engineered Machines] competitions) can draw at will to engineer new life forms and to which they can contribute their own components. From the outset leaders of the field like Drew Endy and Tom Knight have also been groping for suitable legal instruments to ensure that BioBrick™ standard biological parts remain freely available to the SB community. They have been inspired by the open source movement in software development, which uses copyright law in a creative way by devising licenses like the GPL or General Public License ("copyleft") to ensure that newly written software code is not privately appropriated but remains free to use for all. The problem for SB is that legal devices like the GPL that are based on copyright law cannot easily be transferred to the biological field. Due to its "viral" effect a GPL-like license might also be considered too strong in that it would prevent the patenting of any final products such as pharmaceuticals that could be made by SB methods. It is all very well to keep the basic tools and building blocks freely available to the research community, but some synthetic biologists argue that such a viral effect would be undesirable as patents are still a cornerstone in our current system of pharmaceutical innovation.

The legal experts Arti Rai and James Boyle advised the SB community to follow the example of the (public leg of the) Human Genome Project and make new building blocks publicly available as soon as possible: "Placing parts into the public domain not only makes parts unpatentable, but it undermines the possibility of patents on trivial improvements" (Rai and Boyle 2007, 392). This strategy does not provide a watertight guarantee, however, that such parts will be preserved for the public domain or the commons. It is not certain either whether the parts that are already in the Registry are unencumbered by any patent rights. On a workshop held in Berkeley on March 31, 2006, Drew Endy estimated or rather speculated that perhaps one-fifth of Biobricks parts were patented. So it is not unthinkable that in future when SB yields commercially interesting applications in the fields of health, energy or bioremediation, "patent trolls" claiming intellectual ownership of some of the used parts may suddenly turn up to assert their rights. In October 2009 the so-called BioBrick™ Public Agreement (BPA) was proposed as a new legal framework for regulating the rights and duties of the contributors and users of the parts collection. Basically, the Agreement amounts to "an irrevocable promise not to assert any property rights held by the Contributor over Users of the contributed Materials" (http://bbf.openwetware.org/BPA). The BPA is a scalable contract actually made up of two separate agreements, the Contributor Agreement and the User Agreement. Whereas the former binds the contributor of BioBrick parts not to assert IP rights over these parts against any user who has signed the agreement, the latter obliges the user to provide attribution to the contributor, where requested, and to respect biological safety practices and applicable laws. The BPA has no viral effect, so it does not prevent users employing parts from the collection to patent any final products they may develop from these starting materials. One might question whether this proposed arrangement provides sufficient incentives for potential contributors to donate their materials to the Registry (Henkel and Maurer 2009, 1097).

There is no doubt that the synthetic biologists who established the BioBricks Foundation are strongly committed to open-source principles and an ethos of sharing, but they too are forced to accommodate to the realities of an IP-dominated world. Their attempt to carve out a little niche of a commons comprising the building blocks and basic tools of their trade thus continues to rest on a fragile legal base. Another example of the vulnerability of open-source principles in an Age of Intellectual Property is provided by BIOFAB, a production facility in Berkeley for the creation, standardization and characterization of genetic control parts that was established in December 2009 with funding from the National Science Foundation (NSF), Lawrence Berkeley National Laboratory (LBNL) and the BioBricks Foundation. There is a clear tension between BIOFAB's commitment to open-source principles, which it justifies by invoking its mandate to lay the foundation for SB, and the commercial orientations of some of the sponsors and industrial partners. Indeed, for the NSF the long-term strategic aims of its special ERC (Engineering Research Centers) funding program "include cultivating an ethos of commercial application throughout US academic communities" (Bennett 2011, 11). This "ethos" would normally encourage patenting research findings rather than placing them in the public domain. By 2011, the principal sponsoring organizations had not yet decided whether BIOFAB would be allowed to use the BPA (BioBrick™ Public Agreement) or an equivalent legal instrument to place its work in the public domain (ibid., 19).

3.3.2 Craig Venter's Model of Proprietary Science

The BioBricks approach is not the only strand in SB. There is also the "chassis school" represented by Craig Venter and his team. Their favored procedure is to assemble a "minimal genome" (i.e. a microbial genome stripped of all dispensable genes) from synthesized DNA, transplant it into a recipient cell whose own genome has been removed, and use the artificial creature thus obtained as a "chassis" upon which all kinds of economically useful genes can be mounted. On 31 May 2007 the US Patent and Trademark Office caused a stir when it published the patent application that the J. Craig Venter Institute had filed in October 2006 on a new artificial life form called Mycoplasma laboratorium (US Patent Application 20070122826, filed 12 October 2006). The announcement was somewhat premature, because the first artificial creature was only to see the light of day almost 3 years later, on 29 March 2010. However, the claims of the first patent application, to which other applications would follow, were already quite sweeping. They are formulated successively as of increasingly wider scope. Thus the set of 381 essential genes making up a "minimal bacterial genome" is being claimed (claim 1); the synthetic organism that can be made from these genes; any variant of the organism that can produce ethanol or hydrogen (claim 20); any scientific method for assessing the functions of genes by inserting those genes into the synthetic organism (claim 22); and any digital version of the synthetic organism's genome (claim 19). Among the intended applications the creation of synthetic organisms for the production of biofuels like ethanol and hydrogen is particularly emphasized. At present, such applications may sound futuristic, but it seems that Venter wants to signal to the general public that his enterprises (consisting not only of the nonprofit J. Craig Venter Institute but also of the private company Synthetic Genomics, Inc.; patent rights will all be assigned to the latter) intend to play a key role in solving the urgent problems of energy supply and climate change. In his Richard Dimbleby Lecture delivered on 4 December 2007 on BBC One, he went so far as to suggest that SB may save the world and effectively constitute humanity's last chance for survival (Venter 2007).

Contrary to the BioBricks school, which attempts to establish a practice of sharing inspired by open-source models in software development, Venter continues the strategy of aggressive patenting of classical biotechnology with a vengeance. The two strands of SB thus illustrate the tension between the old "IP frame" and the new "A2K frame" (Kapczynski 2008).

The suite of patents that the J. Craig Venter Institute subsequently filed also have very broad claims. John Sulston, Venter's old rival in the race to sequence the human genome, has sounded the alarm on the extremely wide scope of the claims in the patent applications, suggesting that they might, if granted, give Venter's enterprise a monopoly on a wide range of techniques (Chan and Sulston 2010). James Boyle also warned that Venter might become "a monopolist over the code of life" and that the efforts of the BioBricks community to create an open source collection of standard biological parts might be endangered by "the threat of overbroad patents on foundational technologies" (Boyle 2010).

Let us assume, for the sake of the argument, that the plans of Venter's company Synthetic Genomics Inc. to develop highly advanced "fourth-generation" biofuels using carbon dioxide as feedstock will indeed come true and that the new techniques as a matter of course will be heavily protected by patents. This would conjure up the morally problematic scenario in which technological solutions that might be humanity's last hope for survival (as Venter himself suggested in his lecture before the BBC) are locked up in patents that serve to make them inaccessible to any but the most wealthy users. The company will have to tell its impecunious non-clients: "Sorry, you won't be saved, if you are not willing to pay the price of your survival!". But in this case, unlike the users of high-priced patented medicines that are effectively denied to poor patients, the wealthy users of expensive high-tech biofuels won't be saved either. Climate change will not be sufficiently mitigated if only the wealthy inhabitants of the earth use "climate-neutral" energy.

Important medical applications of Venter's SB approach are expected in the area of vaccine development (Glass 2011). In October 2010 his institute and his company set up a new venture, Synthethic Genomics Vaccines Inc. (SGVI), in collaboration with the Swiss pharmaceutical company Novartis, to develop next-generation vaccines. The J. Craig Venter Institute will bring its synthetic genomic research expertise to this venture, "coupled with the intellectual property and business acumen of SGI [Synthetic Genomics Inc.]" (press release October 7, 2010). The direct aim of the venture is to accelerate the production of the influenza seed strains required for vaccine manufacturing, so that the time needed to start vaccine production can be cut short by 2 months (with the so-called swine flu "pandemic" of 2009 serious vaccine production only got started after the peak of the "pandemic" was over). This is a respectable aim, of course (though one might question whether the world might be "prepared" in time if a pandemic outbreak of the rapidity and seriousness of the Spanish flu of 1918 would strike again, even with a time saving of 2 months). There is no doubt, however, that the new venture will pursue a strategy of aggressive patenting. Yet the area of vaccine development for influenza epidemics is precisely an area where intellectual property rights clash with global public health needs (Andrews and Shackelton 2008). Under the rules of the WHO countries affected by flu outbreaks are expected to send samples of viruses to the WHO's collaborating research centers and laboratories, which are all located in the USA, Europe or Japan. These laboratories cooperate with western pharmaceutical companies that take out patents on genetic sequences and vaccines derived from these virus samples (for an expert report on patentability issues related to viruses, see WIPO 2007). Developing countries contributing samples to the WHO are often unpleasantly surprised when they subsequently find out that they cannot afford the patented vaccines that are developed from these materials. No wonder then that in 2007, during the avian flu epidemic, Indonesia refused to further share its H5N1 virus samples if it would not get access to affordable vaccines (Fidler 2008; Hammond 2009). This is a very serious threat as worldwide sharing of virus samples is a vital requirement for the effective working of WHO's Global Influenza Surveillance Network. Within the WHO parties are still negotiating about access and benefit-sharing arrangements for virus samples and vaccines.

As the above examples of biofuels and vaccines illustrate, we have to consider patent issues in the broader context of sustainable development and global health and global justice. Moreover, the traditional justification of intellectual property rights as indispensable incentives for innovation is increasingly challenged as alternative models have emerged in the wake of the open-source movement. Chan and Sulston put the controversy over Venter's patents in the perspective of an epochal confrontation between the IP frame and the A2K frame: "The conflict between private interests in science, protected by patents and cloaked in secrecy, and open access research remains one of the most contentious issues in modern science and affects us all" (Chan and Sulston 2010, 1316; italics mine).

3.3.3 Commodification, Property and Intellectual Property

Jane Calvert has moved the "co-construction" thesis one big step further by arguing, somewhat speculatively, that the requirements of intellectual property law may in their turn also influence the very content of science (Calvert 2008, 2010). She tentatively propounds the bold thesis that SB is following a reductionist engineering approach to biology precisely, or at least partly, with the preconceived aim of making biological systems or parts of biological systems better conform to the characteristics of fungible "commodities", that is, "things" or objects of property that can be exchanged on the market. This aim is promoted by making biological parts discrete and interchangeable, by ensuring modularity, and by realizing reliable and predictable performance of the assembled systems: "In forcing biology into the mould of engineering, by developing discrete and substitutable parts, synthetic biology is simultaneously making biology better fit intellectual property regimes. This is no coincidence, because patent law developed in the context of industrial manufacturing ... It is also consistent with the direction of biotechnology more generally, which can be seen as 'relentlessly pursuing the program of making every element of the world programmable or susceptible to engineering'..." (Calvert 2008, 392–93; quoting Pottage 2007, 340).

There is an obvious objection against this sweeping thesis, which incidentally has not escaped Calvert's notice. How about the synthetic biologists of the BioBricks school who are enthusiastically creating a commons of standard biological parts? Aren't they precisely motivated to keep patents at bay as much as they can, rather than trying to lock up their materials and tools in exclusive property rights? Calvert recognizes that the BioBricks program with its stress on modularity and the use of interchangeable parts makes the biological components more similar to software code: "One advantage of modularity is that several different researchers can work on different parts simultaneously, meaning that the field can develop faster. In this way, modularity is well-suited to open source principles, and many synthetic biologists are ideologically committed to open source, to such an extent that the aspiration to make their work open source is a guiding principle of the field" (Calvert 2010; italics mine). In an earlier publication, however, she argued that open source itself depends on the existence of prior property rights, as in the case of free software where the GPL license is based on copyright: "Rather than being a substitute for intellectual property, open source is perhaps more correctly conceived of as a mosaic of private property [ref. omitted]. For this reason appropriation is just as important in open source as it is in more conventional property rights [ref. omitted]" (Calvert 2008, 392).[4] Since the BioBricks Foundation, after much discussion, opted in October 2009 for a contract-based solution (the BPA) rather than an IP-based licensing agreement, it would seem that this principled argument has lost plausibility as far as the biological field is concerned. One might even dispute the appropriateness of the "open-source" label in so far as the free availability of the online

[4] Amy Kapczynski makes a similar point: "The GPL, of course, also necessarily relies on copyright law for its effects, and it is now frequently pointed out that in this sense, its licensing scheme depends upon copyright law" (Kapczynski 2008, 877). For her, however, this is an illustration of what she calls "law's gravitational pull" and of the framing effect of the dominant IP frame on the adherents of the A2K frame. One is also reminded of the rather hilarious fact that the founder of the free software movement, Richard Stallman, was alarmed by the proposal of the Swedish Pirate Party to limit the copyright term to 5 years only, as this would also undermine free software (Stallman 2009).

BioBricks collection is not assured through legal instruments that rely on IP law (see also McLennan 2012).

Another critical point is Calvert's assumption that so-called "intellectual property rights" (here used as an umbrella term for patents, copyrights, trademarks, breeders' rights and the like) can indeed be considered a proper subset of property rights. Today this is almost a universally held assumption. The meaning of the term "commodities" in the contexts of IP law and of (ordinary) property law is however quite different. In the economic world of Adam Smith and Karl Marx, "commodities" were first and foremost material goods possessing both use-value and exchange-value that could literally change hands on the market, or in other words, objects of real, tangible property (for Marx, "labour-power" was already a very special and exceptional "commodity"; it took a real tour de force to fit that notion into the framework of political economy). It has always been extremely difficult to see what the exact "object" is that is protected by an intellectual property right – such as a literary "work" in copyright law, or an "invention" in patent law. So much is clear that a "work" may not be identified with a particular copy of a book and an "invention" may not be identified with the concrete technical "embodiment" of the inventive idea. The "objects" of IP rights are rather to be seen as "abstract objects" (Drahos 1996). This would make them very spooky "commodities" indeed. In fact, they only become tradable "commodities" of sorts thanks to the granting of exclusive rights, that is, rights of exclusion – and not the other way around, i.e., they do not have to be "commodities" (in whatever sense) to fulfill the requirements of copyright or patent law.

The term "intellectual property" has only come into general use after 1970. The fact that a variety of disparate rights have been successfully lumped together under this general heading is itself a sign of the "propertization" of IP rights (Lemley 2005). The uncritical, taken-for-granted use of the expression "intellectual property" has also contributed to the rise of the "IP frame" since about 1980 due to its powerful framing effects (Kapczynski 2008, 842 ff). In earlier times, the expression was used much more sporadically and not always with the same meanings that are nowadays attached to it. In Robert Merton's sociology of science, for instance, intellectual property rights primarily refer to the recognition and esteem, or academic "credit", which are due to scientific researchers who have made important discoveries, and surely not to any economic exploitation rights with regard to these discoveries (for a more extensive discussion, see Van den Belt 2010).

The question whether patents, copyright and other exclusive rights such as plant breeders' rights are properly treated as a special subset of property is more than a terminological issue. During the patent controversy of the nineteenth century, at the heyday of economic liberalism, the very idea of intellectual property encountered massive resistance among lawyers and economists. The dominant view was then that property in the ordinary sense of the word is based on the possibility of exclusive possession and therefore only applies to material objects; thus there could be no property in ideas (Machlupand Penrose 1950, 12; May and Sell 2006, 17–25). The entry "intellectual property" (geistigesEigenthum) in a German dictionary of economics from 1866 simply read: "Property in ideas, once published, is an insoluble contradiction" (quoted in Machlup and Penrose 1950, 12 note 40). It is also significant that when in 1881 the Dutch minister of justice, Anthony Modderman, introduced a new bill for the regulation of copyright (or authors' right) in parliament, he defended his draft by explicitly rejecting the very notion of "intellectual property rights" (Auteurswet 2006, 59). This historical contrast with nineteenth-century views brings the contemporary "propertization" of IP rights into sharp relief. A different terminology implies a different framing. By refusing to use the expression "intellectual property", our nineteenth-century grandfathers denied patents the respectable dignity of ordinary property rights and reduced them to the status of state-granted privileges. They definitely knew "what's in a name" (Machlup and Penrose 1950, 16).

3.4 Patents, Health, and Global Justice

It is still too early to discuss the potential medical applications of SB and the ethical and legal questions they would raise with regard to patenting in concrete detail. However, an intense international debate is already going on about the ethical implications of patents in the medical area in terms of the human right to health, access to essential medicines and global justice. As the discussion on the ethical aspects of medical SB applications is likely to be placed into this wider debate, it may be useful to sketch the main outlines of this debate in this section of the chapter.

It was the worldwide HIV/AIDS crisis that raised widespread awareness about the morally problematic character of drug patents, especially when western pharmaceutical companies were at first emboldened by the TRIPS Agreement of 1995 to assert their enhanced IP rights with much more vigor than before. A temporary (20-year-long) monopoly on a new drug that a patent affords may help a pharmaceutical company to recoup its investments in research and development. The other side of the coin is that millions and millions of poor patients, especially in sub-Saharan Africa, are doomed to die prematurely while the patented medicines that could save their lives or at least alleviate their suffering are beyond their reach due to high monopoly prices (Forman 2007).

As any economics textbook explains, a monopoly will lead to a static inefficiency or welfare loss that is known as a "deadweight loss". Because the monopoly price is so much higher than the marginal cost price, a patent monopoly on a drug will prevent transactions with all those potential users who are able and willing to pay more than the marginal cost but not the full monopoly price of the patented drug.[5] In the case of patents for essential, life-saving medicines, this "market failure" leads to morally unacceptable situations.

[5]Grootendorst (2009) cites quantitative calculations that indicate that the dead-weight loss in the US pharma market may be no less than 60 % of sales revenues, while other investigations show that the relative size of the dead-weight loss in developing countries might even be much higher. It is clear that, simply in economic terms, enormous amounts are involved.

Since the turn of the century the situation with regard to HIV/AIDS has considerably improved, as a consequence of the heavy moral pressure exerted by NGOs like Oxfam and Médecins Sans Frontières on pharmaceutical companies to lower drug prices, the increased credibility of the threat of compulsory licensing in the wake of the Doha Declaration of 2001, and increased competition from generic manufacturers. In general, prices for HIV/AIDS medicines in developing countries have dropped quite drastically in the last decade.

Although NGOs hold that what has been achieved until now is not nearly enough, others might have doubts about whether continuing to put pressure on companies to lower their prices still further until they come close to the level of marginal costs is the right way to proceed in the search for solutions to global health problems. Pharmaceutical companies wonder why they are singled out for special treatment to contribute to the solution of a problem that they did not create. They also point out that it is incorrect to look at the prices of patented medicines only from a static point of view. After all, patents are temporary monopolies that are precisely intended as incentives to stimulate the search for new medicines. No patents, no innovation. Higher prices in the present (until the competition of generics after the expiration of the patent brings them down) are simply the "price" we all have to pay to enjoy the fruits of progress. A substantial erosion of price margins might well endanger pharmaceutical innovation. Finally, a strategy of differential pricing (i.e. charging low prices in poor countries and high prices in wealthy countries) is also not sustainable, as the low-priced medicines will easily find their way to high-income countries through smuggling.

The German philosopher Thomas Pogge, who has thought long and hard about the working of the international patent system from the perspective of global justice, agrees that one should not consider the problem exclusively from the point of view of static efficiency but also take into account the dynamic role of the patent system to foster innovation (Pogge 2005). However, one cannot simply trade off dynamic efficiency (innovation) against static inefficiency (lack of access to existing medicines). Pogge insists that access to essential medicines is a human right that is to be secured by a just international system. This human right cannot be sacrificed on the altar of pharmaceutical innovation. Even more, when looked at from a dynamic perspective, the international patent system does not meet the requirements of global justice either: it generates innovations, indeed, but it does not generate the right kind of innovations. As financial incentives, patents operate by orienting research towards the needs of the wealthy and the affluent, that is, those who exercise effective demand backed up by purchasing power, and not towards the needs of the poor and needy who are unable to do so. The well-known "10/90 gap" illustrates this defect: "Only 10 % of global health research is devoted to conditions that account for 90 % of the global disease burden" (Drugs for Neglected Diseases Working Group 2001, 10). There are therefore many "neglected" diseases, especially in the Tropics, which fail to receive adequate attention from the international research community. We have seen above that Bill Gates in his speech at the 2008 World Economic Forum in Davos also alluded to the gross imbalance in the global research effort. He saw no reason, however, to question the role of patents in this connection.

Pogge concludes that any proposal for a re-design of the international patent system in the field of medicines has to solve two problems simultaneously: (a) the access problem (cf. deadweight loss) and (b) the availability problem (cf. the 10/90 gap). He has proposed his own institutional solution for dealing with these two problems, the so-called Health Impact Fund, which has been further elaborated with the help of others (see Hollis and Pogge 2008; Singer and Schroeder 2010). Whatever one thinks of the merits of Pogge's reform proposal, he certainly deserves credit for bringing home so clearly that these twin problems define a major part of the task-set for any attempt at institutional re-design.

The idea is that the Health Impact Fund, an international public fund based on contributions from developed countries, should be established to create the possibility of rewarding pharmaceutical companies for developing essential medicines, the size of their reward being proportional to the impact of their invention on the global disease burden. In essence, the scheme means that companies are offered a choice. Once they have taken out a patent for a new drug, they can either attempt to earn money on it in the usual way by exploiting the monopoly and setting prices that affluent markets can bear, or they can choose the option of registering with the Fund and being rewarded according to a formula that is geared to the health impact of the new drug (measured in terms of QALYs, i.e. the number of quality-adjusted life years saved worldwide). In the latter case the drug will have to be made available at an administered price that is set by the Health Impact Fund to reflect average manufacturing and distribution cost. In return the registrant will receive, after market approval of the new medicine, annual reimbursements from the Fund that are proportional to the global health impact of the drug for a period of 10 years. After this period the medicine will be freely available for generic producers. Setting an administered price at roughly the level of average manufacturing and distribution cost will ensure that the problem of access is also addressed, at least for drugs registered with the Fund. (For a detailed exposition of the whole scheme, see Hollis and Pogge 2008).

Several commentators have questioned the political and practical feasibility of the Health Impact Fund. One critical issue is funding. The whole initiative needs initially some 6 billion dollars from governments or other contributors to take off. Will such funds really be forthcoming and can pharmaceutical companies base their long-term R&D decisions with any confidence on government pledges to provide funds over a longer period of time? "Providing public funds to drug companies is unlikely to be politically popular: competing demands will always seem more urgent and desirable" (Buchanan et al. 2009, 21). It has also been pointed out that the measurement procedure for assessing the impact of a new medicine on the global disease burden is rather complex, which would make the assessment vulnerable to corruption (Sonderholm 2010).

Here I would like to draw attention to another critical feature of Pogge's reform proposal, namely the notable fact that the whole scheme still relies very strongly on the "incentivizing" effect of patents.[6] The main problem with the present patent system, in Pogge's view, is that the incentives are geared to (potential) market demand in wealthy countries that is backed up by purchasing power. The "trick" of Pogge's scheme is to leverage the unmet medical needs of the South by backing them up with additional funds, so that they too carry some weight in the market pull directing pharmaceutical innovation. It is all a matter of setting the incentives "straight" – but by the same token the scheme still counts on the role of patents as incentives.

Pogge's reliance on patents dovetails with the received view of the pharmaceutical industry as the preeminent example of a sector where patents are indispensable for innovation, due to high investment costs of R&D and the relative ease to reverse engineer any resulting product. Lately, however, the presumed "incentivizing" effect of patents even for the pharma sector is increasingly called into question. For one thing, the track record of the industry over the recent period is not particularly impressive (even apart from the global imbalance epitomized in the 10/90 gap). Official figures show that in the last three decades "the productivity of the pharma R&D enterprise – the number of new molecules brought to market per dollar spent on R&D – has declined markedly" (Grootendorst 2009, 2). Ironically, according to Grootendorst's hard-boiled economic analysis, it is the patent system itself and the very high profit margins that it generates, which are to blame for a massive waste of economic resources – a lot of effort is simply spilled by patent holders on keeping other rent-seekers at bay.

Thus there is every reason to question Pogge's assumption that patents are indispensable as incentives for innovation. For the adherents of the A2K movement there is, of course, nothing extraordinary in this conclusion. It seems that Pogge got stuck half-way between the IP frame and the A2K frame. Although his Health Impact Fund aims to provide affordable access to the final products of pharmaceutical innovation and to influence the direction of innovative activity, it does not address the fact that most pharmaceutical patents are possessed by only a handful of western drug companies. For the adherents of the A2K movement, however, this concentration of control over innovative activity in the hands of a limited number of big players is a major concern. Access to knowledge, after all, is crucially about participation in the global networked knowledge-and-information economy. The right to actively participate in scientific advancement, not just to passively share in its benefits, is also enshrined in article 27.1 of the Universal Declaration of Human Rights. For the A2K proponents this is a very important human right (Shaver 2009).

[6] As Singer and Schroeder explain: "The Health Impact Fund leaves intact strong incentives for the pharmaceutical industry around the globe, thereby preserving the TRIPS advantages, whilst mitigating its main challenge, namely to block access to life-saving medicines to the poor. By registering a patented medicine with the Fund, a firm would agree to sell it globally at cost. In exchange, the firm would receive, for a fixed time, payments based on the product's assessed global health impact. The arrangement would be optional and it would not diminish patent rights, it therefore aligns the interests of pharmaceutical companies with the interests of poor patients. Such a win-win situation has to be welcomed!" (Singer and Schroeder 2010, 17).

3.5 The Prospect of Wider Participation

Ultimately, the widest possible participation in culture (including science and technology) is also what development is all about. IP scholar Madhavi Sunder formulates this view as follows: "… participation in the production of the world's knowledge is an end in itself. All human beings seek to 'think for themselves', to apply their ingenuity to better their own lives and the lives of those around them, this is what development is for. Amartya Sen's agency-oriented conception of development as freedom recognizes that individuals in the developing world do not simply wish to sit back and be the 'beneficiaries of cunning benefit programs', but rather seek to enhance their capacity to live a life that is happy and fulfilling, to care for themselves, and to interact with others, near and far" (Sunder 2012, 178).

The BioBricks branch of the SB community has promoted wider participation in SB through the organization of iGEM competitions between undergraduate students from different parts of the world (Smolke 2009). Despite the strong element of competition, iGEM also teaches the student participants an ethos of sharing and international collaboration by encouraging them to draw from, and submit new DNA constructs to, the Registry of Standardized Biological Parts. The iGEM competitions are a major mechanism for transmitting the new skills and knowledge of SB to the remote corners of the globe. As Kenneth Oye and Rachel Wellhausen write, "iGEM and other outreach activities of synthetic biologists are models of how to transfer know how by building vibrant international science commons" (Oye and Wellhausen 2009, 138). The participation of Chinese students in the iGEM competitions from 2007 onwards has actually been a unique 'bottom-up' route for the emergence of SB in China (Zhang 2011). Familiarity with iGEM practices may also influence attitudes towards patents. The more young and aspiring SB practitioners imbibe the ethos of sharing as a routine part of their research practice, the more critical they are likely to become of the proprietary strategies of private companies.

SB pioneer Drew Endy, who is also the main architect of the iGEM competition, envisages the whole endeavor in the broad perspective of a more widespread global participation in SB research for the sake of addressing global health needs. He discerns much promise and potential in the fast progress reached by undergraduate students in successive iGEM competitions: "One net positive impact would be to make accessible methods to produce needed chemicals and materials that are now unavailable or too expensive. More specifically, a reduction in capital and research costs associated with biotechnology research and development would allow a greater diversity of teams to work on many now ignored challenges, such as orphan diseases, that mainly affect poorer people who lack significant purchasing power" (Endy 2011). He contrasts the emerging iGEM practice based on two advances, tools and sharing, with "current biotechnology practice, which … is dominated by hoarding of both materials and property rights". It is also notable that Endy does not see the poor in the developing world only as passive recipients of the miracle works offered by modern science and technology. Referring to the well-known poster-child of SB, Jay Keasling's synthetic production of artemisinin, he asks himself: "What if we could enable thousands of artemisinin projects, each hoping to improve the human condition or our environment? What if we could enable the very people whose livelihoods now depend on intensive and expensive methods of manufacturing and production – such as wormwood tree farming – to help conceive, enable, and benefit from transition to a human civilization that is implicitly and responsibly partnered with the living world?" (Endy 2011). Endy is fully aware that the realization of this dream requires "more than technology alone", it also requires "supportive legal, institutional, and commercial environments" (ibid.). The outcome of the contest between the IP frame and the A2K frame in the SB field, with its possible repercussions for pharmaceutical innovation, will in all likelihood also be decisive for the realization of this dream.

References

Andrews L, Shackelton LA (2008) Influenza genetic sequence patents: where intellectual property clashes with public health needs. Futur Virol 3(3):235–241

Auteurswet (2006). Auteurswet 1881: Parlementairegeschiedeniswet 1881 – ontwerp 1884, with an introduction by M. Reinsma. Walburg Pers, Zutphen.

Bennett G (2011) Open technology platforms: (how) should the BIOFAB give things away? (BIOFAB Human Practices Report 3.0). Berkeley

Bliss M (1988) The discovery of insulin. Faber and Faber, London

Boyle J (2010) Monopolist of the genetic code? (http://www.thepublicdomain.org/2010/05/28/monopolist-of-the-genetic-code/). Accessed 28 May 2010

Buchanan A, Cole T, Keohane RO (2009) Justice in the diffusion of innovation. J Polit Philos. doi:10.1111/j.1467-9760.2009.00348.x

Calvert J (2008) The commodification of emergence: systems biology, synthetic biology and intellectual property. BioSocieties 3:383–398

Calvert J (2010) Synthetic biology: constructing nature? In: Parry S, Dupré J (eds) Nature after the genome. Blackwell, Oxford, pp 95–112

Calvert J, Joly P-B (2011) How did the gene become a chemical compound? The ontology of the gene and the patenting of DNA. Soc Sci Inf 50(2):157–177

Chan S, Sulston J (2010) Patents in synthetic biology may hinder future research and restrict access to innovation. BMJ 340:1315–1316

Cook-Deegan R (2011) Gene patents: the shadow of uncertainty. Science 331:873–874

Drahos P (1996) A philosophy of intellectual property. Aldershot, Dartmouth

Drugs for Neglected Diseases Working Group (2001) Fatal imbalance: the crisis in research and development for drugs for neglected diseases. Médecins Sans Frontières, Geneva

Dutfield G (2009) Intellectual property rights and the life science industries: past, present and future, 2nd edn. World Scientific, New Jersey

Editorial (1926) Ethics and patents. Am J Public Health 16(9):919–920

Endy D (2011) On biotechnology without borders. Global Reset. Seed magazine, 3 Mar 2011

EPO (2007) Scenarios for the future. How might IP regimes evolve by 2025? What global legitimacy might such regimes have? European Patent Office, Munich

ETC Group (2007) Extreme genetic engineering: an introduction to synthetic biology (http://www.etcgroup.org)

ETC Group (2012) Synthetic biology: livelihoods and biodiversity – artemisinin (http://www.etcgroup.org)
Fidler DP (2008) Influenza virus samples, international law, and global health diplomacy. Emerg Infect Dis 14:88–94
Forman L (2007) Trade rules, intellectual property, and the right to health. Ethics Int Aff 21(3): 337–357
Gates B (2008) A new approach to capitalism in the 21st Century. Davos, 24 Jan 2008
Glass JI (2011) Synthetic biology: a new weapon in our war against infectious diseases. Conference on Emerging and Persistent Infectious Diseases, Edinburgh, 23–26 Oct 2011. http://www.scienceforglobalpolicy.org/LinkClick.aspx?fileticket=V0Tiy5JoL0g=&tabid=123. Accessed 10 June 2012
Grootendorst P (2009) Patents, public-private partnerships or prizes: how should we support pharmaceutical innovation? University of Toronto, 22 Sept 2009
Hale V, Keasling JD, Renninger N, Diagana TT (2007) Microbially derived artemisinin: a biotechnology solution to the global problem of access to affordable antimalarial drugs. Am J Trop Med Hyg 77(6):198–202
Hamm S (2009) Cheaper artemisinin to fight malaria. Businessweek, 14 Jan 2009
Hammond E (2009) Indonesia fights to change WHO rules on flu vaccines. Seedling, April, http://www.grain.org/article/entries/761-indonesia-fights-to-change-who-rules-on-flu-vaccines
Henkel J, Maurer SM (2009) Parts, property and sharing. Nat Biotechnol 27(12):1095–90
Herper M (2006) Architect of life: Drew Endy aims to reinvent the biotechnology industry. Forbes, 10 February, http://www.forbes.com/free_forbes/2006/1002/063.html
Hollis A, Pogge TH (2008) The health impact fund: making new medicines accessible to all. Incentives for Global Health (IGH), New Haven
Holman CM (2012) Debunking the myth that whole-genome sequencing infringes thousands of gene patents. Nat Biotechnol 30:240–244
Jensen K, Murray F (2005) Intellectual property landscape of the human genome. Science 310:239–240
Kapczynski A (2008) The access to knowledge mobilization and the new politics of intellectual property. Yale Law J 117:804–885
Khalil AS, Collins JJ (2010) Synthetic biology: applications come of age. Nat Rev Genet 11:367–379
Krikorian G, Kapczynski A (eds) (2010) Access to knowledge in the age of intellectual property. Zone Books, New York
Lemley M (2005) Property, intellectual property, and free riding. Tex Law Rev 83:1031–1065
Macfarlane G (1980) Howard Florey: the making of a great scientist. Oxford University Press, Oxford
Machlup F, Penrose E (1950) The patent controversy in the nineteenth century. J Econ Hist 10:1–29
May C, Sell S (2006) Intellectual property rights: a critical history. Lynne Rienner Publishers, Boulder
McLennan A (2012) Building with BioBricks: constructing a commons for synthetic biology research. In: Rimmer M, McLennan A (eds) Intellectual property and emerging technologies. Edward Elgar, Cheltenham, pp 176–201
Oye KA, Wellhausen R (2009) The intellectual commons and property in synthetic biology. In: Schmidt M et al (eds) Synthetic biology. Springer, Berlin, pp 121–139
Palombi L (2009) Gene cartels. Biotech patents in the age of free trade. Edward Elgar, Cheltenham
Pogge TH (2005) Human rights and global health: a research program. Metaphilosophy 36(1/2):182–209
Pottage A (2007) The socio-legal implications of the new biotechnologies. Ann Rev Law Soc Sci 3:321–344
Rai A, Boyle J (2007) Synthetic biology: caught between property rights, the public domain, and the commons. PLoS Biol 5(3):389–393

Reuters (2012) Court reaffirms right of Myriad Genetics to patent genes. New York Times, 16 Aug 2012.
Rutz B (2009) Synthetic biology and patents. A European perspective. EMBO Rep 10:S14–S16
Schwartz J, Pollack A (2010) Judge invalidates human gene patent. New York Times, 29 Mar 2010
Shaver L (2009) The right to science and culture. Wis Law Rev 2010(1):121–184
Singer P, Schroeder D (2010) Ethical reasons for intellectual property rights reform: a report (D1.3) for Innova P2. IGH Discussion Paper No. 7, 16 Feb 2010
Smolke CD (2009) Building outside the box: iGEM and the BioBricks Foundation. Nat Biotechnol 27(12):1099–1102
Sonderholm J (2010) Intellectual property rights and the TRIPS agreement. An overview of ethical problems and some proposed solutions. World Bank: Policy Research Working Paper 5228
Specter M (2009) A life of its own: where will synthetic biology lead us? The New Yorker, 28 September, http://www.newyorker.com/reporting/2009/09/28/090928fa_fact_specter?currentPage=all
Stallman R (2009) How the Swedish pirate party platform backfires on free software (http://www.gnu.org/philosophy/pirate-party.html)
Sunder M (2012) From goods to a good life: intellectual property and global justice. Yale University Press, New Haven
Trafton A (2011) Rewiring cells: how a handful of MIT electrical engineers pioneered synthetic biology. MIT Technology Review. http://www.technologyreview.com/article/423703/rewiring-cells. Accessed 19 Apr 2011
Van den Belt H (2009) Philosophy of biotechnology. In: Meijers A (ed) Philosophy of technology and engineering sciences. Elsevier, Amsterdam, pp 1301–1340
Van den Belt H (2010) Robert Merton, intellectual property, and open science. A sociological history for our times. In: Hans R (ed) The commodification of academic research. Science and the modern university. University of Pittsburgh Press, Pittsburgh, pp 187–230
Van den Belt H, Rip A (1987) The Nelson-winter-dosi model and synthetic dye chemistry. In: Bijker WE, Hughes TP, Pinch T (eds) The social construction of technological systems. New directions in the sociology and history of technology. MIT Press, Cambridge MA, pp 135–158
Van Noorden R (2010) Demand for malaria drugs soars. Nature 466:672–673
Venter JC (2007) A DNA-driven world. The 32nd Richard DimblebyLecture. BBC One. http://www.bbc.co.uk/pressoffice/pressreleases/stories/2007/12_december/05/dimbleby.shtml. Accessed 4 Dec 2007
WIPO (2007) Patent issues related to influenza viruses and their genes. Working Paper
Zhang JY (2011) The 'National' and the 'Cosmos': the emergence of synthetic biology in China. EMBO Rep 12(4):302–306

Chapter 4
Synthetic Biology and IP: How Do Definitions of "Products of Nature" Affect their Implications for Health?

David Koepsell

Abstract Currently, under the law of intellectual property, IP owners may exclude from use or production substances and processes that we would ordinarily consider to be products of nature. This has helped companies monopolize disease genes, and thus diagnostic testing for those diseases, and "biosimilar" products, pharmaceutical materials that mimic biological materials. Extending the current paradigm to the world of synthetic biology and nanotechnology will create further injustices in the delivery of health care to billions of people around the world. As such, I advocate heading this trend off at the pass. Scientists ought to conduct basic research into the building blocks of biology and matter in the open, publishing their results, releasing knowledge into the public domain upstream so that beneficial innovation can be produced without fear of downstream litigation, and so that what ought to remain in the public domain as a matter of right (products of nature) does not become unjustly monopolized.

Keywords Open innovation • Biosimilars • Synthetic biology • Nanotechnology Intellectual property

4.1 Introduction

Currently, under the law of intellectual property, IP owners may exclude from use or production substances and processes that we would ordinarily consider to be products of nature. This has helped companies monopolize disease genes, and thus

---

D. Koepsell
Department of Values and Technology, Philosophy Section,
Delft University of Technology, Delft, Netherlands
e-mail: drkoepsell@yahoo.com

I. de Miguel Beriain and C.M. Romeo Casabona (eds.), *Synbio and Human Health: A Challenge to the Current IP Framework?*, DOI 10.1007/978-94-017-9196-0_4,

diagnostic testing for those diseases, and "biosimilar" products, pharmaceutical materials that mimic biological materials. Extending the current paradigm to the world of synthetic biology and nanotechnology will create further injustices in the delivery of health care to billions of people around the world. As such, I advocate heading this trend off at the pass. Scientists ought to conduct basic research into the building blocks of biology and matter in the open, publishing their results, releasing knowledge into the public domain upstream so that beneficial innovation can be produced without fear of downstream litigation, and so that what ought to remain in the public domain as a matter of right (products of nature) does not become unjustly monopolized.

4.2 The Problem: Products of Nature Are Now Patent-Eligible

The owner of a patent has the right to exclude anyone else from the production or practice of the invention claimed. So, let's consider the above proscriptions as applied to a tricky example, and then see how the courts have hopelessly confused things. Consider Joseph Priestley, who in 1774 discovered oxygen by heating mercuric oxide. He found that the gas released from heated mercuric oxide was quite combustible. He had isolated pure O_2, gaseous oxygen, from a compound. What are the potentially patentable parts of Priestley's activities? There is the process of separating oxygen from mercuric oxide, and there is the product (pure O_2) that is obtained. Under current US and EU precedent, an argument could be made that Priestley could obtain a patent for both the new, useful, and non-obvious process by which the O_2 was created (or isolated from its previous compound state) and also for the product as created by this process (O_2). Patents have been applied for and obtained for the elements Americium and Polonium, both of which are radioactive heavy isotopes that are generally produced by man (although natural processes might make them elsewhere). Patents have also been granted for synthetically produced analogues of naturally-occurring products like insulin and adrenaline. These patents cover not just the processes of creating them, but also the products. So, sorting all of this out requires a rather challenging interpretation of what counts as a law of nature, a physical phenomenon, and an abstract idea, one that, as we'll see, falls apart under scrutiny. All of which poses a particularly interesting challenge to a future in which the material world becomes programmable at the molecular level.

This is how it works out under current law: O_2 is a product of nature, and thus not patent-eligible in its natural state. The reason it is not patentable may be that it is either a 'law of nature' (which it seems it cannot be, since it is a product of nature) or perhaps because it is a 'physical phenomenon' (which seems more likely). O_2 is certainly not an 'abstract idea' since it exists in the universe as something we can experience directly, and do so with every breath we take. The process is less problematic, though it is still somewhat tricky. It is certainly conceivable that mercuric oxide, which exists in the environment in mineral form (as montroydite) has been heated naturally in the past, and released pure O_2 in the process. But humans and other creatures have been producing adrenaline and insulin for eons as well, and yet the courts have held that the 'isolation and purification' of such natural products constitutes sufficient inventiveness to warrant a patent. So what then do the courts do to distinguish O_2 as a physical phenomenon from O_2 as a product of man? The genesis of a particular O_2, insulin, or adrenaline molecule must be what matters. Thus, two structurally identical molecules are different, according to patent law, if one was produced by some human intention, and the other produced through some naturally-occurring process. For patent law, structure and origin of the object matter. If Priestley had obtained a patent for O_2 under current precedent, no one else could isolate O_2 in any manner, since the patent would cover both the process and the product. So even were you to discover that O_2 could be separated from water by electrolysis (it collects at the anode of an electric cell in water), as William Nicholson and Anthony Carlisle discovered in 1800, the Priestley patent would foreclose your new production technique, although you could get a patent on the new, useful, and non-obvious process.

According to the current legal ontology of patent, an object that is morphologically identical to another may yet be considered to be different in a legally significant way allowing the patent on one but not the other. All objects thus must have a structural quality, and a genetic quality, and if both are the result of some human intention, and meet the other criteria of patent (new, useful, non-obvious) then they may be patentable. How this relates logically to the exclusionary qualities 'natural law, physical phenomena, and abstract ideas' is unclear. It is important that we sort this out, because the future of nanotechnology rests upon the production of things at the molecular level, and a complicated web of intentions. Extrapolating from the current state of the law, which calls two identical objects importantly distinct due to their genesis, results in an impossibly complex nanotech future in which each new nanotech component could become patented, and tracking the ownership rights of any useful nanotech-based artifact would become a pragmatic impossibility. Besides the practical problems posed by this scenario, we might well ask whether the philosophical foundations are sound.

What counts as an artifact? This is a long-disputed philosophical problem. From a realist point of view, the world consists of at least two types of objects: artifacts and nature.[1] I have argued that anything in the world which is intentionally created by man is an artifact (Koepsell 2000). But without elaboration, this leaves a fair amount of overlap between artifacts and things we might not necessarily consider to properly be artifacts. Priestley's O_2 would count as an artifact, since he intends to create O_2. Yet O_2 exists in nature, even in isolated and purified form as the product of photosynthesis (by which plants strip the O_2 off of CO_2, synthesize the C for their growth, and excrete the O_2 as a waste product (luckily for us). So is 'synthesized' O_2 an artifact or is it a product of nature, artifactually created?

There are millions of natural phenomena which are duplicated by man. Consider fire. Fire occurs in nature, and yet we much prefer fires that we create and control to

[1] And arguably a third sort of thing we might call 'accidents'.

those created naturally. The 'thing' fire, which is the plasma state of matter undergoing combustion, is therefore in our ordinary experience (with gas stoves, for instance, or fireplaces) a natural product harnessed in some intentionally-generated and controlled process. Each instance of a man-made fire is the reproduction of some natural thing (fire) by means of some artifactual process (like lighting a stove, containing it in a particular place, feeding it with fuel, etc.) which does not alter the fact that the thing itself is natural. It is a physical phenomenon, which should be an exception to patent-eligibility. Does its genesis in human intention matter? It does, and we can recognize the artifactuality of the genesis without conflating the object with its process. In fact, by conflating products and processes we commit a grievous ontological error, as there is no commensurability of products and processes. Things (continuants) persist and are extended in space, and processes (occurrents) act upon them (Simons and Melia 2000; Munn and Smith 2008).

O_2 is O_2, whether it was created due to human intention or not. The process of generating O_2 from some intentional act, like heating mercuric oxide, or through electrolysis, is itself an artifact, a man-made intentional thing, which deserves consideration as patent-eligible. Claiming more, as for instance extending the artifactuality to the product as well as the process, is not ontologically warranted, and as we'll see, becomes a practical problem for intellectual property law, not to mention a nightmare for unraveling ownership issues in a nanowares future. The creation of fire by human means does not create a new type of fire. If this were so, then each instance of fire would have to be characterized by its particular means of generation. This would be a 'match fire,' that would be a 'flint fire,' and the other would be a 'lightning fire' etc. The world should not be populated by so many objects. There are fires, and they owe their origins to different causes, but the physical phenomenon is the same. The occurrents through which each continuant is altered differ, but identical continuants ought not to be split into different sorts of objects due to the acting-on them of various differing occurrents. This would be a muddied ontology, and an overly complicated world.[2] Yet this is exactly what the law as it currently stands demands of us.

Moreover, intellectual property distinguishes between products and processes, and one must make claims in one's patent application for each separately in order to receive protection. Products and processes are mutually exclusive categories. No product is a process, and vice versa. This much, the patent law gets right. We can recognize, in granting a patent for a new, man-made, useful and non-obvious process for creating an otherwise natural product, the genius of the inventor, and encourage and reward that invention with a patent on that process even as we deny that the new product is patent-eligible. The primary reason we should deny it as patent-eligible is simply that it is not in any way new. We need not delve into the various court-recognized exceptions, such as laws of nature, natural phenomena, nor 'abstract ideas.' Two of these exceptions simply reiterate the requirement of 'newness.' O_2 is not new, it has been around for billions of years, is abundant in our

[2]For more on Basic Formal Ontology, see <http://www.ifomis.org/bfo/1.1> [accessed 22 September 2010].

environment, and makes us live. Laws of nature and natural phenomena are, by nature, as old as nature, and pre-date human inventiveness.

All objects are either products (continuants) or processes (occurrents). There are two types of each: man-made and natural, for the purposes of intellectual property law. But this is too simple, as the problem of O_2 makes clear. We must elaborate. There are man-made objects, intentionally produced (all of which might properly be called expressions – the manifestation of some intention). There are accidents, or man-made objects with no intentionality behind them (a sneeze, the metal filings left over after constructing something with a lathe). And there are natural objects and processes, whose existence and form occur by virtue of natural laws or processes, or that are those processes.

Finally, the logical law of identity is one of the three foundational laws of logic identified by Aristotle, and accepted as an axiom in the sciences even today. Simply put, the law states: A=A (Copi 2001). The "isolation as invention" conceit, adopted in patent laws since at least Parke v. Davis, ultimately violates the law of identity. Under the current rule, Joseph Priestley would have been entitled to a patent on O_2 given his discovery of a new process for liberating and isolating O_2 from mercuric oxide. This "isolation" of a naturally-occurring molecule, otherwise morphologically identical to O_2 in other forms, suffices under modern interpretations to produce a patent-eligible product under Section 101. But it defies logic. When Nicholson and Carlisle, a few years after Priestley, succeeded is splitting water into H_2 and O_2 through electrolysis, had we followed the current patent law, their O_2 would have been precluded from patent by Priestley's patent. This is precisely analogous to the recent dispute about the patented BRCA1 and 2 genes. It also illustrates the absurd implications of the "isolation as invention" rule.

As explained above, the patented product encompasses a product that is morphologically identical to the naturally-occurring BRCA1 and 2 genes, (Koepsell 2009, p. 6) just as Priestley's O_2 is identical to Nicholson and Carlisle's, and to O_2 produced naturally by photosynthesis. In essence, under modern patent law, the "isolation as invention" conceit says that A does not equal A, or O_2 does not equal O_2, or BRCA1 and 2 do not equal BRCA1 and 2. The law ought to be consistent at the very least with the fundamental laws of thought, rules of logic that make argumentation both possible and useful, and axioms that underlie all the sciences. By perpetuating this notion, that somehow identical products are not identical, logic is not only strained but broken utterly.

4.3 The Sense Behind the Exclusions

The law of intellectual property is what we could call wholly "positive." It derives from utilitarian concerns, and seeks to bring about utilitarian ends. That is to say, the theory is that without some monopoly incentive, scientists and engineers will not invest the time and energy needed to develop profitable and beneficial new technologies. The IP regime is a trade off that allows for something which is typically abhorred: an artificial monopoly, for a limited time for the sake of some greater good. For about 200 years it has apparently succeeded, if we are to believe that there is some causation behind the correlation of rapid rates of innovation. While this is itself a leap of faith, and no evidence shows causation, let's take it for granted and explore why the law excludes certain things from its monopoly, and then ask whether and to what extent the current trajectory threatens to undermine those values.

Although not explicitly stated in the patent law, which extends protection ordinarily to new and useful discoveries and inventions, certain exclusions have been found to exist as stated above. Namely, abstract ideas, natural laws, and natural phenomena are not considered to be patentable. What might account for this judicially recognized exception? From the utilitarian standpoint, there is a case to be made that allowing patents so far "up stream" would make inventions further downstream harder. Take for example, fission. Fission is a natural phenomenon, and depends upon a law of nature expressed in Einstein's theory of relativity. Fission via nuclear bomb is man-made, but the natural laws and phenomena that make nuclear bombs possible are arguably not. While humans may discover them, their existence depends not upon human inventiveness, though their application through particular devices. Some modern philosophers of science might insist that natural laws and phenomena are as much the result of human inventiveness as any technique or technology. Regardless, utilitarian ends might justify keeping them distinct, and off limits for monopoly, in order to promote inventions downstream.

A natural product not previously known, but discovered though science, might have any number of useful applications, any of which might be encouraged through the promise of an artificial monopoly. The reasoning for excepting these things from monopoly, even if we reject the notion that there is a clear, ontological difference between inventions and discoveries, could well be sufficiently related to the imperative to promote invention, and the danger of hindering it through monopolizing knowledge too far upstream.

Thus, considering fission still, by preventing Einstein from patenting his famous theory, or preventing anyone from patenting the natural process of fission itself, numerous other downstream inventions are enabled without fear or trouble concerning licensing. Particular applications, first through, for instance, the shotgun method and then through implosion devices could each be monopolized as they become invented, but the natural phenomena and laws remain untouched and free to utilize through invention. Fission reactors, bombs, and other applications of natural laws and phenomena would, arguably, proliferate given that there is a monopoly incentive that encourages new and useful applications, even while the laws and phenomena that make them possible remain in the public domain.

But there is another approach, and one which is just as likely behind the legal exceptions to monopoly. Perhaps there is an ontological distinction between that which is discovered and that which is invented. And perhaps the law of intellectual property, which is designed to benefit society by encouraging invention is distinct from whatever encouragements exist that drive basic science. Could the realm of nature, in which we delve to discover phenomena and laws, be justly excluded from monopoly because it is a world apart from the realm of creation?

4.4 The Case for Discovery vs. Invention

Setting aside postmodern notions about the act of observation as invention, and assuming for the moment a more or less scientific-realist perspective taken by most scientists, the world is made up of those things that are not the result of our consciousness, and those things that are. Under this perspective, nature exist independent of our observations of it. This is the world of "brute facts" described by John Searle. On top, or layer upon the world of brute facts is the social world. This is the world of objects we create, including those created by social acts, dependent upon human consciousness. The world of brute facts existed historically before humans, and still exists wherever things exist despite our consciousnesses. The world of social objects only exists because of us.

So is there a way to cleanly delineate between objects that are inventive and those that are discovered in such a way that we can justify the exceptions that have been recognized to patent eligibility? One way is to ask whether something exists both because of human intention and design. We need both of these conditions for something to be "inventive" because many things exist because of some intention, but without any clear design. We might even call these things accidents. While painting a wall, for instance, I spatter paint on a dropcloth. The paint-splattered dropcloth is arguably the product of some intention. I intend to paint a wall, I intend to use a dropcloth to catch the drippings, I do not specifically intend the pattern of paint-splatter, but interpreting the scenario as liberally as possible, the paint-splattered dropcloth is the product of some human intention it would not exist but for human intention, but its particular form of existence is accidental in that no design was involved in the pattern of paint-splatterings. Unlike, say, a Jackson Pollack painting, in producing the paint-splattered dropcloth I employed no degree of design. If we wish to encourage artists to create art, then we might well reward the combination of intention and design, at least to the degree that both are involved in Jackson Pollack paintings, which we need no such incentive, nor would such an incentive be useful in the realm of paint-splattered dropcloths resulting from house painting.

Any discovery of a law or phenomenon of nature involves some degree of intention, some exercise of consciousness. But what it lacks is design. Brute facts may be observed and described, and the act of trying to model or describe them is arguably creative, but science depends upon and succeeds in virtue of the degree to which our descriptions and models hew as closely as possible to nature's "designs," not ours. A successful theory or model reflects as closely as possible that which previously was the case, and remains the case despite our attempts to describe it. Independent attempts to describe or model a natural law or phenomena do not change the nature of the underlying phenomenon. Scientific realism depends upon the idea that by testing, through experiments and empirical observations, we can decide whether some theory or model accurately depicts reality, not merely whether it is somehow instrumentally useful. Simply put, there is a distinction between the inventive and the discovered, and in between is a large grey realm of accidents, but the relevant mental states and states of affairs surrounding the decision about whether something ought to be considered inventive or not are easy to describe, if not always easy to agree upon ex post facto. The relevant inquiry is: but for the intention and design of someone, would the thing (or process) exist as it does?

4.5 Justice and Invention

Taking for granted the contestable notion that innovation demands limited monopoly schemes for inventors, is there a sense in which justice might demand limitations too to the realm of objects for which monopolies might be allowable? Assuming that limited monopoly rights are justified on some utilitarian grounds, and that although they impede basic rights to free expression these impediments are deemed to be outweighed by their overall value to society in the long run, one could argue that limiting the subject matter to things which are actually human creations is justified by some Lockean notion of mixing labor with nature (Locke 1690). That is to say, one way in which property rights are often justified over land and moveables is by recourse to the Lockean notion that improvement creates a right to ownership based upon possession. Our legal schemes that recognize that legal ownership is often grounded in valid possession plus some use or improvement are essentially Lockean in this respect. It is just, then, to exclude from use by others some tangible thing, a token as opposed to a type, over which we have exerted our will in use and improvement. Conversely, it is unjust to deprive anyone of possession where their claim to ownership is grounded in peaceful acquisition, use, enjoyment, or improvement. What then grounds a right to exclusion of others from reproduction of a type, and which types may not justly be excluded?

Assuming that the process of invention is a type of labor, some argue that "improvement" of types, through the creation of new objects and processes, justifies a valid claim via patent to exclude others from use of that type through reproduction of some object or use of a process without recompense to the inventor. Extending the IP monopoly to discoverers, instead of only inventors, may be unjust if the realm of discovery cannot be justly monopolized. I have argued that the realm of science, which includes types not created by man, such as natural laws and natural products, is a "commons by (material/logical) necessity." it cannot justly be enclosed. No amount of labor creates it, nor improves it. Scientific programs reveal it, but unlike the world of objects, it exists as it does despite human intention or design.

Our scientific pursuits at the realm of the very small, by way of synthetic biology and nanotechnology, necessarily tread closely to the realm of nature. Molecular components, both organic and non-organic, are sometimes the creations of man, existing only because of human intention and design, and sometimes the work of nature. Justice may well demand that we recognize the distinction and not grant rights over those things belonging to the commons by necessity. Utilitarian concerns aside, good reasons may exist to draw clear distinctions early and often as we improve our abilities to manipulate matter at its most fundamental levels and scales, even while utilitarian reasons would alone suffice.

Promoting invention and recognizing inalienable rights of all to the commons by necessity are not mutually exclusive aims, and a patent system can legitimately acknowledge and accommodate both. Legal tests based upon sound ontological principles, rather than merely ad hoc or aimed to achieve policy grounds, are most apt to survive the test of time in courts. A simple and effective test is this: ask whether the object or process over which some patent is sought exists but for both some human intention and design. We need not speculate as to whether nature itself could have devised the thing or process, but rather what actually occurred. This makes the inquiry fair and achievable, and draws a legally-friendly bright line between invention and discovery, acceptable to most who respect scientific realism, which includes most practicing scientists. It also leaves plenty of room downstream for creation, real innovation that combines intention and design in the development of things and processes that are truly new, useful, and non-obvious.

In order to avoid the injustices that come from moving the line of patent-eligibility too far upstream, and preventing the monopolization of both valuable new health technologies, and products of nature herself, we should take account of the current status of the law as described above, its full present implications, and the consequences, both utilitarian and deontological, for human health if not checked by applying some sound logic and reason as I propose herein.

References

Copi I (2001) An introduction to logic. Prentice Hall, New Jersey

Koepsell D (2000) The ontology of cyberspace: law, philosophy, and the future of intellectual property. Open Court, Chicago

Koepsell D (2009) Who owns you: the corporate gold rush to patent your genes. Wiley Blackwell

Locke J (1690) Second Treatise of Government, edited, with an Introduction, By C.B. McPherson. Hackett Publishing Company, Indianapolis/Cambridge, 1980

Munn K, Smith B (2008) Applied ontology: an introduction. Ontos Verlag, Frankfurt, p 268

Simons P, Melia J (2000) Continuants and occurrents. Proc Aristot Soc Suppl Vol 74:59–75, 77–92

Chapter 5
Synthetic Biology, Biotechnology Patents and the Protection of Human Health. A Consideration of the Principals at Stake

Anna Falcone

Abstract Synthetic biology offers our society huge possibilities in the large-scale prevention and cure of numerous medical conditions and physical deficits. However, it also involves serious legal and philosophical dilemmas. This paper tries to offer a critical vision of the legal framework related to this issue, paying special attention to the principles at stake. On one hand, it points out the legal necessity to separate the legitimate protection of the invention from the arbitrary monopolization of the discovery. On the other hand, it highlights that a general reorganization of the regulation of patents might be needed, so as to avoid some of the dysfunctions that this regime provokes in terms of justice.

Keywords Synthetic biology • Biotech patents • Pluralism and freedom of scientific research • Right of access to medical genetic • Genetics open source

5.1 The Impact of Biotechnology on Genome and Human Health: From OGM to Synthetic Biology

Biogenetic interventions using human genes, plants and animals offers our society previously unimagined for possibilities in the large-scale prevention and cure of numerous medical conditions and physical deficits. Until now, the genomes of living organisms have been the major source of natural biogenetic material, the known base from which to decode, and therefore replicate and modify, the genetic information of living organisms. Thanks to biotechnology various genetic information can be reproduced in the form of *biotech* applications for use in agriculture, industry,

---

A. Falcone
Department of Legal Sciences, University of Calabria,
Rende (Cosenza), Italy
e-mail: anna.falcone@unical.it

I. de Miguel Beriain and C.M. Romeo Casabona (eds.), *Synbio and Human Health: A Challenge to the Current IP Framework?*, DOI 10.1007/978-94-017-9196-0_5,

diagnostics and for therapeutic ends. But it has been during the evolution of biogenetic processes, in the decoding of the human genome and of many other living organisms, the knowledge of DNA structure and the various genetic sequences that possibilities that go way beyond these have appeared. Today the avant-garde of genetic engineering has gone much further than the modification of genomes in order to make them more resistant, adaptable and durable. The new horizons of biotechnology, fruit of the synergy between molecular biology, chemistry, information technology and electronic and genetic engineering, have created the possibility to construct *ex novo* original genetic systems or models, assembled using portions of genomes, both those copied from natural sequences as well as those born from artificial sequences created in the laboratory.

'Synthetic Biology' is the new sector of incredibly innovative research that using existing genome models and the mechanisms of combination, interaction and replication, allows the construction of 'artificial genes' and new 'genetic systems'. From a single functional genetic unit or 'base brick' – the so called "BioBrick" – capable of expressing diverse functions and characters, today it is possible to not only to replicate existing portions of genomes, but to give life to complex and original biomolecular systems, the fruit of an artificial biology project, or to install synthetic genes in organisms or natural genomes in order that they are able to better carry out their natural function. Through the study of biogenetic systems, the comprehension of the genes' expressive potential in the different genomic sequences and functional contexts, their activation and the possible results of a reciprocal interaction, synthetic biology is an area in which completely new scenarios arise in the creation of new of human, animal and vegetable models, but also in the area of raw materials, bio-combustibles, immunizations, pharmaceuticals, and, in a less welcome light, but both possible and probable, chemical weapons and relative defense agents.

For these reasons the legal regulation surrounding the discovery and access to genetic data, the possibility of using the base functional units that codify particularly relevant genetic characters (think for example of the 'oncogene – cancer gene') is one of the hottest topics which experts and operators in the field have been called upon to address in recent times. The legal regime that ends up being adopted – whether it is more open or more restrictive – will depend in fact on the evolution of the research and on the *biotech* products themselves, and on the optimization of the possible benefits and the number of people that are able to reap these benefits. Given the different speeds at which scientific progress travels, and capacity of the law to understand and respond to such phenomenon, dealing with these legal ethical questions is both crucial and urgent. Attempts to do so in an open, laical and pluralist light – which searches both to protect the dignity of the human person as well as to preserve the biosphere and all of its life forms – should guide the development, the diffusion, and the maximum access to those advantages that these biotechnological innovations provide.

The most delicate issue is that regarding the application of synthetic biology to the human being to better protect life and human health: if developed correctly the available knowledge could represent revolutionary solutions for the diagnosis, prevention and treatment of many medical conditions. Other than the direct possibility to 'repair' the genome through the insertion of 'correct' artificial genes, or to compensate for an inherited or acquired functional deficit, it is possible to imagine the creation of artificial vaccines or genetic pharmaceuticals, or the creation of synthetic organisms for the production of biological substances that can be used for therapeutic ends. The potential for synthetic biology to treat what up until now have been considered incurable conditions, the therapies' effectiveness, and the potentially low cost when compared to traditional treatments, lead us to hope for the greatest diffusion possible of these new techniques. The universal principle of equity asks and augers that such revolutionary treatments, particularly those that are lifesaving, are able to be accessed by everyone, or at least by the greatest number of people possible, irrespective of their concrete socio-economic conditions. It is also essential that new discoveries in such a cutting edge and constantly evolving field are made available to the scientific world as a whole in order to aid the progress of other studies, the expansion of research in the same subject and the usefulness of the 'codifying unit' in new and more efficient products and biotechnology therapeutic protocols. As such the development of the *biotech* and synthetic biology sector calls for an orientation, also legally speaking, towards a model that is as open as possible, in which discoveries and scientific results are shared freely between members of the biotechnology sector. A regulative structure that facilitates the use of Bio-bricks and codifying sequences in as many research and biomedical projects as possible, rather that the shrouding of information motivated by exclusive ownership and commercial aims. In exact contrast to this position, since the entrance of the first OGM products onto the world market, *biotech* companies have given high priority to the business of patenting and the protections offered by intellectual property laws for all of the organisms studied and genetic sequences used in the biotechnical applications bound for commercialization. The prospective for the economic exploitation of the genetically engineered product marketplace and the scale of their commitment has spurred a frantic race between big industry players and multinationals to buy up the planet's genetic resources, and the subsequent imposition of patent rights on this genetic information, both those derived from animal and vegetable life forms and those derived from synthetic biology processes. With substantial ensuing misrepresentations.

It has been exactly the rise of synthetic biology, and the need demonstrated by the research and development of new '*biotech* products' for increased quantities of the 'bricks and base information' required for the construction of these products, that shows how the legal instrument of a patent – studied and designed to both recognize the inventive property of its creator, guaranteeing the right to gain financially from the application and the diffusion of discoveries and innovations that follow – can no longer withhold the challenge of time. Even more, in the *biotech* sector its pervasiveness risks creating an obstacle to the very means it was created for, for many and various reasons. Above all else, in an oligolistic regime the instrument of a 'patent' is no longer useful in protecting the 'scientific paternity' of a discovery and its application, and those economic rewards that follow in terms of a single scientist or researcher (under the condition as already noted, to make discoveries and new applications public) rather than more pragmatically guaranteeing the exclusive rights to the economic benefits, real and future, to the company that holds the title to the laboratory. To this we can add that this hoarding of resources does not take place under the conditions of a 'free market', where equal opportunity and the plurality of different laboratories that operate in the *biotech* sector exists. Instead, the extremely high costs of research and operation in the sector mean that only a few companies – those with the greatest economic resources- are able to progressively privatize the planet's genetic resources, the human genome included, and to utilize this knowledge of these genetic traits for the creation of synthetic products. Which has the effect of transforming genetic resources into a sort of private heritage, available only to those who are able to pay the requested royalties, when genetic resources, which, by their very nature rightly belong to all humankind. Even the intrinsic ability of genes to be passed on from generation to generation according to the nature of inheritance, should qualify them legally as 'common inter-generational property' and, as such, non-excludable heritage. The same can be said for BioBricks, which carry out the same role in biochemistry as a genetic characteristic or sequence.

Many international documents have uniformly affirmed this position: that in the field of biogenetics genetic resources, both those with natural origins and those created in the laboratory, should be considered as 'common concern of humankind' and the international community. According to UNESCO's *Universal Declaration on the Human Genome and Human Rights* genetic information is heritage that should be passed down intact from generation to generation. This definition does not regard only the human genome, but should be logically extended to cover all of the material on which hereditary information is stored. To this the base components of genetic information (nucleobases organized in genes) can be added, that are common not only to all of humankind but also to all living beings. The same genes do not demonstrate differences according to their natural or synthetic origin. A particular gene sequence and a particular amino acid have an identical appearance both when taken from a natural genome and when artificially produced in a laboratory. That is, what distinguishes different genes is the combination of the base elements, the order of these bases and their interaction at a bio-molecular level. In turn genetic sequences and their capacity to express character traits and living matter follow laws that are still the subject of research, and not the human desire to constrain them to co-exist with determined artificial models of genes. Therefore even the eventual creation of artificial genes, hypothetically capable of codifying new character traits, would be considered more a 'discovery' – as such not patentable – than an 'invention'. Which is different to 'products' and 'processes' that are fruit of original and innovative biology projects that can lay full claim to the title of *biotech* 'invention', in as much as they are the result of an 'innovative idea' or of 'artificial human creativity', and in this way are able to be patented. Nowadays, on the opposite, about 20 % of the human genome has been patented. Most of the genetic patents are markedly different to other works of human genius covered by patents, those that involve a level of inventiveness and creativity, in that they are fruit of the discoveries around DNA and regard the function of single genes or parts thereof. Even the patents that cover artificial genetic sequences are often completely or in part copied from human genes modified and adjusted to the match functions requested of the *biotech* product.

5.2 The Nature of Patent Protection and Particularities to Synthetic Biology

Outside of the ethical question in which biotechnology, in reproducing the human body or a single part thereof – must not degrade the 'subject' into an 'object' – thus annulling the human dignity that should eminently guide all research, availability or intervention on the human genome – what we are interested in here is how much an economic-regulative system that is based on patents and intellectual property can assist the function of and rapid development of the synthetic biology sector, resulting in the greatest possible benefit-sharing, and the highest protection of human life and health, and in the end, also the best possible response to the needs of an open and pluralist market. In addition, in the light of the necessary requirements for the patent of a new product or process, it is worth asking what exactly, in the field of synthetic biology, can be considered a 'patentable invention' and what should instead be excluded.

The standard criteria for the patenting of a product are: the newness (novelty), the innovative step involved in the invention, and its industrial application. Compared to the application for and publicity for a patent (or rather in the detailed description of the process/product) the holder of the patent (that in the *biotech* and pharmaceutical sectors is often not the inventor) has the exclusive rights to the economic gain from the commercial sale of the product for a period of 20 years. But the application of this model to the peculiar reality of the synthetic biology brings up several discretions that demonstrate how poorly adapted this instrument is to the regulation of an industry, that of the biotechnology applied to the human being, in which the various interests in play are in potential conflict. It is noted in fact that:

(a) Synthetic biology and its products, that are the result of research in various disciplines (biology, chemistry, IT, genetic engineering, etc.) and knowledge that, shared between them, do not lend themselves to being adequately covered by the legal patent system. The competition between different forms of 'know-how' that make up the development process of synthetic products makes it difficult, if not impossible to individuate under which level of legal protection each element of the product is protected. Even more arduous is the rendering compatible the legal protection by which both the processes involved and the single components (BioBricks) are covered, with that which the protection of the final *biotech* product. Given its potential 'multi-functionality', the legal protection of a gene, or of any base bio-molecular unit, does not cover all of the levels of its possible *biotech* applications. Therefore, in a legal context, it gives rise to various problems in the interpretation of the patent and its application and effectiveness in different countries and, therefore, its liberal use, or less, for new synthetic products or processes. Not least, also thanks to the different criteria in the registration of a patent followed by different patent offices and the non-homogenous protection that patents guarantee around the world, which then becomes a much greater legal obstacle the smaller the research laboratory that adventures into the synthetic biology sector. This issue involves a potentially insurmountable limit for individual researchers who wish to study those sequences protected by patents but find themselves confronted by difficult legal codes, with the end result being the loss of potential discoveries and scientific applications useful to the health of mankind.

(b) The possibility of subjecting to patent every single component/BioBrick would lead to, with the progressive patenting of human and other genetic material, an escalation of the production costs of *biotech* products that result from their assembly and recombination. In particular for those products that end up being applied as genetic pharmaceuticals, or that are used in therapies that use synthetic products or processes. In a global market without controls or moratorium regarding the price of patented pharmaceuticals and most avant-garde therapies, this could render those forms of therapy, medicines and types of cure that utilize synthetic biology completely out of reach for many people. The same products and therapies, if they were allowed free access to human genes and all of the BioBricks important for potential medical and diagnostic applications, would on the contrary, have the power to represent not only extremely advanced forms of prevention and cure, but also relatively economically, as they would be able to spread the cost of research and development across the highest number of possible users. Obviously, to have already registered over 40,000 patents of the human genome does not help affirm the view of the market as open and orientated toward maximum accessibility. At least, not until the growth of the base of the market coincides with the strategies of the market, and with the economic strategies of the patent holders. An arbitrary position that is sincerely unacceptable, especially when the patents concern lifesaving medicines and therapies.

(c) The 20-year life span of the patent of an innovation in the *biotech* field seriously conditions the access to information crucial for the evolution of scientific studies in the area and the ability to come up with new cures, pharmaceuticals and biogenetic therapy. Enough to say that even just access to the biologic samples, both natural and artificial, deposited with the request for a patent are subject to the consent of the depositor, even if such access is sought only for research motives and not as a means to financial gain. To this we add that the duration of the patent, even if from one side is directly proportional to the increase in company profits for each "BioBrick" patented, on the other hand impedes the construction of new synthetic products by other companies in the sector who would like to use the same component. In this way it promotes a system in which the crossroads are always blocked between those patent holders which – in the most extreme consequences – could seriously limit, if not block completely, the development of new products/pharmaceuticals/synthetic therapies by third parties, and therefore also future profits for the entire sector. Even when they are conceded, access to the functional unit under patent is conditioned by the payment of very high royalties, of which the amount, in a monopolist regime, is determined entirely by the holder of the patent who becomes a sort of 'umpire' in the use of an often crucially important genetic resource. Again the effects are twofold: from one side there is a noticeable increase in the price (variable) of the final product, and from the other the consequent drop in potential buyers and in the possible number of people that are able to benefit from the innovation.

Here there is a crisis within the legal-economic function of the patent itself, or rather the maximization of the general well-being expected to come from it, a negative outcome of the attempt to balance incentive with disclosure, the patent's temporary guarantee of exclusive economic gain and the limit in the creation of monopolies. The application of a system of patents for BioBricks, in fact, not only favors the constitution of 'mountain monopolies' – thanks to the high costs of both research and access to the intellectual property legal system and of the commercial exploitation of their products – but also of 'valley monopolies' – given the irrefutable advantage of concentrating the patents for the base components on which synthetic biology is founded in the hands of few, and therefore limiting the access for their utilization for other *biotech* products. All of this in a sector where, evidently, both research and the consumer would benefit from greater competition and plurality of the players involved. The patent is a legal-economic asset that gravely conditions the potential for development in the *biotech* sector and in synthetic biology in particular. A limit that would become unacceptable if dropped into the so called "red biotechnology", the sector dedicated to the development of genetic engineering technology for the medical treatments and biomedical processes such as antibiotics and pharmaceuticals.

In the balancing of the interests between the monopolist protections of economic law and the expectations of treatment by those suffering from serious pathologies that these breakthrough treatments could cure, it becomes difficult to justify a system that gives pre-eminent, if not exclusive, protection, to the first rather than the second group – and therefore to relative rights, rather than to fundamental rights. This system of legal protections is moreover, in the area of synthetic biology, revealed as outdated and unsuited to the needs of the market, because it is constructed out of a system of roadblocks in the area of research and development, slowing down the realization of new *biotech* products and contrary, in the long run, to the commercial interests of the industry itself. Even more gravely, it is unable to provide the protection of human life and well being that these same biotechnological innovations have the possibility to aid. In light of these considerations and in the most recent normative evolutions in the field, it is worth noticing how such a rigid model for the protection of intellectual property is still legally founded on and compatible with legislation which at both an international and European level, also in the biotechnology sector – and according to current progressive approach – relies upon the pre-eminent safeguarding of the right to life and human health, the right to access the best possible cure, the classification of the human genetic information as a shared heritage which is the property of 'all of humanity'. No less, the protection of this non-excludable heritage and fundamental rights implied by the acts of the disposition of the human genome appears constantly more closely tied to and conditioned by the availability and free circulation of genetic information codes and knowledge in the biotechnology area.

In a society that has evolved from a legal-economic system based on 'ownership' to a global model of development based on the 'knowledge economy', the safeguarding of 'common heritage', the pre-eminent protection of the human person over the market or its economic-speculative interest in the human genome and the genetic resources of the entire planet, is also a response founded on merit and reason. The freedom of movement of both discoveries and other subject matter, as never seen before in another sector, demonstrates an interest that overtakes the single benefits, and projects itself into the future in the interests-rights-obligations of humanity. A wider viewpoint is, in fact, the essential premise that we must preserve the genetic resources of both mankind and the planet, both for the current generation and for future generations, thus guaranteeing for all access to the benefits derived from biotechnology and the consequent improved protection of life and human health.

5.3 General Principles for the Protection of Human Genetic Heritage to Emerge in International and EU Documents Relevant to the Biotechnology and Synthetic Biology Fields

A set of regulations, specific to the biotechnology and synthetic biology field, does not yet exist at any regulative level. The disciplines in this subject area are governed by a combination of: (a) regulations, directives, and European recommendations in the OGM sector, biomedicine, biosecurity, chemical products, protection and terms of patents, with various legal obligations and significance; (b) general dispositions made by the World Trade Organization (WTO) and the World Health Organization (WHO); (c) international documents in the area of bioethics and human rights; (d) national transposition norms (often with relevant modifications) of the legal background and specific laws pertaining to the protection of health, environmental security, research and the protection of intellectual property, obviously unique to each different legal system.

At the moment, all synthetic biology is approached using genetic modification/manipulation techniques, regulated by the EU with a series of acts and regulations introduced from the start of the 1990s and amended over time. For member states these ordinances are binding, but with various differences surrounding the nature of the obligations imposed on each individual sector (medical devices, pharmaceuticals, food products etc.) and variable as a result the integration of national laws. EU law therefore provides a legal point of reference and common minimum guarantees that each state is free to elevate according to national law and terms bound by the constitution. In a general and not overly exhaustive overview of this we are able to extrapolate those principles that should guide the use and exploitation of human biotechnology, and therefore also synthetic biology, in both an international and EU environment.

5.3.1 International Documents

At an international level, important indications emerge: from the *Convention on Biological Diversity*, that repeats the principle of the sustainable use of genetic resources and the equal distribution of the benefits derived from them; to *UNESCO's Declaration on the Responsibility of the Present Generation towards Future*

Generations, proclaimed on the 12 November 1997, that reminds the first group to safeguard the interests of the latter (art.1) "continuing efforts towards the maintenance and the perpetuation of humanity out of respect for the dignity of the human person", without bringing judgment "to the form of human nature" (art.3) and in particular to the human genome (art.6); and to the *Universal Declaration on the Human Genome and Human Rights*, unanimously adopted at the General Conference of UNESCO the 11 November 1997, that established the principle of non-excludable heritage and proclaims the human genome as "the heritage of all human kind" (art.1) inviting all States and relevant national organizations to co-operate in preparing the most suitable measures with which to contrast those practices at odds with respect for human dignity. This last document in particular, approved by the General Assembly of the UN on the 9 December 1998 in the context of the celebrations for the 50th Anniversary of the *Universal Declaration of Human Rights* constitutes the primary instrument for the Universal regulation of bioethics, based on legal and ethical principles that give pre-eminent respect to the dignity and the solidarity, also inter-generational, between human beings that, it affirms, must guide the progress of genetic research and its application, in order to safeguard its development from the dangers that could derivate from biomedicine. In particular the fundamental principles of the Declaration regard: respect for the dignity and the rights of each individual in relation to his or her genetic characteristics (art.2); the outlawing of the use of the human genome as a source of economic gain (art.4); the subordination of the research of the human genome and its application to respect for the dignity, the rights and the fundamental freedoms of every individual or human group (art.10); the liberty of research and the solidarity in the sharing of the advantages and progress made within biomedicine, especially with developing countries (art.12); the ethical and social responsibility of the researchers involved in the study of the human genome (art.13); the responsibility of the states in implementing the directives of the Declaration (art.14,15,16).

Among those acts made by the Council of Europe there is the *Recommendation n.934/1982 on genetic engineering* and various other acts that are however without legal value. The *Convention for the Protection of Human Rights and the dignity of the Human Person with regard to biologic applications and medicine* (better known as the *Oviedo Convention* or *Biomedicine Convention*) of 4 April 1997, signed in Paris 12 January 1998, already binding for signatories. Today the Convention constitutes the most advanced of the documents that deal with the safeguarding of the human genetic heritage. It affirms: the right of every human being to their own identity and integrity with regard to the biologic applications and medicine (art.1), the supremacy of the human being respect to the interests of society and science (art.2) and the outlawing of any form of commercialization or utilization of the human body or its parts, including the genetic heritage as a means to profit (art.21). Notwithstanding the binding nature of the Convention (in light of its ratification by the majority of states and also given the necessary instruments that the ratification provides) the Convention of Oviedo has not proved a sufficient instrument with which to correct the imbalance between the protection of products in the discipline through the use of *Biotech* patents. Not being a source of binding legislation for the EU, or external countries, it is unable to exercise real control even if tacitly abrogative. It is able however, to provide a more efficient limit for the legislative control of *Biotech* patents within single national legislations in which the Convention is legally binding.

5.3.2 European Union Regulations

Various documents have been produced over the years at the EU level that regard the subject of genetic engineering and biotechnologies as applied to humans. At the end of the 1980s, the European Parliament pronounced, with the *Resolution 16/03/1989, on ethical and legal problems surrounding genetic manipulation* (doc. A2/327/88), that, whilst confirming the liberty of science and scientific research, it asks that society is responsible for the expression at a legal level of the necessary limitations required for the safeguarding of the rights of third persons and society as a whole that could be damaged by biotechnological applications (art.8), by giving pre-eminent respect to the dignity of the individual and of the entire human race (art.9). The definition according to such confines is regarded as "work that cannot be given up by the legislator" (art.10) and cannot be extended, according to the extensive interpretation, to those who use or exploit *biotech* products or innovations for means that are outside respect for human dignity and the inviolable human rights.

These principles, emphasized in the *Convention for the Protection of Human Rights and Dignity of the Human Being with regard to the Application of Biology and Medicine* of 20 September 1996 and in a series of other resolutions relating to human cloning, also inspire other normative documents developed by the EU. Let us remember a title of exemplary merit: the *Fifth Framework Programme (1998–2002) "Quality of Life and Management of Living Resources"* (1998–2002), and the more recent actualization by the EU of the *"Bonn Guidelines" Access to Genetic Resources and Fair and Equitable Sharing of the Benefits Arising out of their Utilization* – in a Communication from the Commission to the European Parliament and the Council of 23 December 2003, repeating the importance of the maximum distribution of the possible benefits in every further biotechnological development. The most recent EU norm in the area of OGM is inspired by the guarantee of "an elevated level of protection of human life and well-being" – *Reg. n. 1829/2003 of the European Parliament and of the Council of 22 September 2003 on genetically modified food and feed* – thus using the principle of caution as a priority – *Reg. 1946/2003 of the European Parliament and of the Council of 25 July 2003 on Transboundary Movements of Genetically Modified Organisms.*

But the most important indications for the Synthetic Biology industry come from the *EU Charter of Fundamental Rights*, in as such that it is binding for all member states and has a strong influence over all European Courts. Its integration in the Lisbon Treaty and the value that these norms assume with respect to other EU normative fonts, make it an important instrument, even in the area of *Biotech* patents, in restoring the equilibrium, at least in EU legislation between the protection of fundamental human rights and the economic rights of the *Biotech* multinationals. The preamble of the *Charter* declares that the enjoyment of all rights must "promote responsibility and duties with regard to future generations", intended also in relation to the use and availability of genetic resources. Another indication comes from art. II-63, on the "Right to the integrity of the person", that expressly prohibits at comma 2, Lett. C), "of making the human body and its parts as such source of financial gain". It is blatantly evident how this prohibition is at odds with the possibility to patent human genes isolated from the body or artificially replicated. The indication of an open and pluralist model for the management of genetic resources gives the pre-eminent orientation to respect for human dignity, the fundamental right to life and well-being, and to equality and equal opportunity in access to these rights, declared also in the articles: Art.II-61 *Human Dignity* – "Human Dignity is inviolable. It must be respected and protected"; Art.II-62 – *Right to Life*: "Every individual has the right to life"; Art.II-73 "Freedom of arts and sciences: "The arts and scientific research shall be free from constraint. Academic freedom is shall be respected"; Art.II-81 – *Non discrimination*: "Any discrimination based on any grounds such as gender, race, skin color, social or ethnic origin, genetic features, language, religious or personal beliefs, political or other opinions, pertinence of a minority group, heritage, birth, disability, age or sexual orientation, shall be prohibited". Again, when recognizing the right to good health in Art.II-95 the *Charter* binds the EU to "guarantee a high level of protection for human health" – configuring also the right to access the best possible cures, including those biotechnological ones already present – thus imprinting this objective in all EU politics and activities in the field.

An analysis of the aforementioned principles, reinforces the means for which the Charter of Rights was born – *"to strengthen the protection of fundamental rights in the light of society's evolution, of social progress and scientific developments, make such right more visible in a Charter"* – and highlights an important aspect in relation to the evaluation of the conflict (evident as never before at the EU level) between fundamental rights and modern biotechnology, the patentability of the human genome and base components of genetic information and the commercial exploitation of *biotech* discoveries and innovations. From here should follow, with the refusal of all those activities that are potentially harmful to human well-being, the reversal, even only tacit, of those norms that legitimize the reduction of human resources to mere merchandise, that limit the access to these resources and knowledge, and that reserve for a few the benefits derived from biotechnology, which relies on these resources for the creation of its products.

5.4 Weak Principles and Strong Interests: International and European Discipline on the Legal Protection of Biotechnology "Inventions"

The ever increasing international documents and charters of rights dealing with the protection of the human genome and genetic resources, created to promote the fair and equal use of biotechnology, are however not enough to overcome the vulnerability that underlies the sector: the non-binding nature of the International acts, the limited and only relatively obligatory nature of EU regulation, and the substantial incapacity to cut through national and super national legislations to create a uniform discipline at least in terms of setting limits for the patentability of genetic information. The European case is emblematic of this fragility: the recognizing of human rights, both present and future, with regard to the exploitation of genetic resources, contained at an international level by documents from the Council of Europe to EU legislation, cited also in many regulative acts and discourse by European institutions, is not able to make inroads in the area which has the greatest sway over the genetic resource industry and its management: that of the patentability. Even the intervention of more important acts, such as the EU's Charter of Fundamental Rights, that indicates specific prohibitions in the area, have not proved enough to cover more adequately these principles in the discipline of intellectual property and the commercial profit from products that are based on the human body, and therefore also DNA and genetic information contained in single or entire units of genetic code.

5.4.1 The Directive 98/44/CE and Legislation on 'Biotech Patents'

Regulation of the legal protection of biotechnological innovations and genetic material in Europe is covered by the Directive 98/44/CE, which integrates the *European Patent Convention*, signed in Munich 5 October 1973, while at an international level it descends from the TRIPS agreement – *Agreement on trade related aspects of intellectual property rights*. The patent system delineated allows patent rights to be imposed on parts of genomes, or entire genetic sequences belonging to a particular living organism, under the condition that they are associated with a biotechnical process, capable of isolating and reproducing them for industrial use, and that this process has a specific application. The TRIPS agreement sets a common standard at the international level that, by overcoming the limits, the differences and eventual *aporia* of national regulations in the patent field, aim to uniformly control the sector in order to efficiently regulate the global intellectual property market. Biotechnology is not mentioned expressly, but the discipline is also applicable to biotechnological inventions, in as much as its norms do not exclude the possibility and are considered compatible. The TRIPS agreement allows the patenting of almost any invention that demonstrates: newness, creative activity, or industrial application. According to a literal interpretation of the agreement, simple discoveries would be excluded from patenting, but given the dubious nature of 'technological innovation" the mere 'discovery' of genetic information has the potential to be transformed into a real and proper 'invention'.

The agreement also contains a disposition (art.25) that allows member states to exclude from patenting inventions that are contrary to public order or decent behavior, in order to protect human well-being, plant or animal life, or that aim to avoid grave damage to the environment, but the variance of the cited criteria in the different national contexts (and also within them) has impeded the formation of an unequivocal approach in the area. In each way the vague approach of both US and European institutions and legal systems suggests the need for much better international co-ordination. This could happen, for example, through the revision of the TRIPS agreement, from which an improved certainty of the rights in those legislations privy of specific regulation for this area – that would provide – auspiciously – shared solutions for particularly complex profiles, as is the case with synthetic biology.

The *EU directive 98/44/CE on the legal protection of biotechnological inventions*, which was the fruit of the "*biotech* lobby's" insistent pressure at the EU level, was born out of the *Biotech* multinationals quite open objective to assure themselves of the economic exploitation of patent rights, even of the discoveries themselves, before they had even been applied to *biotech* products. The discipline introduced, in fact, warping the semantic meaning of 'discovery' and 'invention', excludes the first from patenting, but allows it for the second, but then goes on to clarify in art.3 that "biological material which is isolated from its natural environment or produced by means of a technical process may be the subject of an invention, *even if it previously occurred in nature"*. With regard to the human body, art.5 specifically states that "the human body, at the various phases of its formation and development, and the simple *discovery* of its elements, including the sequence or partial sequence of a gene, cannot constitute patentable *inventions*", but at the same time adding that "an element isolated from the human body, or otherwise produced by means of a technical process, including the sequence or partial sequence of a gene, may constitute a patentable invention, even if the structure of the that element is identical to that of a natural element"; and again "the industrial application of a sequence or a partial sequence of a gene needs to be disclosed in the patent application". This means that the human body is not patentable and nor is the genome in its entirety, nor single genes, or parts thereof, as long as they remain in the organism, but they become (patentable) as soon as they are separated from the body or "copied" using a technical process. In this case both the appropriation, through the granting of the patent, and the commercial exploitation are consented to. The successive articles 8) and 9) insert an additional extension of legal cover for patented genetic material for any product that is derived, or in which the patented material is inserted (genetically modified plant or animal).

This mechanism consents, in fact, to the progressive imposition of patent rights on a potentially enormous number of natural genomes, and therefore on plant and animal organisms, even those pre-existing in a natural state, "privatized" thanks to the insertion of a genetic characteristic covered by a patent. Therefore if an already existing plant or animal in its natural state is not patentable, the same organism, enriched by a gene covered by a patent, becomes in turn patentable.

What drastically contrasts with the concept of 'invention', and therefore with the assumptions on which the legitimacy of the patent protection is founded, is the possibility to patent a gene or organism as a result of almost any human intervention of an 'inventive' nature on the same organism, or as a result of an intervention that affects the expression of genetic information of the living matter. No qualitative difference exists, in fact, between the natural sequence of a gene and an exact copy created in a laboratory; the mere discovery of the codification of a gene is in itself an invention. One can consider, moreover, that every single gene is potentially multi-coding; or rather it can manifest itself as various and diverse hereditary characters. The assumption is flawed because it misunderstands the interactivity of genetic material in every genotype and the potential variety of variability of the information coded in genes. It had come close, in the qualification of the genome and the genes, to the prospect of 'epistemological and genetic reductionism' as the necessary condition in order to define a good, to limit it, to weigh it, to give it a value on the market, a pass resulting as for the founding the legitimacy of the exclusive right to exploit a 'genetic resource' that needs to be delineated in its function and in its application. The clear legal acknowledgment of the multi-codifying character of genes would impede, on the contrary, the legitimization of the request for a patent for the genetic sequence or for an artificial copy, and therefore the imposition of patent rights on the biological support, other than on the decodified genetic information and its application.

In reality the ambiguity between 'discovery' and 'invention' that is found right through the Directive 98/44/CE, aims to cover this silent knowledge on the part of the *Biotech* companies that so strongly desired its approval. These companies, well informed as to the expressive potentiality of each single gene, through the extension of the patent for industrial application to cover genetic material which holds this information, have in this way guaranteed for themselves *pro future* the exploitation of any other type of genetic information that may be coded into the 'privatized' gene that they own the patent for, or other expression in which it is involved. Which is like saying: with the discovery of Kinetic energy and the patenting of the bicycle, every other mode of transport that uses this type of energy would then fall under the original patent.

5.4.2 Limits and Problems Regarding the Imposition of Patent Protections on the Human Genome and Base Genetic Components. The Legal-Economic Crisis Around the Patenting of Synthetic Biology

Two elements are peculiar to the directive with regard to legal protection of the biotechnological and relative inventions: (a) the ultractivity of the patent of an organism/biological material in which it is inserted; (b) the automatic extension of the patent to all of the possible functions of the gene/BioBrick, that have intruded on the reality of synthetic biology, which survives on the combination/contamination of natural and artificial genetic models, and represent the greatest regulative blocks to the development of the sector and are more than anything else the factor that favors the rigidity of the patent system and the construction of monopolies. How binding the regulations are is very debatable legally, if not clearly in contrast with the patent's function and with many fundamentals of EU legislation and often sanctioned at an international level. In the area of synthetic biology also the norm dealing with transparence in art.13 of the Directive 98/44/CE turns to guarantee the right of third parties to access the 'deposited biological material': given that synthetic biology products are the fruit of a combination of knowledge, not necessarily traceable to one biological sample, the access to this sample does not guarantee the publicity of the invention and the knowledge behind it.

The persistence of such regulation is an obvious obstacle to the freedom, but also to the transparency of scientific research of synthetic biology, the pluralism of scientific contributions, the diffusion of knowledge in the subject and the access to the sector by the entire scientific community. Even more seriously, the generalized imposition of *biotech* patents on organisms and genetic resources, both natural and artificial, leads to the construction of immovable 'monopolies of knowledge' that allow very few *biotech* companies to bully their way into the governance of the planet's environmental and biological resources. By now it depends on them, not on individual states, to make decisions around the politics of the sector, the possible applications and the diffusion of the benefits. The situation that is emerging in the *biotech* market poses a problem in the protection of insuppressible fundamental rights, in front of which an arrogant and distorted use of intellectual property rights is unable to ask for or find legitimate legal protection.

5.4.3 Regulative Conflicts and Emerging Limits in the Area of Patentability and Economic Gain from Human Genetic Resources

The pre-eminent protection of economic rights, and of industrial property rights with respect to fundamental rights such as life, human well-being and the freedom of scientific research is not legally justified also in light of the new political 'mission' in Europe that through the insertion of the Charter of Fundamental Rights as a primary font has modified the relationship between economic interests and the rights of human beings, to favor the latter. The directive, in fact, has been strongly criticized and contrasted, at both an EU level and within various national contexts, as a result of the evident contrast between the principles that guide the protection of human dignity and the safeguarding of genetic resources sanctified at a European and international level. But what has caused more of an uproar, following the ratification of the Charter, is the continued and clear violation of the principle of the non-excludability of the human body, or parts thereof – expressly communicated in art II-63 – and of the prohibition of the commercialization and economic gain from any of its parts.

After much resistance the directive 98/44/CE was transposed in the legislation of the member states, with some modifications. Given the vagueness of the norm on the limits of patentability (art.6) many of the modifications regarded the integration covered by 'safeguarding clause' provided for in the same norm, that in a generic way, excludes from patentability those inventions whose commercial sale "goes against public order and decent behavior". It is exactly the operating leverage of the safeguarding clause provided by art. 6 and on the principles taken from art. II-63 of the Charter of Fundamental Rights that the European Court of Justice has recently sanctioned the non-patentability of "a procedure which, utilizing a sample of **stem cells** taken from a human embryo at the blastocyst phase, will destroy the embryo", in this way opening the way for a particularly promising interpretation of the directive. As can be read in the sentence C-34/10, the court is not called to confront questions of a medical or ethical nature, but that it should limit itself to the legal interpretation of pertinent dispositions of the directive'. In response to this, according to the Court "the fact of giving an invention a patent implies its industrial and commercial exploitation". Therefore, "even if the scope of scientific research is distinctly commercially motivated, the utilization of human embryos cannot be covered by a patent". As a consequence, the Court concludes that "scientific research that requires the utilization of human embryos cannot obtain the protection of patent rights", with this affirming the principle with which human embryos cannot be utilized/sacrificed for commercial motives. From this we can deduce also the human body and its parts, including its genetic heritage and the information contained in it.

Further legal evolution in this direction is the hoped for key in resolving once and for all the question of what is patentable and what is not, and with this the regulatory contrast between regulative fonts that guaranteed the principle of the 'non-excludability' of the human body, the pre-eminent safeguarding of life and human well-being, the freedom of scientific research and those normative fonts that protect intellectual property.

5.5 The Reorganization of Intellectual Property Law on Genetic Heritage: The Affirmation of an 'Open Source' Model for BioBricks and Synthetic Biology Base Components

Notwithstanding the limits that have emerged, especially with the advent of biotechnological inventions and synthetic biology, there has been no modification of the multilevel discipline of the patent to make it more adequate in the protection of the needs of this innovative sector, which is so crucial to its development. Even more, the guarantee of intellectual property rights and the centrality of the patent continue to play essential roles in the attraction of private investment in the *biotech* sector, sustaining its development and therefore consenting for the future benefit sharing and the increased protection of fundamental rights in the area of health, alimentation etc. Even in the most advanced international documents the desire to put the interests of humankind, present and future, and the qualification of non-excludable human resources ahead of those that are object of excusive private rights, is yet to triumph. But this does not justify public institutions' compliance, when faced with pressure from economic interests, and indifference to both old and new protections of fundamental rights, the human person and the freedom of scientific research.

More recently, other more far-sighted approaches reflect and affirm the model in which genetic resources and Bookracks are shared in the same way as software is shared (already proven efficient) in the 'Open Source' model, and on the guarantee of the rights to economic gain via the final products of synthetic biology. According to this model the regulation of technological discoveries and innovations should be inspired by a mixed model, justified by the fact that some very relevant discoveries and inventions can only be considered part of the common heritage of humanity, therefore they not be made the subject of any form of commercial exploitation. This premise would imply that the 'inventions' of biotechnology or synthetic biology in particular, can be classified in the following way: (a) that which belongs to the common heritage of humankind should not be patentable or used as a means to financial gain, and should be made available to all; (b) particularly relevant '*biotech* inventions', for example pharmaceuticals and lifesaving vaccines, should be made available to the public, so that everyone is able to use them and share them as a 'common good'; (c) all the other 'inventions' should be protected at the discretion of the inventor by a system of intellectual property suitable for the protection of the paternity, but at the same time encouraging of invention.

The first category should include the human genome and those large projects concentrating on the human genome, and the discovery of single genes and chromosomes, both in their natural state and artificially replicated. The second category should include those inventions that are called 'pre-competitive', that would in any case have high associated costs that need to be spread across the population, but that at the same time need to be made accessible at a low cost, or at least sustained by the public sector. BioBricks are included in this category, or the base code units that are required for the creation of new *biotech* products or living organisms. For their fair and equal diffusion new types of standards and licenses should be developed that are open to the interaction between systems developed both by engineers and geneticists. The third category should include the processes and the final products of biotechnology and synthetic biology, for which the inventors themselves are able to choose between patenting and an open license, in order to favor the accessibility and constant improvement thanks to the contribution of other scientists.

To repeat a crucial point: the protection by patent of any invention, including biotechnological inventions, is the legitimate right of whomever contributes to scientific and technical progress, that consists of a product, a new use for a product, a procedure or a method, in which the requirements of novelty, implication of inventive activity and industrial application. In giving full legitimization to the granting of a patent for a product, its new application, a biotechnological method or procedure that satisfies the prerequisites, but does not include that this protection can be extended to material such as BioBricks. The logic behind the maximization of profits from every biogenetic discovery that evidently sustains this regulatory choice, cannot legitimately found the one-way protection offered to *Biotech* companies that invest in the sector. It is sustainable to justify using the high costs of research that need to be covered by subsequent profits. The high cost of investment is however more than compensated for by the sale of *biotech* products, which are put on the market in conditions of monopoly, often at prohibitively high prices, chosen freely by their produces in order to maximize profits. The imposition of patents on BioBricks and other base components of synthetic biology, both material and immaterial, ends up creating an obstacle to the vitality of the entire sector and places serious limits on the development of other products.

It is for this reason that the application of the "Open Source" model, or a type of open license, would represent for these products, in the light of this analysis, the most solution most coherent with synthetic biology and offering the best protection of the commercial and scientific interests at play. At the same time giving full respect to the human health and wellbeing, as well as guaranteeing the greatest possible access to the *biotech* products. A system that operates in this way cannot, however, be realized without the strong support of both private and public sectors, of independent laboratories and public research institutes capable of conditioning, thanks to the constitution of a critical mass, an open model in which information and genetic data are shared sufficiently to give rise to this new and predominant system. Without this premise, it will be difficult to convince European and international institutions to modify the current regulations in the patent and *biotech* areas.

5.6 Freedom and Pluralism in Research: The Advantages of a Mixed Public-Private System and the Reframing of the Patent as a Human Right of the Person. Conclusions

It is evident that the concentration of capital favors the possibility of investments in the *biotech* sector and, therefore, increases the probability of reaching more quickly and easily the desired scientific results. It is not true, however, that 'only' the multinationals have or can guarantee the means with which to achieve these results. The research associations across different states are testament to this, and also the network of public and private independent laboratories are alternatives not to be overlooked. This does not detract from the fact that an effective interest on behalf of different nations to give incentives for research in the area should translate into the adequate public financing of this research and to stimulate the most promising lines of investigation in the promotion of improved public health. The 'special treatment' that the multinationals have until now enjoyed, also influencing the regulative choices in the sector, seems more a result of the pressure of the huge economic interest of the sector than to the effective merit of the protection accorded to the *biotech* giants.

Private companies and laboratories, in as much as they are economic subjects that operate for financial gain, also make large investments in the research programs that are able to guarantee the rapid usability of the discoveries made and the profitable commercial of the resulting products. Pure research and other lines of research that appear not to offer great economic rewards are therefore destined, in a system monopolized by private companies, to find little support. Over and above this, the need to maintain credibility and continued financial support on the part of investors, or to 'pass off' on the market their bio-industrial products, does not guarantee adequate transparency in the scientific results of private research. Only the adequate investment in and development of the public sector and the reconstitution of a plural system of laboratories, seems capable of guaranteeing, in an open and free competitive system, the conditions of liberty, pluralism and scientific transparence that are capable of advancing science, the market, and the protection of human rights.

The patent institutions have ended up bowing to the enormous pressure of the private economic interests of the biotechnology sector and that have warped the ratio between economic and social function. The patent, which was conceived as a legal instrument for the protection of the personal rights of the scientist/inventor to the economic gain resulting from his invention, has ended up as the legal-economic justification of monopolistic interests that have nothing to do with the rights of the person who physically creates a biotechnological 'invention'. It is sadly noted that even the best "brains" in the industry, in their assumption by the *Biotech* giants, are tempted by attractive contracts and advanced facilities, and are forced to renounce any claim to the future economic exploitation of the applications that are fruit of their own discoveries. This means, in the majority of cases, that the real artifices of biotechnological innovation are excluded from the enjoyment of the financial benefits that result from their inventions. In the most fortunate of cases they are able to enjoy a slice of the profits, a percentage that is most of the time laughable. In light of the re-visitation of the legal instruments that regulate the sector, there is the need to ask whether it is possible to continue to legitimize the separation between the right to economic gain from the invention – in favor of the company that has provided resources and capital – and the personal right of the inventor in recognizing his intellectual paternity of the invention. If in fact a mechanism for the division of the benefits between scientists and their employers who have both lent weight to the realization of the invention can be considered fair and equal, it can be considered illegitimate the a priori expropriation by the *biotech* companies of the rights to innovations at the expense of the inventors. The recognition of patent rights, at the same time as ownership, can be justified if it obeys its political social function, or if the title to the right remains principally with the inventor, and not otherwise.

In this sense the thesis by which the patent is redefined as a fundamental and personal right, appears co divisible in as much as it is unavailable and therefore incredible in its totality. To take the patent and the discipline surrounding it back to its nature as a "human right of the person" would be a coherent and transparent legal operation between means and ends, useful in reinstating the equilibrium between scientists/inventors and companies, and even more, in the reorganization of the hypertrophy of the latter's rights to the *biotech* applications and the heritage from which they are derived. The acceptance of such formulation would offer a dual advantage: above all it would allow for the creation of more equal and equilibrated contractual relations between companies and the authors of inventions, in which the former would see themselves guaranteed the recognition of the fair profits for the investments made and the author would maintain the ownership to the patent; secondly it would obtain the important result of avoiding the abnormal concentration of patents in the hands of a few multinationals. This would allow, moreover, every time that a patent regarded products/methods/techniques essential for the protection of primary goods, and the consideration in politically and legally more serene and equilibrated terms of the conflict, and the careful balancing, between the patent rights of the individual scientist and the fundamental rights of people, of the survival, health and development of the population and all of humanity. All the more reason why it would not be legitimate to endorse, in the case of conflict, the prevalence of rights derived from the companies' economic exploitation over the rights of people to access lifesaving cures or therapies, or the conservation of natural ecosystems.

A final essential note, in the context of the reform of the institution, regards the legal necessity to separate the legitimate protection of the invention from the arbitrary monopolization of the discovery. In the reorganization of the regulation of patents, to return them to the protection of goods that can be legitimately considered as such does not mean eliminating the attractiveness of the sector, but only returning the profits of private capital to that which can be legitimately considered the object of remuneration: the biotechnological inventions and the techniques and methodologies used in the interventions on genetic heritage, and not the discovery of the same genetic heritage, that is a heritage common to all of humanity, and as such unavailable and insusceptible to privatization as a means to selfish economic gain.

Bibliography

AA.VV (2006) Il gene invadente, Milano: Baldini-Castoldi-Dalai

AA.VV (2011) Romeo Casabona CM (ed) Los nuevos horizontes de la investigacion genetica, Comares, Bilbao-Granada

Baker D, Church G, Collins J, Endy D, Jacobson J, Keasling J, Modrich P, Smolke C, Weiss R (2006) Engineering life: building a fab for biology. Sci Am 294(6):44–51, PMID 16711359

Balmer A, Martin P (2008) Synthetic biology: social and ethical challenges. http://www.bbsrc.ac.uk/web/FILES/Reviews/0806_synthetic_biology.pdf

Bifulco R, D'aloia A (2008) Un diritto per il futuro. Teorie e modelli della responsabilità intergenerazionale. Jovene, Napoli

Bifulco R, Celotto A, Cartabia M (2001) L'Europa dei diritti, Il Mulino, Bologna

Bologna G (1996) I contenuti della sostenibilità, Ed. Ambiente, n. 1

Boschiero N (ed) (2006) Bioetica e biotecnologie nel diritto internazionale e comunitario: questioni generali e tutela della proprietà intellettuale. Giappichelli, Torino

Bovenberg JA (2006) Mining the common heritage of our DNA: lessons learned from Grotius and Pardo. 5 Duke Low & Technology Review 1–20

Calvert J (2008) The commodification of emergence: systems biology, synthetic biology and intellectual property. BioSocieties 3:383, London School of Economics and Political Science

Campiglio C (1999) I brevetti tecnologici nel diritto comunitario, in Dir Comm Int 849

Casaburi C (2005) Le biotecnologie fra diritto comunitario, Corte di Giustizia e inadempimento italiano. Foro Interno IV:408

Casonato C, Piciocchi C, Veronesi P (eds) (2011) I dati genetici nel biodiritto. Cedam, Padova

Cassier M, Gaudillère JP (2004) Le génome: bien privé ou bien commun? Biofutur 10:204

Cavalli Sforza L, Menozzi P, Piazza A (1994) The history and geography of human genes. Princeton University Press, Princeton

Ciciriello MC (1996) Dal principio del patrimonio comune al concetto di sviluppo sostenibile, in Dir Giur Agr Amb n. 4

Danchin A (2008) Synthetic biology: discovering new worlds and new words. EMBO Rep. doi:10.1038/embor.2008.159
Davies K (2001) Il codice della vita. Genoma: la storia e il futuro di una grande scoperta. Mondadori, Milano
De Miguel Beriain I (2010) Biología sintética y propiedad intelectual, una relación complicada, Perspectivas en Derecho y Genoma Humano. n.16, 2, Bilbao
Ducor PG (1998) Patenting the recombinant products of biotechnology. Kluwer Law International, London
Eigen M, Schuster P (1978) The hypercycle. Springer, Berlin
Elowitz MB, Leibler S (2000) A synthetic oscillatory network of transcriptional regulators. Nature 403(6767):335
Falcone A (2005) La tutela del patrimonio genetico umano nel processo di individuazione e codificazione 'costituzionale' dei diritti fondamentali dell'Unione Europea. In: Scudiero M (ed) Il Trattato costituzionale nel processo di integrazione europea. Jovene, Napoli
Francioni F (ed) (2001) Human rights & international trade. Hart, Oxfrod
Gestri M (2006) La gestione delle risorse naturali d'interesse generale per la comunità internazionale. Giappichelli, Torino
Ghidini G, Hassan S (1990) Biotecnologie, novità vegetali e brevetti. Giuffrè, Milano
Grandoni G (2001) La nuova direttiva sugli organismi geneticamente modificati, Riv Dir Agr 427
Habermas J (2002) Il futuro della natura umana. I rischi di una genetica liberale. Einaudi, Torino
Heller MA, Eiserman RS (1998) Can patents deter innovation? The anticommons in biomedical research. Science 280(5364):698. doi:10.1126/science.280.5364.698
Henkel J, Maurer SM (2007) The economics of synthetic biology. Mol Syst Biol 3:117
Henkel J, Reitzig M (2008) Patent sharks. Harvard Business Review, 129
Jonas H (1987) Creazione dell'uomo, il Mulino (XXXVI), Bologna, 615
Juengst ET (1998) Should we treat the human germ-line as a global human resource? In: Agius E, Busuttil S (eds) Germ-line intervention and our responsibilities to future generations. Kluwer, Dordrecht, pp 85–102
Kaznessis YN (2007) Models for synthetic biology. BMC Syst Biol. doi:10.1186/1752-0509-1-47
Kumar S, Rai A (2007) Synthetic biology: the intellectual property puzzle. Tex Law Rev 85:1745
Leduc S (1912) La Biologie Synthétique. A. Poinat Editeur, Paris
Lewontin R (1993) Biologia come ideologia. La dottrina del DNA. Bollati Boringhieri, Torino
Lucarelli A (2013) La democrazia dei beni comuni. Laterza, Bari
Martín Urganda A (2003) La protección juridica de las innovaciones biotecnológicas. Comares, Bilbao
Menesini V (1996) Le invenzioni biotecnologiche fra scoperte scientifiche, applicazioni industriali, preoccupazioni bioetiche. Riv Dir Int I:399
Miller AR, Davis MH (2000) Intellectual property: patents, trademarks, and copyright in a nutshell. West Group, St.Paul
Mohan RS, Waxman MMJ (1970) Synthetic biology patent applications expected to present new challenges. Life Sci Law Ind Rep 2(12):473
Monod J (1970) Il caso e la necessità. Mondadori, Milano
Moufang R (1989) Patentability of genetic inventions in animals. IIC Int Rev Ind Prop Copyr Law 20(6):823
Murphy SD (2001) Biotechnology and international law. Harvard Int Law J 41:47
Pavoni R (2004) Biodiversità e biotecnologieneldirittointernazionale e comunitario. Giuffrè, Milano
Pérez Bustamante G (1998) Patentes de invención Biotecnológicas: un análisis jurídico-económico, Revista de derecho y Genoma Humano, 8/1998, 159
Rai AK, Boyle J (2007) Synthetic biology: caught between property rights, the public domain, and the commons. PLoS Biol 5:58
Rifkin J (1998) Il secolo biotech. Il commercio genetico e l'inizio di una nuova era. Baldini & Castoldi, Milano
Ritter WE (1919) The unity of the organism. Richard G. Badger, Boston

Rodotà S (2011) Il corpo giuridificato. In: Rodotà S, Zatti P (eds) Trattato di Biodiritto, vol I. Giuffrè, Milano, AA VV
Romeo Casabona CM (2002) Los genes y sus leyes. El derecho ante el genoma umano. Comares, Bilbao
Strickberger Monroe W (1992) Trattato di genetica. Piccin, Padova
Szostak JW, Bartel DP, Luisi PL (2001) Synthesizing life. Nature 409:387–390
Van Overwalle G (2002) Study on the patenting of inventions related to human stem cell research, Luxembourg Office for Official Publications of the European Communities
Zanghì C (1998) Pour la protection des génération futures, Boutros Ghali Amicorum Discipulorumque Liber, II, 1459. Bruylant, Bruxelles

Chapter 6
Patents and Living Matter: The Construction of a Patent System Attractive to Biotechnology

Ana Paula Myszczuk and Jussara Maria Leal De Meirelles

Abstract This paper discusses adjustments in the intellectual property system, necessary to the construction of a system attractive to Biotechnology. For this, the paper was divided into two parts. The first part does an historical analysis of this process, from the inclusion of non-human living matter, to the possibility of patenting human genes. The second part does a brief analysis on most important leading cases on the human genes patent issue and highlights some new perspectives that come with the Brüstle v. Greenpeace Case.

Keywords Biopatents • Human living matter • Patents and human DNA • Intellectual property system and human dignity • Patents and living organisms • Patents and biotechnology

6.1 Introduction

The race is now on to patent living matter, both general and human. From microorganisms to vegetables, animals and human beings, there are numerous cases of patent applications. Science advances rapidly, leading to many benefits but also ethical, moral and legal disputes. It may be that the system is not sufficiently well prepared

A.P. Myszczuk (✉)
Academic Department of Economics and Managment, PUCPR, Paraná, Brazil

UTFPR – Universidade Tecnológica Federal do Paraná, Paraná, Brazil
e-mail: anap@utfpr.edu.br

J.M.L. De Meirelles
Law Department, UFPR, Curitiba, Brazil

Pontifícia Universidade Católica do Paraná, Paraná, Brazil
e-mail: jumeirelles29@gmail.com

I. de Miguel Beriain and C.M. Romeo Casabona (eds.), *Synbio and Human Health: A Challenge to the Current IP Framework?*, DOI 10.1007/978-94-017-9196-0_6,

to solve all the legal problems created by these new phenomena, nor would it be fair to expect it to be, but it is necessary to discuss the issue.

In the wake of all this controversy, the possibility of patenting inventions based on living human matter has been widely discussed, with ardent defenders and opponents all over the world. A large number of patents have already been granted. Although there is no worldwide agreement regarding the possibility of patenting living human matter, there is a consensus that the patent rights system has to be adapted to be able to analyze living human matter as something patentable. Furthermore, it is necessary to establish requirements and set limits on the granting of such patents.

It should be mentioned that patents were originally meant for the exclusive protection of inanimate inventions. Over a century would go by before living matter could be considered patentable, and even so it was always with considerable modifications to protect new inventions resulting from the human intellect. In this context, Synthetic Biology introduces a highly controversial variable into this debate, making the determination of what is human an even more complex issue. Therefore, the study of the consequences for patenting rights of biotechnological inventions has become even more important. This study will discuss the adaptations necessary for the patenting system.

6.2 Patents and Living Matter: Adjustment in the Intellectual Property System

The first patent of a living organism was granted to Louis Pasteur in 1781 in France and 1783 in the USA for isolated yeast free of organic germs that was obtained through an improvement in beer manufacturing. However, there was considerable resistance to granting patents for living matter because the intellectual property system was intended for the mechanical rather than the living, and complex adaptations were required.

To include biotechnology in the patent system, (Brody 2006, p. 02) understands that four distinct components were required: complete ownership of living products that arose naturally (including natural living organisms and isolated or purified products found in living organisms); complete ownership (patent) for the first inventors (USA) or applicants for patents (Europe); complete exclusionary rights (use by third parties requires that a royalty be paid to the inventor) and free interpretation of the traditional patent requirements (novelty and non-obviousness) to enable a perfect revelation of the invention and an intelligible request.

6.3 Patents and Non-human Living Matter

In the United States, the Patent Act of 1793, as modified by Thomas Jefferson, is the basis of the American patent system. It enables the granting of patents to "any new and useful art, machine, manufacture or composition of matter, or any new or useful improvement thereof" (USA Patent Act 1793, SEC. 2),[1] with no mention of patenting living matter. Thus, in 1889, the US Commissioner of Patents denied a request to patent an isolated pine needle fiber. This decision was based on the "product of nature doctrine". In other words, that which is invented to extract what exists in nature is patentable, but what already exists in nature is not as there is no inventive activity involved (Kevles 2002, p. 02).

This doctrine was first questioned in 1891, especially in the case of modified plants. In 1930, through the Plant Patent Act, the United States Congress recognized that improved plants are artificial and, thus, man-made inventions. Given the difficulty in describing the creation process of the new variety, the members limited the protection of plants to those reproduced asexually (budding, grafting, inarching or division). The Plant Patent Act only forbade the unauthorized use of the name of the plant variety described in the patent in advertising. As a result, few patents were requested (911 over the next 20 years) (Kevles 2002, p. 13).

In 1940, questions were raised as to whether bacteria were covered by the protection of the Plant Act, given that scientists classified bacteria as plants. But the USPTO understood that bacteria were not covered by this law. In the case of Funk Brothers Seed Co. v. Kalo Inoculant Co., in 1948, the request for a patent of natural products with added bacteria was overruled because it was seen as an aggression to the species rather than an invention (Poland 2002, p. 269). It was not until 1970, with the enactment of the Plant Variety Protection Act (PVPA) that sexually reproduced improved plants became eligible for protection in the form of patents. The battle for the complete ownership of living products that arose naturally was won by the biotechnology industry.

In the early 1970s, a great legal battle (Diamond v. Chakrabarty) began, with the granting of the first patent of a modified microorganism (Pseudomanas bacterium, genetically modified to destroy crude oil components in seaweed). Two questions came under discussion: whether the researchers were inventors or had merely interfered in normal metabolic processes, and whether the possible patenting could or should be centered on the transformation of matter by human activity, irrespective of it being living matter.

The initial patent application was rejected based on the understanding that the bacillus was a product of nature and that the insertion of plasmids, despite modifying it, did not result in the creation of a new species. The request was also rejected because living matter was not patentable as there was no legislation or legal precedent that could permit it. In 1974, following the rejection of an appeal, Chakrabarty appealed to the Board of Appeal of the U.S Patent Office, claiming that the bacillus he had created was not a product of nature, seeing that it had been fundamentally modified by the inventor and was therefore an invention. In May of 1976, the Board of Appeal understood that the bacterium was not a product of nature, but rejected the application for a patent because in their understanding a bacterium was not patentable because it is a living organism. The Board concluded that:

[1] http://ipmall.info/hosted_resources/lipa/patents/Patent_Act_of_1793.pdf. Accessed on 22.10.2011 at 21:00.

> To adopt a broad interpretation of phrases such as "new composition of matter" would "open the flood gates to patentability for all newly produced microorganisms as well as for all newly developed multi-cellular animals such as … chickens and cattle". The Board's ruling reiterated Tanenholtz's warning and added that if patents could be granted to single-cell organisms with added plasmids, so might they be given for "multicellular organisms (including human beings)" with transplanted livers or hearts. Chakrabarty's bugs might not occur naturally, but the Board chose to emphasize "that a human being with a transplanted liver or heart is also not naturally occurring. (Kevles 2002, p. 17)

Chakrabarty decided to appeal the decision, seeking a legal precedent that would enable him to patent his invented process and products. However, this case became entangled with that of Malcolm E. Bergy, an associate researcher at the Upjohn Company. Bergy had created a process for obtaining purified strains of a newly discovered fungus (*Streptomyces vellosus*), which metabolized chemicals producing the antibiotic lincomycin. In 1974, Upjohn had applied to patent both the product and the process. The application was denied as the product in question was understood to be natural. In 1975, Upjohn appealed to the Board of Appeal. In 1976, the Council rejected the application on the same grounds that it had rejected that of Chakrabarty: the fungus was living matter. Upjohn then appealed to the US Court of Customs and Patent Appeals, and both cases were restricted to the matter of when a living organism can be patented in accordance with the American Patent Act.

In October of 1977, the Court ruled in favor of Bergy, understanding that there was nothing in the Patent Act to deny the granting of a patent only because the product in question is a living thing and its use lies in the fact that it is a modified living thing. In the case of Chakrabarty, the Court ruled in his favor in 1978 by three votes to two. However, fearing that the patents granted could be invalidated by the federal courts and that the matter might to taken to Congress, the USPTO, represented by its commissioner Sidney Diamond, appealed to the Supreme Court.

In April of 1978, the Bergy and Chakrabarty cases were appealed and in June of 1980 the Supreme Court ruled in favor of the patents by five votes to four. The Court understood that the bacterium in question was a new product or a new material manufactured as a result of human inventiveness, and this allowed the inventor to request a patent. Furthermore, the Court understood that the scope of Jefferson's Patent Act was broad enough to allow them to rule on fields of science that were unforeseen at the time, such as biotechnology. The focus of analysis is whether the process or product is an invention of human intelligence or something that exists in nature rather than whether the thing is living or not.

The Patent and Trademark Law that was passed by the US Congress in 1980 sparked cooperation between universities and industry. The universities plunged into the commercial world and the biotechnology industry incorporated academic features that were considered necessary to attract and hold top class researchers. Since the 1980s, it has been possible to patent invented living matter (Miralles and López Gusmán 1999, p. 282).

In 1984, marine biologists Standish K. Allen Jr., Sandra L. Dowing and Jonathan A. Chaiton filed a patent application for an improved version of a Pacific coast oyster (Crassostrea gigas). This served as a precedent for the patenting of a larger animal. The USPTO initially denied the request. An appeal was filed with the Board of

Appeal and the patent for the polyploid oyster was granted in 1987. In the understanding of the Board, the oyster did not exist in this form in nature. In the same year, the USPTO decided that non-naturally occurring and non-human multicellular organisms are patentable and that patents on human beings are forbidden by the Constitution. But in this case, the biotechnology industry had won an important victory: the complete ownership of living organisms had been extended to multicellular organisms.

On 13 September 1988, the United States Congress passed the Animal Patent Bill. It exempted farmers who purchased transgenic animals and used them for reproduction with their own non-transgenic animals. The bill also explained that it was the responsibility of the USPTO to request a deposit of biological material from patented animals. It also stated that human beings could not be patented. By not defining a human being, the act allowed some leeway for this definition to be left to the USPTO, researchers or applicants for patents. This could lead to a very broad definition, including creatures considered as higher animals, or a very narrow definition, excluding modified creatures and the concepts of morality and humanity that protect them (Fishman 1989, p. 473).

In 1990, the first genetically modified higher animal was patented. This was the oncomouse, a transgenic rat with cells capable of developing breast cancer, developed in the 1980s by two Harvard researchers, Philip Leder and Tim Stewart. The main focus of the request was to protect the animal itself, since through other methods a similar animal could be created. The USPTO granted to Harvard University a patent on any transgenically engineered non-human mammal to incorporate into its genome an oncogene linked to a specific promoter (Kevles 2002, p. 47).

6.4 Patents and Living Human Matter: Moore v. Regents of the University of California

John Moore worked in Alaska and was diagnosed with a rare and potentially fatal form of leukemia. He was treated by Dr. David W. Golde at the University of California Medical Center in August 1976. The case offered a unique opportunity for research and the doctor recommended the removal of his patient's spleen. This operation was performed in October with the patient's consent. His condition was stabilized and the spread of the disease arrested. Moore returned to the Medical Center on a regular basis from 1976 to 1983. Samples of his blood, skin, bone marrow, sperm and blood serum were taken. The medical justification for these procedures was that his body elements had "unique characteristics" that were of interest both in terms of research and for the "improvement of humanity".

When Moore told the doctor that he could no longer afford the trips from Seattle to Los Angeles and that he would have to seek treatment in Seattle, the doctor offered to pay his expenses, putting Moore up in what he described as "a luxury hotel" in Beverly Hills (Bergman 1992, p. 130). In 1983, when asked to grant to the university the rights to his cell lines and any other product obtained from his body for research purposes. Moore refused to sign and sought legal advice (Myszczuk 2005, p. 78–79). His attorneys then discovered that in 1979 the researchers had immortalized the cells taken from his spleen in a new cell line, known as the "Mo cell line". With these cells and using recombinant DNA techniques they could produce lymphokines indefinitely. The researchers hoped that this product would be of commercial value both as a research tool and for therapeutic use. The attorneys also discovered that in the same year, the UCLA and Golde had applied for patents on sub-products of the Mo cell line for the production of certain proteins. The application was amended in 1983 and granted in 1984. This patent was licensed to the Genetics Institute and Sandoz Pharmaceutics. The doctor became a paid consultant at the Genetics Institute, being awarded shares in the company and other benefits in exchange for exclusive access to the results of his research.

Moore sued the UCLA, Dr. Golde and Shirley G. Quan, a UCLA researcher, claiming the right to a share in the profits gained from the production of drugs and the sale of products to pharmaceutical industries that were created from his genetic material (Brody 2006, p. 16). The court ruled in favor of the UCLA, claiming that there were no caveats in the consent forms signed by Moore when he agreed to surgery and medical procedures at a university research hospital. This gave the doctor authority to perform his tasks, even for commercial, in addition to medical and scientific, purposes. The majority opinion of the Court of Appeals was that surgically removed human tissue was "the personal property" of the patient. Therefore, without the express permission of Moore, the use of his tissue by the university constituted misappropriation (Rabinow 1995).

In 1990, the Supreme Court of California identified two problems: (1) when potential donors must be informed, within the process of obtaining informed consensus, that their biological material can be used for commercial purposes and when they should be compensated for flaws in this process; (2) and whether, in cases of no informed consent, donors have ownership rights over their biological samples and derived products and whether failure to inform the patient entitles him to reverse his decision.

The Supreme Court of California was divided. In the majority vote it was stated that:

> a physician who adds his own research interests to this balance [burden and benefits] may be tempted to order a scientifically useful procedure or test that offers marginal, or no, benefits to the patient. [In a footnote, the Court noted that Moore had alleged just that with regard to the drawing of blood and other material after this treatment.] The possibility that an interest extraneous to the patience's health has affected a physician's judgment is something that a reasonable patient would want to know in deciding whether to consent to a proposed course of treatment. It is material to the patient's decision and, thus, a prerequisite to informed consent. (Brody 2006, p. 16)

The Supreme Court of California decided that there were no precedents for holding people responsible for misappropriation of human cells for medical research. This would mean hindering research by restricting access to the necessary raw materials. Scientists would have to track down the genealogical consent for every sample of human cells used in research to avoid their research being deemed illegal.

Furthermore, ownership of the genetic code of lymphokines could be attributed to Moore, even though their biochemical constitution is the same in all human beings. On this point, they also decided that Moore had a cause against the doctor, who failed to reveal that beyond the therapeutic aspect of the treatment he had personal interests at stake (Rabinow 1995). The majority of judges decided that Moore had no ownership rights over the cells removed from his body because this could hinder the flow of biological material among researchers. They stated that each sample of a patient could turn into a litigation "lottery ticket" and that as a result investments in this field could dry up.

Another matter discussed in the doctrine is whether Moore had the genetic information found in the cells of his spleen, the T-lymphokynes. Each of us is the owner of our own body, but we do not own the information it contains: the "model" of the body. A copy of the "model" is possessed, but not the "model" itself, this intangible information (Moore 2000, p. 107). In this way, a precedent was established that donors have no right to a share of the economic benefits that result from samples taken from their bodies. The battle for complete ownership for the first inventors or applicants for patents was won by the biotechnological industry.

6.5 Patents and Human DNA

In 1991, J. Craig Venter, a biologist at the National Institute of Neurological Disorders and Strokes in the USA sequenced random fragments of cDNA, the EST (expressed sequence tags), which are complementary parts of the encoded regions of genomic DNA derived from parts of the brain. The researcher and the National Health Institutes requested a patent of the EST sequences, the whole sequence of the gene and the protein produced by it, even though only a part of the had been sequenced. The justification for this request was that it would protect future research and development.

James Watson, who at that time was head of the Human Genome project of the NIH was a harsh critic of this move. He claimed that the sequencing was purely mechanical and did not deserve to be patented. He added that the granting of patents for ESTs at this early stage of research would lead to researchers keeping secrets from one another and would reduce international cooperation. This argument cost Watson his job and he resigned in 1992. In the same year, the USPTO rejected the patent application, claiming that it did not meet the requirements for novelty, non-obviousness and utility.

In 1996, Lawrence Goffney, the Acting Deputy Commissioner of Patents and Trademarks at the American Association for the Advancement of Science, announced that the USPTO had decided that it would accept patent applications for collections of ESTs, based on their utility as a research tool. This led to a series of technical debates that culminated in an exchange of letters between the NIH and the USPTO and the preparation of guidelines for possible patenting. In 1997, the USPTO declared that the mere allegation that sequences are a useful research tool without revealing for what purpose would be insufficient information to warrant a patent. But the revelation of the utility of a sequence of ESTs with their scientific identification, anatomic type or origin, chromosome maps, chromosome identification or as a marker of a gene with a known and useful function could be considered sufficient (Brody 2006, p. 108). The proposition of applications for patenting collections of ESTs depends on whether these are "specific, substantial and credible".

The USPTO decided that human genes are patentable as long as they can be isolated, purified, characterized and put in useable form in the development of tools, diagnoses or therapy (Terry 2003, p. 379). The component of free interpretation of the traditional patent requirements to enable a perfect revelation of the invention and an intelligible request was settled.

6.6 A New Component: Human Dignity and the Oliver Brüstle v. Greenpeace Case

In 1997, Oliver Brüster, a neurologist, applied to the German patent office to patent isolated and purified neural precursor cells processed from embryonic stem cells at the blastocyst stage for therapeutic use. The patent was granted but was challenged in 2006 by Greenpeace EV, who claimed that the grant was in violation of Article 2 of the German Patents Law and Article 6(2)c of Directive 98/44/EC, in that the patent violated the principle of human dignity. Brüster appealed to the European Court of Justice, questioning the application of the principle of human dignity on inventions based on stem cells. He posed three questions on the matter: (1) how should human embryos be defined according to Article 6(2)c of Directive 98/44? Are the stages of development of the human embryo considered from the time of its fertilization or should other requirements be added? Are embryos organisms such as unfertilized human ova into which the nucleus of a mature human cell has not been transplanted or which have been stimulated to continue developing by parthenogenesis until the blastocyst stage? (2) What does the use of human embryos for industrial or commercial purposes mean? Is scientific research an exception as it is susceptible to commercial exploitation? (3) are inventions not patentable when the use of human embryos does not in itself constitute the technical information protected by the patent, but a necessary requirement for the application of information since the patent is for a product whose preparation requires the prior destruction of embryos or because the patent is for a procedure for which this is necessary as a base material?

The European Court of Justice ruled that in order to apply of Directive 44/98/CE it is necessary to have a common understanding in Europe of what an embryo actually is or how a patentable embryo should be defined. In response to the first series of questions, the Court adhered to a broad concept of embryo, understanding that a human embryo is the entire human ovum from the time of fertilization and the unfertilized ova into which the nucleus of a mature human cell has not been transplanted or which have been stimulated to continue developing through parthenogenesis until the blastocyst stage is an embryo. However, the Court ruled that it fell to each national jurisdiction to determine whether a cell obtained from a human embryo at the blastocyst stage is an embryo in accordance with the Directive. In response to the second series of questions, the Court ruled that patentability refers to industrial, commercial and scientific application and that the latter is excluded only if the purpose is for therapeutic or diagnostic purposes. In answer to the third series of questions, the Court ruled that Article 6 excludes from patentability any inventions for which the patent applications requires the prior destruction of human embryos or their use as base material.

This decision is important to set that the human gene has a twofold nature. It is a chemical compound or information, but it is also part of a human being, his most basic identity. It should be stressed that DNA, gamete or an embryo from a biological viewpoint, is part of the bodily structure of a person and, as such, is part of the dignity of each individual, which corresponds to the human body as a whole. Thus, inventions that are based on any living human matter have to adapt to this multiple identity, adding to the patent system the same protection requirements given to human beings.

6.7 Final Considerations

Even though there has been an effort to raise and maintain a suitable level of human dignity, there have been many cases in which the essence of human beings is no longer considered valuable in terms of dignity and humanity. Instead, they are valued for their genes and the information that these genes may contain. This problem is especially evident when it comes to patenting inventions derived from living human matter. The pressure from the market for investments made in the biotechnology sector to be rewarded with exclusive rights to exploit products and procedures often clashes with the more serene analysis of requirements for a certain "invention" to be patented. Furthermore, there is currently no consensus as to whether living human matter should be used by private interests and exploited economically. Synthetic biology adds even more factors to this discussion.

In addition to this, for the current patent system to accommodate the possibility of patenting inventions based on living human matter, many alterations are required than those made during the twentieth century. It is worth mentioning that one of the characteristics of the Patent Act is exactly this flexibility that allows it to constantly respond to and keep up with economic needs, advances in science and the challenges these present when it comes to protecting the fruits of human ingenuity. Thus, new adaptations are required.

This system must adapt to human characteristics regarding their multiple nature. It is not right to reduce live human matter, even if synthetic, to something inhuman, a simple chemical compound, as this is not the legal nature of this "input". This would be a definite step toward the reification of a human being, reducing them to the atomic scale, a simple chain of chemical reactions bereft of any human nature or potential, a simple chemical program. Therefore, it cannot be forgotten that human dignity limits the freedom of the researcher. Human dignity requires that for patents to be granted, people must be respected, both for the need for their full development and in the drive for improved quality of life for human beings. This inclusion means that a technical analysis of patents must ensure that people are protected by national and international systems.

References

Bergman HR (1992) Case comment: Moore v. regents of the University of California. Am J Law Med 18(1–2):127–146, Boston

Brody B (2006) Intellectual property and biotechnology; the U.S. internal experience – part I. Kennedy Inst Eth J 16(1):01–38, Baltimore: The Johns Hopkins University Press

Fishman R (1989) Patenting human beings: do sub-human creatures deserve constitutional protection? Am J Law Med 15(4):461–482, Boston

Kevles D (2002) A history of patenting life in the United states with comparative attention to Europe and Canada. Council of Europe Publishing, Strasbourg

Miralles, A. López Guzmán, J (1999) Biotecnología y patentes: reto científico o nuevo negocio? Revista Cuadernos de Bioética. v. 10, n. 38, p. 282–287.

Moore AD (2000) Owing genetic information and gene enhancement techniques: why privacy and property rights may undermine social control of the human genome? Bioethics 14(2):97–119, Oxford

Myszczuk AP (2005) Genoma Humano. Limites jurídicos à sua manipulação. Juruá, Curitiba

Poland, SC (2002) Genes, Patents, and Bioethics: Will history repeat itself? In: Kennedy Institute of Ethics Journal. Vol 10, nº 3, p. 265–283.

Rabinow P (1995) Cortando as amarras: fragmentação e dignidade na modernidade hoje. http://www.anpocs.org.br/portal/publicacoes/rbcs_00_23/rbcs23_05.htm. Accessed 14 Feb 2013

Terry PF (2003) PXE International: harnessing intellectual property law for benefit-sharing. In: Knoppers BM (ed) Populations and genetics. Legal and social-ethical perspectives. Martinus Nijhoff Publishers, Lieden, pp 377–393

Chapter 7
Patents Originating in Human Tissue and Data: Questions on Benefit Creating and Benefit Sharing, on Morality and Property

David Townend

Abstract Synthetic biology poses interesting iterations of familiar legal and ethical questions raised in modern biotechnology. These are particularly interesting in relation to patents, privacy, and property. These questions ask us whether there are inconsistencies in our approach to safeguarding individuals and, at the same time, encouraging innovation. The first issue explored here is about the procedural inclusion of morality within the patenting process. Morality is a seemingly different question from legality and there seems to be reluctance in many places to embrace morality as a full and appropriate part of the patent granting agenda. However it is arguable that the patenting process has to change to include a more effective evaluation of the morality of innovations. A second tension arises when one considers the regulation of privacy alongside the patenting process over innovations with their origins in human data and tissue. Considering this tension opens up the question of what the concept of property should be that is used in the regulation of innovations in modern biotechnology. This requires us to consider the social context of the definition of property. The paper then considers these discussions in relation to the broader human rights debate, and particularly how a more extensive application of the human rights agenda is necessary to ensure consistency in the regulation of modern biotechnology.

Keywords Synthetic biology • Biotechnology • Patents • Human rights • Property • Privacy • Morality

---

D. Townend
Department of Health, Ethics and Society, CAPHRI School of Public Health and Care

Faculty of Health, Medicine and Life Sciences, Maastricht University, Maastricht, The Netherlands
e-mail: d.townend@maastrichtuniversity.nl

I. de Miguel Beriain and C.M. Romeo Casabona (eds.), *Synbio and Human Health: A Challenge to the Current IP Framework?*, DOI 10.1007/978-94-017-9196-0_7,

7.1 Introduction

Ultimately, synthetic biology seeks to go beyond engineering with already known biological components to creating the component parts of genetics and cell biology from chemical raw materials; the goal is understanding and then creating life from first principles (Alleyne 2010). How far this could go towards the creation of organisms, and at what level of organism, is contested, and, indeed, safety arguments and concerns may be the greatest regulatory objection and block to the full development and realization of this biology should the potentials of the higher-level work be remotely approached. However, the possibility of these developments challenges not only the operation of modern intellectual property law in the area, but it invites us to consider once again the fundamental concepts that underpin intellectual property. Synthetic biology arguably does not require us to consider particularly new ethical and legal principles, but like other new developments in biotechnology, it challenges our established ideas from a new perspective. The question is whether or not we will take that challenge and revisit those fundamental principles: questions, within a free economic market, of individuality and dignity, of free expression, of the extent of the concept of property, of privacy and private life and of each person's rights and responsibilities in relation to full and equitable participation in one's society. They are challenges about the rights in benefit creating and benefit sharing.

Three problems about intellectual property are often posed in this area, problems that are visible in the case law: the regulatory regimes for the collection and use of samples and data seem to operate with a presumption that there are no property rights for the donor of the sample; intellectual property is allowed to place monopolies over the science of developments rather than over the products resulting from applications of the science of the developments; and, the increased commodification of elements of the natural sciences introduces, at one end of the process, caution about undertaking fundamental research into areas where the science has been captured by patents, and, at the other end, reluctance to explore scientific lines of interest that do not have an obvious potential income stream. From this, the suggestion can follow that modern biotechnology is being hampered by the distortion that comes from the intellectual property regime - particularly by the initial impulse to see intellectual property as necessarily expanding to fit every development's claim for inclusion, rather than starting from a position of considering whether the development is within the principles of intellectual property and property more generally, and, if not, to consider the social implications of extending the regime rather than simply chasing the immediate economic interests.

On one hand, these criticisms are misplaced. The role of intellectual property is to provide a simple monopoly within which innovation can be encouraged by protecting original and inventive investment through a market opportunity. That individual innovators in modern biotechnology seek to make use of this environment is not the fault of them or the system in which they operate. Indeed, there might be no moral or social tension presented by synthetic biology, or any other innovative development. However, the question must be raised as to whether such questions are asked by new developments, particularly whether new developments point to inconsistencies within different aspects of our normative landscape that are unsustainable and that require a reorientation of our expectations and normative responses. In this paper, five possible inconsistencies are introduced with a view to asking if they produce unsustainable inconsistencies.

7.2 The Procedural Morality Tension

European intellectual property law is required to consider the moral and social implications of its operations. Under the European Patent Convention, a patent should not be granted for a novel, innovative product with the potential for industrial application, the exploitation of which is against morality or ordre public,[1] and yet at the granting stage there is arguably little systematic investigation into this requirement.[2] A presumption seems to operate that the market, rather than the regulator is the appropriate forum in a democracy to challenge the moral or social validity of the application. This is at one level absolutely correct: it is fully appropriate to open the consideration of the patentability of patent applications to social scrutiny as civil servants are not moral guardians in modern democracies. However, the moral and social issues posed by applications, particularly those in the modern biotechnology industries, should arguably be considered specifically, robustly and systematically before the grant of the patent, rather than relying on the idea that morality is determined by whether or not members of the public purchase the item when it is released for sale and whether the grant is challenged through litigation.

Limiting the consideration of morality to the scrutiny given by purchasers in the market rather than by separate investigation in the patent granting process may give an appearance of the democratisation, but it is only an appearance. On one hand, it ignores the cost of litigation, which is prohibitively expensive making this route to moral scrutiny unrealistic except in exceptional cases. More fundamentally it fragments the debate about the morality from the patenting system to the morality of individual patents in their interactions with particular consumers; it locates the question on an individual product, rather than on either general trends and developments in innovation, or on the suitability of the innovation reward paradigm for new developments and social perceptions. So the first question that is raised by each new development in patenting is, where is the proper place to discuss its morality (or perhaps more easily, the social desirability) of pursuing new opportunities?

---

[1] European Patent Convention, Article 53 (a). See also Universal Declaration of Human Rights, Article 29 (2). European Patent Office (2010); UN General Assesmbly (1948).

[2] It is difficult to pin down evidence of this. However, the suggestion is made on the basis that (1) there are few formal challenges to a decision not to grant a patent on the basis of Article 53; (2) there are few Article 53 challenges to patents that have been successful; and, (3) there is an argument that those engaged in the patent granting process are not equipped to make judgments under Article 53. One might also point to the sense of novelty that has attended the Norwegian Patent Office's work with the National Research Ethics Committee to develop a patent ethics board (see Forskningstetiske Komiteer 2008).

There is an argument that the place for this debate is not at the point of considering the grant of patent monopolies, as the grant does not function as a 'permission' in that sense; it is not, it is argued, a moral or other normative approval to go to the market (although arguably it is difficult to assert that a licence from the State does not carry with it an implied approval). And it raises the question of whether, because some individuals wish to purchase a commodity or service in the open market, that desire makes it morally acceptable in society. So, this argument this argument is made as, 'shouldn't this be a matter for parliaments and legislators?'

Clearly parliaments are the seats of democratically elected representatives who are charged with considering and reflecting the moral tone of their societies in legislation. However, the level at which the incremental developments in innovation operate – the invention-by-invention nature of the development – makes legislative responses inappropriate to regulate particular inventions; legislators operate at the meta-level, and the determination of the morality of the particular invention is at the micro-level. In our example, synthetic biology is not, of itself, inappropriate, but some of the particular developments within the it might be questionable. Therefore, despite the discomfort that it causes, Article 53 and the requirement to consider the social and moral impact of patent applications seems to be the necessary compromise; the place to discuss the moral and social impact issues of a particular invention is within the patent granting process. Given that this presents difficulties, the question returns to 'how should this requirement operate?'

The inclusion of morality in European patent law acknowledges a fundamental difference between law and morality. Functionally, law sets a boundary, an outer limit on the appropriateness of action. It is a response to a question: 'can I do this?' It says to its society, 'in this aspect of life, you can do this, but you cannot do that'. It is in this respect a negative, binary boundary. Law's meaning is continuously challenged to see how far one can push the meanings defining the boundary line; law is defined by the question, 'is this action in or out of the realm of the (legal) sanction?' Morality, however, is a response to a very different question: 'should I do this?' Morality demands that every action is placed under a scrutiny of whether (in the particular circumstances) it is appropriate, be it legally sanctioned or not. Thus, morality challenges the boundary of law, in that it speaks a 'should?' to the 'can I do this?' boundary; it challenges the actions that the law accepts as acceptable or rejects as unacceptable, asking 'although you can (or can't) do this at law, should you do this?'

The inclusion of this second question – the 'should I'? as well as the 'can I?' question – in intellectual property acknowledges that every application to patent law is a novel challenge not simply to the established definition of the law, but to the previous order of society. Intellectual property is concerned with innovation and each application is about things that were previously unconsidered. Intellectual property is charged by society to be the place where these twin boundary questions of 'can I do this?' and 'should I do this?' are merged.[3] And they are not simply questions posed by the individual consumer, but they are posed on behalf of all citizens; the 'should I do this?' is also a 'should we do this?'

Part of the difficulty that this presents is perhaps about the resolution of contests between theories. Law, created in democratic parliamentary systems has an internal

[3] In jurisdictions that adopt the option in Article 27 (2) of the TRIPS agreement.

dispute resolution mechanism. The passing of a law, or the creation of a law under delegated power from a primary statute, answers those who disagree with the content, thus: 'your opinion has been heard, but the democratic process has produced a different result from the one you would wish'. It is, of course, open to revisit the point or challenge the operation of the process, but the resolution is catered for in the procedure. Morality is different. Morality is contested, in that there is disagreement about the understanding of the morality to use both at a theoretical and practical level. Morality, however, unlike law, does not contain within it an agreed mechanism for the resolution or accommodation of the contest. It is therefore perhaps unsurprising that Article 53 is deficient, when it neither points to a particular morality to apply (and competing moral theories can produce diametrically opposing views on the same point), or a mechanism within which to resolve the contest between moralities. Morality's inclusion then as a condition for patentability in Article 53 is problematic for (legal) systems that are accustomed to relying on the internal authority of the rules and procedures that are to be applied.

It is not, however, sufficient to say that courts, lawyers and patent officers are not trained in morality or the resolution of questions of morality so the issue is not appropriate in such fora, and then to leave the issue without consideration or resolution. The need is to ensure that there are fora that engage individuals who do have the familiarity with the mechanisms to make moral and ethical judgments. There is a real need to develop patent ethics committees, in the manner of research ethics committees and clinical ethics committees in other areas of health governance, where Article 53 morality questions can be seriously explored as part of the patent granting process. Indeed, the Norwegian Patent Office has taken steps to develop such a process.[4] However, this does not seem to have been enthusiastically followed by other patent offices. So here there are difficulties, if not inconsistencies, but there are possible solutions that could be employed that are used elsewhere in governance structures for similar problems.

7.3 Patents Originating in Human Tissue and Data: A Regulatory Tension

If synthetic biology reminds us of an unresolved and continuing procedural difficulty, it also reminds us of substantive patenting issues relating to privacy and the right to a private life.[5] Within modern biotechnology, there are increasing areas of patents that are based on material and data that are derived from humans (for example, from stem cells or from genetic information). Equally, there are emerging areas, as seen in synthetic biology, where there is an interaction between artificially created biological material and individual humans. These later developments could be seen as following a line from prosthetic devices such as artificial hip joints, but equally arguably, they have a significant difference in that they have a much greater

[4] See Forskningstetiske Komitteer 2008.

[5] Universal Declaration of Human Rights, Article 12; European Convention on Human Rights, Article 8.

interaction with the human; the aim is to effect biological (typically microbiological) change through the operation of the product, or for the product to become (or even to be) the person. These developments are undertaken within commercial environments, and there is a desire to seek patent protection for these biological inventions and innovations.

The regulatory framework for these areas of modern biotechnology originating in human tissues and samples is constructed through two arguably different regimes: on the one hand the human rights based tissue and data regulation, and on the other the commercially-oriented intellectual property regulation. The two regimes operate for very different purposes, and from very different starting assumptions (not least in relation to the different concepts of 'property' that are employed in each). These biotechnological innovations require human tissue and genetic information (often in an on-going relationship with the research participant, enabling the raw genetic information to be considered against the participant's changing environment).

The regulatory regime that has emerged concerning the use of such tissue and data is robust.[6] Its primary aim is to produce a governance environment that gives the public confidence to participate in medical research and treatments (the key elements of its benefit sharing strategy). Its focus is on the ethical gathering, storage, use, and destruction of the samples and data. It also concerns the sharing of the material with others. In the case of tissue (often through the licensing of those who work with human tissue and heavy non-compliance sanctions), it regulates the institutions and individuals who can have access to the material. In both tissue and data regulation, the safeguard of informed consent from the participant (and to some extent the 'anonymisation' of samples and data) is crucial. Because of this rather 'front end' focus (rather than focusing on the applications of the products derived from the processing of the samples and tissue), the legislation tends towards a rather public or administrative law approach, safeguarding the procedures of protection. Issues such as property rights in the sample and data are not central to these purposes. Indeed, there is some confusion around the property issues posed by tissues and data.[7]

Many regimes, although not all, follow a presumption that 'ownership' of a human body by the individual human whose body is in question is inappropriate. Based on a Lockeian approach that property is justified from the added labour and effort invested in raw materials rather than the raw materials themselves, and a sensitivity against the implications of the commodification of the human

[6] In relation to the regulation of personal data in Europe, see particularly the Data Protection Directive 95/46/EC. For a discussion of the regulation of the use of human tissue in research see Wright et al. (2010).

[7] It is arguable that the intellectual property regime has a similar 'front end' approach, concentrating on the granting of the right rather than on the use of the property generated through the operation of the monopoly.

body by the human in question,[8] there is often a prohibition on the classification of the relationship between the human and his or her own body in relation to the rest of the world as a 'property' right. However, at the same time in this area, there is an extraordinarily strong property language of 'donation' that underpins the process. The idea that a participant 'donates' his or her sample or data suggests, at least at a popular level, that there is property that is being given and received.

The intellectual property regime, on the other hand, is all about creating property. Here, the regime is again a gateway regime in as much as it regulates the types of products and processes that will be accepted to become property, but a property that is a market lead time in which the owner of the property has an opportunity to make the most of a monopoly situation for his or her product. The elements of the assessment are: that the product of the process is novel (i.e. could not be found in the 'prior art', the information known in the particular area); that it is innovative (tested by asking if the notional individual with a perfect knowledge of the state of the art who is devoid of imagination would look at the product or process and say whether it was obvious or not); that the product or process has an industrial application; and, that the product or process is not excluded from patentability.[9]

There is an inconsistency between the regulation of the human tissue and data that is used in the biotechnology that forms the basis of the innovation and the basis of the (intellectual property) interests created in the innovation. This is an inconsistency of approaches to the property involved in each element – in the tissue and data, and in the innovation. This gives rise to two further property based difficulties: the presumption against the property ownership by the individual in his or her own body (especially because of dignity arguments) is inconsistent with the commodification of the same material by others once the material or data are removed from the individual; and, the continuation of the use of patents as the basis for the availability of, or access to, the products denies the medical and social significance of the products. These inconsistencies will only be resolved if the underlying concept of property is addressed.

[8] For example, that an individual might be able to sell his or her kidney.

[9] These are the requirements long established in Patent Law, but expressed today in Article 27 of the TRIPS agreement, Article 52 of the European Patent Convention and variously in domestic laws (see, for example, the UK Patent Act 1977, Section 1). World Trade Organization (1994).

7.4 The Property Tension

Article 53 of the European Patent Convention indicates that it is concerned with a broader question of morality than simply if the invention is, of itself, moral. Article 53 demands that the 'commercial exploitation' of the invention is moral (or in line with *ordre public*). This on the one hand might entail a technical question about how far 'up-stream' science should be patented. However, more importantly for biotechnology, and the developments of synthetic biology, the exploitation of the 'property' in the intellectual property might give rise to the moral question not simply of benefit creating, but also of benefit sharing.

I have written elsewhere, both alone and with Djims Milius (Townend 2003, 2012; Milius and Townend 2008), about the concept of property. It is important, to contribute the two central arguments in the context of this collection about synthetic biology, namely, that property is a moral issue, and that property is a social construction. Property is a moral issue first in a popular sense. The control of resources is a major determinant in individuals' access to fundamental human requirements. Food, drugs, therapies, all determine the length and quality of an individual's life; the foods, drugs and therapies that are developed, and whether particular individuals can gain access to them, determine life chances. Intellectual property creates property rights, rights about controlling access to these commodities, and this raises moral questions about benefit sharing. It asks, is there a necessary link in cases of all commodities, and in biotechnological cases in particular, between benefit creation and determining the terms of benefit sharing?

Secondly, property is a moral issue because it is the relationship between people about things. This is the more technical or theoretical reason for the claim that property is a moral issue. Morality concerns the proper ordering of relationships between human beings; property concerns that part of the ordering that relates to 'things'. Property is therefore a moral issue. We are bound to ask, is the order that we seek to impose upon our relationships about these commodities (that we value in society) morally acceptable?

In a colloquial sense, the potential for these questions is difficult to grasp. There is a conditioning that 'property' is a fixed, paradigm in our society, an unquestionable given. However, it is worth remembering in this collection of essays about intellectual property that property is a social construction that, as Macpherson reminds us, has changed over time. Macpherson reminds us that the dominant paradigm before the present private, industrial revolution property paradigm was the feudal paradigm, with its concept of property resting not in ease of transfer or citizenship right, but in property being given in return for social duties (Macpherson 1975). He points to the change from feudal property (where property rights are conferred within a strictly hierarchical social structure in return for social obligations), to private, industrial revolution property (based on individual rights to own property on the basis of added value, and conferring transferable rights devoid of social duties). He envisaged that the future would see a shift from the private, industrial revolution property to a concept of property based around rights to work and social benefit (see also Reich 1964 on this particular change), and then changing again to political rights.

Macpherson was writing before the atrophying effect of 1980s neo-liberal politics and economics upon thinking about property concepts. However, the central message of Macpherson was not simply the type of concepts that property would change into, but that property is not conceptually fixed: 'property' is a dynamic concept that is responsive to social needs. The historical developments in the concept of property reflect changes in the dominant social organisational morality. The question is what are the catalysts for change? The moral questions that underpin the benefits sharing debate and the evidence of the effects of the extension of the private, industrial revolution property paradigm into biotechnology are arguably contemporary catalysts for change. And these are debates that are real, international, and on the mainstream political agenda. However, arguably, they fail because there is a reluctance or even inability to see property as a challengeable paradigm.

There is an inconsistency in our treatment of the concept of property: as a concept it is a social construction that is changeable because of moral or social pressure, but it is treated as absolute and unchangeable (arguably because of economic pressure). Synthetic biology gives another opportunity to revisit the concept of 'property' that we wish to advance as the basis for modern biotechnology in the 'information age' because individuals are not only the beneficiaries of technology but they are its raw materials, radically shifting their moral and social position within the paradigm in relation to the inventor's claims.

7.5 Social Consistency and Property in the Human Body

If the construction of the concept of property produces an inconsistency, then the practical expression of that concept also produces inconsistency, particularly in relation to the treatment of property in the human body. Once tissue is removed it can become property in the hands of another, but whilst still in the donor it is not property. If this is to suggest that the tissue is in some way special because there is not a separation of the individual and the body, we must be saying this until there is a physical separation of the parts. If we admit that, on physical separation, then there is a commodity in certain circumstances, the reason to exclude the originating human being must be to avoid that person making a choice to separate the particular tissue for profit. However, because property is not an absolute right with a fixed and necessary set of characteristics, it does not follow as an inevitable consequence that creating a property right in the donor's body will necessarily allow (or remove the ability to restrict) that individual to sell his or her organs. The sale for profit by an individual of his or her organs could be outlawed within a property right if that was considered morally or socially inappropriate.[10] However, resolving a legal inconsistency is not the prime reason for addressing the property concept here.

[10] Indeed, we are fully used to restrictions being placed upon our 'property', again because property is a social construction, for example in compulsory purchase, restrictive covenants, or other licensing requirements.

The more compelling argument concerns social consistency. Individuals talk in terms of property rights in relation to their interaction with medical research; their concerns are about improper commercialisation and commodification, and about exclusion (Gaskell et al. 2006 and 2010). Creating property rights for the donor in these circumstances would enhance the individual's dignity because it would recognise the 'donor' nature of the participation, it would recognise someone giving something of their property to another. Because the property is given without cost, this challenges the basis, extent and use of profits made downstream from that initial donation, or at least it allows individuals easier arguments for contractual shares in the benefits.[11]

Because property is a social construction, recognising an individual's property in his or her own body would also require the broader consequences of the reframed relationship to be considered. For example, the value of public investment in the up-stream science that enables the technology can be examined,[12] the right to be told about incidental health findings in research might be renegotiated. This move could enhance public trust and confidence in the medical research and biotechnology industries because it could open up the governance of those institutions and companies to the ethical considerations of the citizens upon which it they depend. Realigning property rights in this area would give all members of society an opportunity to negotiate the practical meaning of Article 53 of the European Patent Convention, and to frame an equitable and appropriate benefit sharing in the area of patents using human tissue and data. On the basis of such an opportunity for participation in the whole enterprise, individuals may well then take a more active and enthusiastic interest in this important medical science.

This, however, is perhaps not an argument that is sustainable within the existing political paradigm. It requires a number of steps away from the current law, and away from modern economic thinking, and therefore it is unlikely to succeed of itself. Certainly, property is a social construction and there is a moral argument that suggests that a new 'benefit creating: benefit sharing' balance should be struck, but that is only one approach and the competing morality of the 'industrial revolution, private property' market is another (and that is the dominant paradigm). There is, however, one line of argument that exists within the current legal paradigm that does require an answer and cannot be dismissed as easily as mere appeals to alternative moralities: the human rights agenda requires a more inclusive 'benefit creating: benefit sharing' paradigm. It can be argued that the appeal that is made currently to support the patent regime does not adequately take into account the full range of human rights; it is an appeal based on a selective argument, and that is its weakness.

---

[11] For an example of how this can be argued, see Beyleveld and Brownsword (2002) *Human Dignity in Bioethics and Biolaw*. Oxford: Oxford University Press, pp. 173–175.

[12] Hubbard and Love are keen to point out this investment (see below).

7.6 Using the Human Rights Agenda

The Human Rights agenda is perhaps the only remaining and acceptable 'grand narrative'. It is, as O'Neill indicates, problematic, not least as it places emphasis on rights-holding rather than duty-giving (O'Neill 2002). That lack of responsibility in its rhetoric, despite its obvious necessity, makes the human rights imperative to equitable benefit sharing more obscure. However, the human rights agenda is problematic in another way: it is applied rather selectively. Intellectual property, despite the potential in Article 53′s wording about the morality of the exploitation of the invention, has, arguably, focused on one right only, the right to personal property in intellectual property. However, within human rights, as they are presented, for example, in the Universal Declaration of Human Rights or the European Convention on Human Rights, and in the subsequent developments, for example the International Covenant on Economic, Social and Cultural Rights, there is a range of rights that together form an agreed basis of human dignity.[13] Taken together, they require a balance in benefit creation and benefit sharing. And they must be taken together, and not individually for one's own interests if the human rights agenda is to mean anything significant in its second 50 years as the acceptable agenda for international justice.

The right to ownership of personal property is certainly present in the human rights canon.[14] Equally, the ownership of intellectual property is also sanctioned.[15] These, along with the right to free expression,[16] form a strong case that the individual inventor has a right to the benefit of his or her creation. However, these are tempered by the right to participation in the social advances of one's society,[17] particularly when this is coupled to the social and economic rights, particularly the rights to an 'adequate standard of health and well-being' under the Universal Declaration[18] and to 'the highest attainable standard of physical and mental health' under the 1966 Covenant.[19]

A response to this could be that all that is intended here is to create a right to participate in a free market; that whilst there should be no bar to participation in the market for reason of race or gender, or perhaps even age, human rights do not imply a right in relation to economic discrimination. The rights do not imply anything in relation to one's ability to pay to participate. However, another response could be

---

[13] Universal Declaration of Human Rights *supra*. UN General Assembly (1948); Council of Europe (1950); UN General Assembly (1966).

[14] Universal Declaration of Human Rights, Article 17; Protocol to the Convention for the Protection of Human Rights and Fundamental Freedoms, Paris, 20 March 1952, Article 1.

[15] Universal Declaration of Human Rights, Article 27 (2).

[16] Universal Declaration of Human Rights, Article 19; European Convention on Human Rights, Article 10.

[17] Universal Declaration of Human Rights, Article 27 (1).

[18] Universal Declaration of Human Rights, Article 25.

[19] International Covenant on Economic, Social and Cultural Rights, Article 12 (although this would require a broad reading of the four duties placed on the signatory States under the Article).

that these would be hollow rights to participation if they did not attract some duty from the community of rights-holders to solidarity amongst its members.[20] So as a first consideration, the interpretation of Article 53 and the meaning of the exploitation of the patent could look to the importance of the invention in society, and the mechanism by which it will be exploited and made available in society. This is not to suggest that the inventor should be denied reward, although this is not without precedent in either invention or intellectual property.[21] However, at a second level, it must be an impetus for finding alternative reward structures to ensure that the patent system facilitates benefit sharing and not simply benefit creation.[22]

7.7 Conclusion

There are clearly a number of procedural and substantive inconsistencies in the current law relating to synthetic biology. These are not new but are common to much of biotechnology and other innovations. Within the current patent law, there is a need to take the morality clause of Article 53 seriously, perhaps through patent ethics committees. There is arguably a greater need to revisit the concept of property that operates in relation to synthetic biology and all aspects of biotechnology, particularly to create a better balance between benefit creating and benefit sharing because in the new innovations individuals are not only the beneficiaries of biotechnology but are also its raw materials. Whereas moral and social arguments could be the catalyst for such a debate, the human rights agenda, because of its prominence in modern international law, could be a more effective arena for such a debate. Indeed, because the human rights agenda already contains elements that support both benefit creation and benefit sharing, if it is to maintain its credibility as the driving force to justice it must be the place where this debate is vigorously pursued.

[20] Article 2 of the Universal Declaration of Human Rights states that "Everyone is entitled to all the rights and freedoms set forth in this Declaration, without distinction of any kind, such as race, colour, sex, language, religion, political or other opinion, national or social origin, property, birth or other status". Article 14 of the European Convention on Human Rights has the same scope. 'Property' could arguably extend to one's financial or economic status.

[21] See for example the development of the 'world wide web' and the attitude of Sir Tim Berners-Lee towards his invention. See also the treatment of Trade Marks that have become generic terms (and are thereby outside protection).

[22] See, for example, the work of Hubbard and Love on reward systems in the area of innovation in pharmaceuticals for 'orphan' diseases and the provision of drugs in developing countries: Hubbard and Love (2004); Love and Hubbard (2007).

References

Alleyne R (2010) Scientist craig venter creates life for first time in laboratory sparking debate about 'playing god'. The Daily Telegraph, 20 May 2010

Beyleveld D, Brownsword R (2002) Human dignity in bioethics and biolaw. Oxford University Press, Oxford

Council of Europe (1950) European Convention for the Protection of Human Rights and Fundamental Freedoms, as amended by Protocols Nos. 11 and 14, 4 November 1950, ETS 5, available at: http://www.unhcr.org/refworld/docid/3ae6b3b04.html (last visited 19th February, 2013)

European Patent Office (2010), Convention on the Grant of European Patents (European Patent Convention) 14th Edition applicable since December 2007

Forskningstetiske Komiteer (2008) (ed.) Patentnemnd uten Portefølje? En analyse av etiske utfordringer ved patentinering Publikasjon nr. Jul 2008. Oslo: De Nasjonale Forskningstetiske Komiteer (Norwegian National Research Ethics Committee) Oslo, pp 76–96

Gaskell G, Stares S, Allansdottir A, Allum N, Corchero C, Fischler C, Hampel J, Jackson J, Kronberger N, Mejlgaard N, Revuelta G, Schreiner C, Torgersen H, Wagner W (2006) Europeans and biotechnology in 2005: patterns and trends. Final report on Eurobarometer 64.3. http://ec.europa.eu/public_opinion/archives/ebs/ebs_244b_en.pdf. Accecesed 19 Feb 2013

Gaskell G, Stares S, Allansdottir A, Allum N, Castro P, Esmer Y, Fischler C, Jackson J, Kronberger N, Hampel J, Mejlgaard N, Quintanilha A, Rammer A, Revuelta G, Stoneman P, Torgersen H, Wagner W (2010) Europeans and biotechnology in 2010: winds of change? Brussels: European Commission DG Research. http://ec.europa.eu/public_opinion/archives/ebs/ebs_341_winds_en.pdf. Accesed 19 Feb 2013

Hubbard T, Love J (2004) A new trade framework for global healthcare R&D. PLoS Biol 2(2):e52. doi:10.1371/journal.pbio.0020052

Love J, Hubbard T (2007) The big idea: prizes to stimulate R&D for new medicines. Chi-Kent L Rev 82:1519

Macpherson CB (1975) Capitalism and the changing concept of property. In: Kamenka E, Neale RS (eds) Feudalism, capitalism and beyond. Edward Arnold, London, pp 104–124

Milius D, Townend D (2008) Thoughts on the scope and operation of morality clauses in patent law. In: Forskningstetiske Komiteer (ed.) Patentnemnd uten Portefølje? En analyse av etiske utfordringer ved patentinering Publikasjon nr. Jul 2008 Oslo: De Nasjonale Forskningsdtetiske Komiteer, Oslo, pp 76–96

O'Neill O (2002) A question of trust? Cambridge University Press, Cambridge

Reich CA (1964) The new property. Yale Law J 73(5):733–787

Townend D (2003) Who owns genetic information? In: Sandor J (ed) Society and genetic information: codes and laws in the genetic era. CPS–Central European University Press, Budapest, pp 125–144

Townend D (2012) The politeness of data protection: exploring a legal instrument to regulate medical research using genetic information and biobanking. Universitaire Pers Maastricht, Maastricht

UN General Assembly (1948) Universal Declaration of Human Rights, 10 December 1948, 217 A (III), available at: http://www.unhcr.org/refworld/docid–/3ae6b3712c.html [accessed 17 February 2013]

UN General Assembly (1966) International Covenant on Economic, Social and Cultural Rights, 16 December 1966, United Nations, Treaty Series, vol. 993, p. 3, available at: http://www.unhcr.org/refworld/docid/3ae6b36c0.html (last visited 19th February, 2013)

World Trade Organization (1994) Agreement on Trade-Related Aspects of Intellectual Property Rights. 1869 UNTS 299; 33 ILM 1197

Wright J, Ploem C, Śliwka M, Gevers S (2010) Regulating tissue research: do we need additional rules to protect research participants? Eur J Health Law 17:455–469

Chapter 8
Patenting SynBio in Anglo-America and Europe: Chaos or Opportunity

Amina Agovic

The two worst strategic mistakes to make are acting prematurely and letting an opportunity slip (Paulo Coelho)

Abstract This chapter describes patentability requirements for Synthetic Biology related inventions in Anglo-America (Australia and the US) and Europe, including an outline of any ethical challenges that may arise with respect to patenting such innovation. As Synthetic Biology and its research related patents are still in their early developmental stages, Craig Venter Institute's patent is used as a primary example to assess key tensions that may develop with patenting Synthetic Biology and the impact such patents may have on Synthetic Biology's overall progress. In drawing comparison to extensive ethical problems that struck patentability of human embryonic stem cells, the paper suggests a pressing need for the patent system to tackle any ethical anxieties around Synthetic Biology innovation pro-actively rather than to subject this latest technology to the same arduous and cumbersome path of human embryonic stem cell inventions.

Keywords Synthetic biology • Stem cells • Patents • Ethics • Anglo-America and Europe

8.1 Introduction

Over the past few decades, evolution of biotechnology (biotech) as an industry has skyrocketed and branched out into many different fields. Biotech's latest brainchild comes in form of synthetic biology (SynBio). This type of scientific adventure deals with designing and building new biological parts and systems, or with modification of existing ones in order to program them for specific tasks. It is a promising new

A. Agovic
Faculty of Technology and Society, Malmö University, Malmö, Sweden
e-mail: amina.agovic@mah.se

I. de Miguel Beriain and C.M. Romeo Casabona (eds.), *Synbio and Human Health: A Challenge to the Current IP Framework?*, DOI 10.1007/978-94-017-9196-0_8,

area of biotech research enthusiastically described as a field which is 'moving from reading the genetic code to writing it' (UK Parliamentary Office 2008). SynBio's future goals vary from producing new medicaments, therapies, environmental biosensors to novel methods of creating food, drugs, chemicals and even energy (UK Parliamentary Office 2008).

However, the availability of patent protection is of paramount significance in securing a strategic market position and economic advantage for the biotech industry per se. Without the ability to rely on patent protection, investors may be hesitant to invest which in turn could result from failure to develop and exploit new technologies to greater calls placed on governments worldwide to increase researchers' funding.

Unsurprisingly, as SynBio advances, its appetite for patents is bound to expand. And, as SynBio patents become more commonplace, an array of concerns in respect of granting and subsequent exploitation of these patents will pose increasingly critical challenges not only to the research itself, but also to patent systems and economies worldwide.

At present, most debates regarding SynBio research evolve around ethical concerns to environmental worries and fears of bioterrorism. However, the relationship between patent law and SynBio innovation is one area that has largely been left unexplored. First question that arises in that respect is whether SynBio can be compared to other forms of technology in order to be regarded as subject matter for patent protection. Second, in view of tremendous problems with patenting genes and human embryonic stem cells (hESCs), one cannot but wonder whether SynBio is to face similar if not identical future to hESC and gene patents. In addition, SynBio's complex definition is more than likely to resurrect the question of whether ethics could and/or should play any role in patent examining procedures.

Given the calamity over hESCs patents in Europe and to an extent in the US, a sense of urgency to engage all relevant parties in the discourse on how best to approach patenting SynBio should become a highly favoured patenting priority. Otherwise, SynBio patent applications risk turmoil, uncertainty and bewilderment just as their bio 'predecessors' have.

The article begins with a brief introduction to SynBio's present confusion concerning the relationship between intellectual property rights (IPRs) and SynBio. The paper proceeds by describing patentability requirements for SynBio related inventions in Anglo-America (Australia and the US) and Europe, including an outline of any ethical challenges that may arise with respect to patenting such innovation. As SynBio and its research related patents are still in their early developmental stages, Craig Venter Institute's patent is used as a primary example to assess key tensions that may develop with patenting SynBio and the impact such patents may have on SynBio's overall progress. In drawing comparison to extensive ethical problems that struck patentability of hESCs, the paper suggests a pressing need for the patent system to tackle any ethical anxieties around SynBio innovation proactively rather than to subject this latest technology to the same arduous and cumbersome path of hESC inventions.

8.2 SynBio and Intellectual Property

8.2.1 The Science and IP Protection

SynBio is considered an emerging field that entwines biotech, software and electronics. This science is defined as the 'design and construction of new biological systems' which do not exist in nature. It is a promising new area of biotech research enthusiastically described as a field which is 'moving from reading the genetic code to writing it' (UK Parliamentary Office 2008). Its potential influences on different sectors stem from biofuels, anti-pollutants and textiles, cosmetics to diagnostic and therapeutic tools, vaccines, drugs food and feed ingredients (European Group on Ethics 2009). Some examples include, a live polio virus 'created from scratch using mail-order segments of DNA and a viral genome map that is freely available on the Internet' (Ball 2008, p. 624). Scientists have also created a bacteria programmed in a way that allows it to take photos or form visible patterns (Basu et al. 2005, p. 1130; Levaskaya et al. 2005). Overall, SynBio is said to take genetic engineering a step further. Instead of isolating a pre-existing gene from its natural environment like in the recombinant DNA and transferring from one species to another and similar, SynBio aims to create these very genes.

As a scientific category, SynBio includes, but is not limited to (a) engineering DNA-based biological circuits, including but not limited to biological parts; (b) defining a minimal genome/minimal life (top-down); (c) constructing protocells, i.e. living cells, from scratch (bottom-up); etc. (Bennerand and Sismour 2005; O'Malley et al. 2008; Schmidt et al. 2009). Its potential influences on different sectors stem from biofuels, antipollutants and textiles, cosmetics to diagnostic and therapeutic tools, vaccines, drugs food and feed ingredients (European Group on Ethics 2009).

Although SynBio per se, is a not a new concept, recent developments as to its ability to develop whole genomes and organisms creates all sorts of research based but, also intellectual property (IP) related concerns. IPRs have become more important than manufacturing goods or dealing in commodities (Thurow 1997) and their crucial importance to rapidly advancing biotech has raised a number of issues. As a result, many wonder as to whether and how one should apply certain IPRs to SynBio research results. The mere nature of SynBio and its cross between many industries make it unclear as to which IPR will affect it the most. To some, SynBio has the characteristics of software from certain aspects, while others deem the software categorisation as overstated and that the technology should primarily be treated as patentable subject matter (Edwards 2010). Moreover, some believe that the IP law may not even have the correct system in place to fittingly address protection of SynBio. For example, Rick Johnson, head of an OECD group on SynBio referred to this type of scientific exploration as 'an IP law professor's dream final examination problem'. Johnson mentions that design rights, often used in Europe and Asia but hardly in the US, could potentially be utilised as a form of IP protection for SynBio inventions. Using such method of protection would avoid the obstacles life sciences and biotech experienced with patents (Edwards 2010).

Nevertheless, the paramount worth of patent protection to other areas of biotech indicates that SynBio is a technology for which patent activity is likely to be high and one which will require careful evaluation (Edwards 2010). In fact, not only are patents seen as a sort of a life-line to the biotech industry but the ability to rely on patent protection for biological inventions is considered as 'central to protecting scientists' work…' (European Group on Ethics 2009). And judging by rather broad applications already filed at patent offices, the race to patent SynBio has begun (Recent patent applications 2009).

8.2.2 Emerging Problems with SynBio Patents

The rise of new and emerging technologies brings about a key question of whether the patent system, traditionally designed to protect mechanical and electronic innovation, is adequately equipped to address emerging technologies such as SynBio. Even more importantly, the issue of patenting emerging technologies raises the issue of whether the patent system is capable to promote the encouragement of new technologies.

The basic idea of the patent system rests in the bargain theory where a patent is deemed a trade-off between a temporary monopoly reward to the inventor and the society which gains access to protected inventions via patent disclosure (Bently and Sherman 2004).

As a result, the core of conflict over biotech, including SynBio patents relates to fears that patents on material of human and living origin risk upsetting the delicate balance between the economic and public benefits of patent law in favour of economic gain (Bahadur and Morrison 2010). This is particularly relevant as SynBio produces life forms of which there are no similar versions in nature. The existing laws which regulate genetically modified organisms, life sciences, stem cell (SC) research are overall unsatisfactory and inadequate. At present, there is no established body of work which will be efficient to deal with designer organisms as they develop and this in itself creates a whole set of controversy. Yet, the economic impact of this field of scientific exploration might be huge. Whether patents are issued or not for SynBio inventions, they will nonetheless have a huge say as to how and in which direction the technology advances.

On the other hand, once patents in this area begin to issue en masse, there are several issues which are viewed as particularly problematic to biotech patents and easily might translate to the up and coming SynBio patents. For example, overly broad patents issued would only replicate the very same problems experienced with the BRCA1/2 genes (Etheridge 2005; Willison and MacLeod 2002), hESC patents and similar. This is disconcerting as broad patents may impede further innovations and research in the area of SynBio, not to mention impediments to the access to healthcare. In fact, the US patent office (USPTO) has been heavily criticised for awarding broad patents in respect of biotech and genetic research related inventions (Shulman 2001). Many suggest that 'to ensure that promising future lines of research are not impeded' … 'patent claims and any claims allowed in the future ought to be interpreted narrowly' (Scherer 2002, p. 1364).

Second issue which might arise with SynBio patents concerns the cumulative nature of the invention. There is a strong need to balance the incentive between early patent holders like Craig Venter (U.S. Patent Application No. 20070264688) versus later innovations which may be blocked by these earlier patents (Dent and Lim 2009). Although cross-licensing agreement could easily resolve this problem in theory; in practice as proved by the lawsuits against Myriad's BRCA1/2 gene and WARF's SC patents (Use of embryos/WARF), this is far more difficult to achieve.

Third problem that might arise with SynBio patents relates to the anti-common effects. For instance, should there be a diverse and multiple number of SynBio patent holders, these owners have the right to exclude others from further innovation which in turn may result in none having an effective way to utilise on patented inventions (Heller and Eisenberg 1998, p. 698; Gallini 2002, p. 131). Therefore, a potential lack of will on behalf of upstream SynBio patent owners (i.e. Venter and similar) to licence out its patented inventions would prevent a downstream innovator (i.e. a healthcare provider) from being able to make use of its innovation (Verbeure et al. 2006, p. 115).

These issues are not discussed in the public domain yet. Nevertheless, given the nature of this potentially world changing technology, there is a requirement and almost a need for a much broader discourse on these very issues among much broader groups of people. In particular, there should be a discussion revolving around the original goals of the patent system (that of a balance) and ethically sound science.

At present, patent attention is very limited in the area of SynBio patenting. Likewise, political and social attention is rather small and this is likely due to the fact that SynBio is still in its infancy. However, this appears to present an ideal time and opportunity to engage in a pro-active approach to understanding the potential impacts that SynBio patents could and are likely to have on the society, scientific progress and subsequent SynBio innovation on the European soil. Given the tremendous problems experienced with patenting genes and hESCs, one cannot but wonder whether SynBio is to face similar if not identical future. In addition, SynBio's complex definition is more than likely to resurrect the question of how ethics could and/or should apply in the patent examining procedures.

8.3 Patentable Subject Matter

8.3.1 Patenting Requirements

Prior to the US Supreme Court landmark decision of Chakrabarty (Diamond v. Chakrabarty), life forms were deemed 'products of nature' rather than patentable human inventions. Although the decision confirmed that phenomena of nature in their natural states continue to be unpatentable, the Court ruled that a major exemption exists should the products be isolated from their natural state through human intervention. This extraordinary decision heralded a new era of patenting living organisms, and paved the way for the European and international patent offices to issue life patents (Chapman 2009, p. 267). In fact many credit the patent system's ability to adapt to biotech with the development of new and dynamic life science technologies (OECD 2002, pp. 7–8).

By nature, a patent is a negative right. It is an exclusive right to prohibit all others from exploiting (i.e. use, sell, make…) the patent holder's patented product or process for a limited period of time.

International treaties on IP law have an important influence on the shape of Australian, American and European patent laws. All three strive to be in compliance with the more particular elements of the international instruments. The TRIPs Agreement prescribes minimum standards (TRIPs Agreement, art 1.1.3; Blakeney 1996, p. 39) for patentability of inventions to be complied with by each of the World Trade Organization (WTO) member state. Minimum patentability requirements can be found in the Article 27.1 of the TRIPs which states that 'patents shall be available for any inventions, whether products or processes, in all fields of technology, provided that they are new, involve an inventive step and are capable of industrial application'.

The European Patent Convention (EPC), Article 52(1) sets forth the criteria for patentability by stating that, 'European patents shall be granted for any inventions, in all fields of technology, provided that they are new, involve an inventive step and are susceptible of industrial application.'

The EPC Regulations allow patents for a biological material which is isolated from its natural environment or produced by means of a technical process even if it previously occurred in nature (Implementing Regulations, r23c(a)). This is only relevant if such material has been isolated from its natural environment or produced by means of a technical process; for example it has been made technically available.

In Australia, under section 18 of the Patents Act 1990, an invention is patentable if it:

(a) *Is a 'manner of manufacture' – that is, the invention is appropriate subject matter*;
(b) *For patent protection*;
(c) *Is novel*;
(d) *Involves an inventive step or innovative step*;
(e) *Is useful*; *and*
(f) *Has not been used secretly within Australia before the priority date of the patentapplication.*

Some jurisdictions in Australia still retain the term 'manner of manufacture' derived from the English Statutes of Monopolies 1623 (Patents Act 1990 (Cth) s 18(1), sch 1; English Statute of Monopolies s 6).

Thus, Australia can issue a patent for inventions claiming synthetic genes or DNA sequences, mutant forms and fragments of gene sequences, novel expression systems among others (IP Australia, Australian Patents). However, there have been suggestions that some inventions concerning specific genetic materials or technologies may not, or should not, meet the legal criteria for patentability (Australian Law Reform Commission No 27).

On the other hand, the US Constitution grants the US Congress the power to enact laws with respect to patents. There, the Article I, section 8 states that, 'Congress shall have power… to promote the progress of science and useful arts, by securing for limited times to authors and inventors the exclusive right to their respective writings and discoveries.' Patent rights are available to anyone who, 'invents or discovers any new and useful process, machine, manufacture, or composition of matter, or any new and useful improvement thereof… subject to the conditions and requirements of this title' (Patents Act, 35 U.S.C. § 101). Therefore, the burden of proof rests with the USPTO to show that an applicant does not meet statutory patentability requirements. The invention must be 'useful' in a practical sense, 'novel' and 'nonobvious' to one of ordinary skill in the relevant art. The fourth criterion is that of 'enablement' which requires that the invention must provide a sufficient disclosure to enable any person skilled in the art to practice the invention (Patents Act, 35 U.S.C. § 101).

Following the decision of Diamond v. Chakrabarty, the USPTO issued a statement confirming that 'non-naturally occurring, non-human multicellular living organisms, including animals, to be patentable subject matter'(USPTO, Manual). Despite the fact that a level of ambiguity in the US as to the nature of what is being patented remains, so far, the USPTO and the American courts agree that the isolation and purification of naturally occurring products is patentable (Chapman 2009, p. 267).

Overall, with respect to SynBio innovation, the main challenge appears to be providing the appropriate framework which will encourage and promote investments in SynBio without stifling research and/or restricting benefits. At present, patents seem to be one and almost the only way of achieving such. Thus, SynBio inventors can apply for patents directed at:

- Methods, techniques or technologies;
- Specified sequences of DNA (UK Parliamentary Office 2008).

8.3.2 *Exclusion on Ethical or Moral Reasons*

Patent law has a long historical pedigree of moral and ethical limits imposed on the patentable subject matter. Specifically, it has drawn distinction between the useful and fine arts based on economic but also social and practical reasons. Although the dominant objective of the patent system is the promotion of innovation and dissemination of technology, so clearly enunciated in the TRIPs, it is important to acknowledge the social impact on patents. Article 7 of the TRIPs Agreement calls for patent rights to operate in a manner that is conducive to social and economic welfare. The TRIPs as such does not only speak of the economic rationale for the patent system, but also of the social and ethical considerations.

In addition to having to fulfill standard patentability requirements, SynBio inventions may be subject to ethical or moral exclusions. In particular, the TRIPs Agreement allows (but does not require) exceptions to patentability based on ordre public and morality (TRIPs Agreement, art. 27.2). This principle is founded on a lengthy tradition in patent law, especially in Europe (European Patent Convention 2000, art. 53(a)). In Europe, the so called 'morality clause', Article 53(a) states that:

European patents shall not be granted in respect of:

(a) *Inventions the commercial exploitation of which would be contrary to 'ordre public' or morality; such exploitation shall not be deemed to be so contrary merely because it is prohibited by law or regulation in some or all of the Contracting States;*

Article 53(a) EPC is reflected in the European Parliament's Directive on the Legal Protection of Biological Inventions (Biotech Directive). The Biotech Directive provides a list of specific inventions that cannot be patentable on the grounds of ordre public or morality (Implementing Regulations, rr. 23(b) – 23(e)).

The European Technical Board of Appeal at the European Patent Office (EPO) in T-315/03 said that in order to rely on the morality clause and prevent the patent to issue, the exploitation of the invention needs to be contrary to public order or morality (Transgenic animals/HARVARD, [4.2]). Furthermore, it is said by the same Board of Appeal in another case (Plant Cells/Plant Genetic Systems, [6]) that in order for the subsequent use of the invention to be viewed as contrary to morality as according to Article 53(a) of the EPC, it has to offend against 'common European standards of morality'.

In practical terms, the applicability of the morality clause has so far proved extremely controversial in fields of biotech inventions and hESC research in particular. Having a complex definition to start with, SynBio inventions may prove to be as hotly contested as hESCs have before the EPO (Use of embryos/WARF, Order [2]), the Court of Justice of the EU (CJEU) (Oliver Brüstle v. Greenpeace) and the USPTO (U.S. Patent No. 5843780; U.S. Patent No. 6200806; U.S. Patent No. 6280718).

Moreover, the present patenting system in the US seems to deal with any ethical concerns post-issuance of the patent. It is, thus, unsurprising that the US law on patents fails to contain any express prohibition on inventions claiming human beings or the processes for their generation, equivalent to section 18(2) of the Australian Patents Act (Cth) or the European Article 53(a) EPC. To be fair though, the USPTO does have a long standing policy not to grant such patents but little sizeable consideration appears to have been given to whether such policy encompasses hESCs (Australian Law Reform Commission Discussion Paper No 68, [16.31–16.53]). The US does not in general acknowledge ethical concerns as relevant to IPRs policy and norms (Chapman 2009, p. 264).

However, the American courts have established the concept of rejecting inventions contrary to order public which are 'frivolous or injurious to the well-being, good policy, or sound morals of a society' before the adoption of the TRIPs. The US Supreme Court refused to take any ethical issues into account in determining the patentability of a genetically engineered bacterium capable of degrading multiple components of crude oil in Chakrabarty. Contrary to the petitioners arguments that a broad interpretation of § 101 to allow patents on genetically engineered organisms might result in a 'gruesome parade of horrible', the Court justified its position by exclaiming that such 'contentions now pressed on us should be addressed to the political branches of the Government, the Congress and the Executive, and not to the courts' (Chapman 2009, pp. 261, 316–17). Further, the Supreme Court added that:

> [w]hat is more important is that we are without competence to entertain these arguments – either to brush them aside as fantasies generated by fear of the unknown, or to act on them. The choice we are urged to make is a matter of high policy for resolution within the legislative process after the kind of investigation, examination, and study that legislative bodies can provide and courts cannot. That process involves the balancing of competing values and interests, which in our democratic system is the business of elected representatives (Diamond v. Chakrabarty, p. 317).

In Australia, SynBio inventions should beware of section 50(1)(a) of the Patents Act, which may be closer to the European morality clause. Section 50(1)(a) provides that the Commissioner of Patents has the discretion to refuse an invention on the grounds that its use would be 'contrary to law' (Patents Act 1990 (Cth) s 101B(2)(d)). This is a discretionary power which is to be applied in the clearest of circumstances (IP Australia, Patent Manual, [2.9.6]).

Thus for example, an invention 'contrary to law' which 'one the primary use of which would be a criminal act, punishable as a crime or misdemeanour' would always be refused protection. Second, an invention with one unlawful use would have to be considered on a case by case basis (Official Rulings 1923 C) since the section 50(1)(a) should be invoked only against claims where an unlawful use and no lawful use has been described (IP Australia, Patent Manual, [2.9.6]). This means that this section will likely have limited application to inventions involving genetic materials and SynBio technology primarily because a patent applicant will be able to identify a lawful use for such invention (Australian Law Reform Commission Report No. 68 [7.15]).

Australia, however may have an implicit exception to patentability on ethical grounds by nature of section 6 of the Patents Act which states that an invention should 'be neither contrary to the law, nor mischievous to the state by rising prices of commodities at home, or hurt of trade, or generally inconvenient'. Obiter dicta of the High Court and Federal Court decisions suggest that this 'generally inconvenient' phrase incorporates public policy considerations and is possible to refuse an application by its invocation (Advanced Building Systems Pty Ltd v Ramset). However, just like the American judiciary, the Australian courts have stated that 'making law about patents' is a matter to be addressed and determined by the Parliament, rather than courts (Advanced Building Systems Pty Ltd v Ramset).

8.4 SynBio vs Stem Cells

8.4.1 Venter's Synthia

Patents by nature may be speculative and broad, especially when claims are directed at new technologies still undergoing rapid changes. However, recent SynBio developments as to its ability to develop whole genomes and organisms have begun ringing all sorts of research based but also patenting alarm bells.

An argument has now developed as to whether all or some parts of SynBio innovation should form part of patentable subject matter for the commercial benefit of 'inventors'. Furthermore, slowly but steadily, concerns of ethical nature are expressed over the ability to afford patent protection to SynBio inventions.

For example, the biggest uproar to date appears to be raised over Craig Venter's SynBio patent. Venter's 2007 patent application (U.S. Patent No. 20070264688) claims rights to a gene sequence representing the 'minimal requirements for life' for a synthetic, self-replicating version of a bacterial species. The functional version is yet to be produced, but the patent application already seeks a fairly broad coverage over the creation of any synthetic genome. Venter's patent application makes claims that inventors contemplate that their method will be applied from constructing all manner of genomes, including a 'eukaryotic cellular organelle' to anything that 'is substantially identical to a naturally occurring genome', etc. In addition the application claims products such as 'an energy source' (undefined in the patent specification other than by reference to 'hydrogen or ethanol'), and, 'therapeutics and industrial polymers' (U.S. Patent No. 20070264688).

Venter's invention has one of the smallest genomes of any known bacterium, yet its patent claims to cover any method of 'constructing a synthetic genome' using nucleic acid cassettes'. In this case, Venter's patent claim directed at the technological field of making a synthetic genome, howsoever this is performed, sounds all too reminiscent of the SC patent issued to WARF claiming unmodified hESC lines per se, regardless of their 'creator' (U.S. Patent No. 6200806).

Albeit, many are quick to label Venter's invention as the first example of artificial creation of life, of man interfering with God, etc., what Venter achieved in practice is a 'chemically synthesized genome' (Gibson et al. 2010). This 'organism' is created in a way where synthetic genome was introduced into a 'pre-existing living bacterial cell, where the former hijacked the host's machinery (including its proteins, ribosomes and membranes) to decode its own information and thereby substitute the host machinery in its entirety, by what one may term as the process of 'infinite dilution" (Gowrishankar 2010, p. 152). In reality, besides the synthetic version of this natural bacterium, it is almost identical to the natural one. The only difference seems to be creating the synthetic version in a laboratory with an exception that the genome has been tweaked in order to incapacitate it from infecting humans. Whether this makes the synthetic bacterium sufficiently different to a natural bacterium and whether it satisfies the threshold established by the US Supreme Court decisions of Brogdex (American Fruit Growers v Brogdex) and Chakrabarty and in view of the recent breast cancer genes' patents decision (Association for Molecular Pathology) can be debatable. Tweaking the genome so as to render it harmless to humans may not be enough to make the difference between the synthetic and natural versions distinguishable either in 'form, quality or property' (Gibson et al. 2010) nor the kind of functionality that would be 'markedly different characteristics to any found in nature' (Diamond v. Chakrabarty, [III]).

Another problem with Venter's application revolves around a claim which focuses on the technical platform for the production of a synthetic 'energy source', but fails to disclose any information as to the way to achieve so.

Hence, it comes as no surprise that the first opposition steps to Venter's patents have already been taken. Canadian nongovernmental organization, the Action Group on Erosion, Technology and Concentration (ETC Group) announced it was challenging the two patent applications (U.S. Patent Publication No. 2007/0122826A1) filed by investigators at the Craig Venter Institute on 'the world's first-ever human-made life form' (Patenting the parts 2007, p. 822).

On the other hand, another challenging 'phenomenon' to face this field of research may be a SynBio patent recently issued. A patent claiming a minimized Escherichia coli genome (U.S. Patent No. 6989265), a bacterium commonly used in biological research is said to have a potential impact of hindering SynBio research. E. coli is the type of chassis that could be useful for the SynBio community and the patent claims here could cover any synthetic cell derived from an E. coli genome. The significance of this patent was not lost on corporate investors where a start-up Scarab Genomics founded as a result of this IPR, has already begun offering a 'minimized version of E. coli K12 (15 % of the genome deleted) with enhanced genetic stability and improved metabolic efficiency for gene cloning and heterologous protein expression applications' (Patenting the parts 2007, p. 822).

8.4.2 Stem Cell Lessons

As new entrants into the patent world, new and emerging technologies and their associated patents are more and more subjected to a rather intense public and political scrutiny that either adversely or positively affects them. However, SC related innovations seem to take the lead in patent controversies. In order to derive hESCs, an embryo is generally destroyed and this has made both the EPO and the CJEU (Oliver Brüstle v. Greenpeace) rather apprehensive about the social and ethical implications of advances in SC knowledge and techniques. This in turn, has resulted in ample legal and public controversies.

For instance, the EPO's leading decision on SCs, known as the WARF (Konskiand Spielthenner 2009, p. 725) patent application, EP-A 0770125 claimed a monopoly for a cell culture comprising primate ESCs which are capable of proliferating in vitro for over 1 year and so forth. The EPO ruled that: if the invention relies exclusively on a method which necessitates the destruction of a human embryo from which the said products are derived, no patent will issue. WARF confirms that this ban stands 'even if the said method is not part of the claims' (Use of embryos/ WARF, Order [2]).

Similarly, Oliver Brüstle director of the Institute of Reconstructive Neurobiology at Bonn University applied for a German patent (DE19756864C1) in December 1997. Claims included isolated and purified neural precursor cells, processes for their production from ESCs and the use of neural precursor cells for the treatment of neural defects (Oliver Brüstle v. Greenpeace, [15]). The Greenpeace filed opposition to the patent which resulted in the Bundespatentgericht (Federal Patent Court) invalidating the patent on grounds that it covers precursor cells obtained from hESCs and processes for the production of those precursor cells. Brüstle appealed against the judgement to the Bundesgerichtshof which then referred a number of questions to the CJEU for a preliminary ruling in late 2009 (Oliver Brüstle v. Greenpeace, [19]). The CJEU upheld the EU's advocate-general opinion (Opinion of Advocate General Bot 2011) and took it even a step further by barring any procedure that involves hESCs from patentability if the hESCs were derived from the destruction of human embryos. The ban applies retrospectively and it is deemed irrelevant how distant any downstream products using these lines are from the original derivation of the hESC line (Oliver Brüstle v. Greenpeace, [49]).

There are no further legal appeals available to Brüstle. Unsurprisingly, SC scientists are deeply troubled about the impact that this decision may have on the SC technology and innovation in Europe. The CJEU decision appears to have left Europe's leading SC scientists short-handed and caught off guard. For many, the CJEU ruling equated to suicide. For Brüstle, the decision suggests that '…years of translational research by European scientists will be wiped away and left to the non-European countries' (Kemp 2011).

For a renowned SC researcher, Professor Austin Smith of the Wellcome Trust Centre for Stem Cell Research at the University of Cambridge, the decision 'leaves scientists in a ridiculous position. We are funded to do research for the public good, yet prevented from taking our discoveries to the market place where they could be developed into new medicines. One consequence is that the benefits of our research will be reaped in America and Asia' (Kemp 2011). In Brüstle's words, the CJEU ruling is 'the worst possible outcome and it's a disaster for Europe' (Callaway 2011, p. 441). For a private industry, patent clarity was desired but the effect of the Brüstle case is that, trade secrets might take over patenting in this area (Abbott 2011, p. 312).

The CJEU ruling does not bar the scientists from engaging in hESC research experiments but it does remove 'a key commercial incentive for biotech and pharmaceutical companies to back stem-cell research in Europe' (Gautam 2011). What this translates to is that, 'of all the intellectual work being done in Europe, if something is successful it will now be [commercialized] by a company outside Europe where patent protection is available. Europe is basically exporting its research – it is unfortunate' (Gautam 2011).

8.5 SynBio's Patent Opportunity

The nature of the economy has dramatically changed over the past few decades resulting in unprecedented changes in patentable subject matter. Until recently, the patent system dealt with manufacturing methods and mechanical inventions, whereas nowadays patent protection is required for materials and in new areas such as SynBio. Many believe that biotech is only the latest variation of technology which instrumentalises animate nature and turns organisms into manufactures, just as the mechanical and chemical sciences instrumentalised inanimate nature (Pottage and Sherman 2008).

Nonetheless, like none other, biotech manages to wreak unprecedented havoc within the patent system. The emergence of new technologies raises the question of whether the patent system is suitable to protect inventions in fields as new as SynBio. Due to the fact that patenting biotech seems to involve vital moral issues, the patent law has been turned upside down displaying the system's inability to fit the peculiarities of life sciences into the traditional patentable subject matter scope. As a result and despite breathtaking promises of SynBio, one cannot but wonder about the existence of costs of such developments.

To be quite clear, one of the patent system's reasons for its long lasting success rests in its applicability to 'any technology' (Rutz 2009, p. 14). In addition, the overall problem of new technologies is not the patent system as such but, in some circumstances, patents issued may exacerbate the situation due to its failure to consider ethical issues when conducting a patent examination. Overly restrictive licensing and smotheringly broad patent interpretations (i.e. US WARF Patents) as well as constant confusion as to ethical concerns when patenting inventions in Europe (i.e. WARF) could literally make a shambles of SynBio as an emerging technology.

The patent system's dual nature of balancing social welfare with the aim to promote and further research and development in science and technology requires some serious and well overdue attention. The past decade has proved intensely controversial with governments worldwide struggling in their attempts to adequately address moral issues that arrive with patenting new technologies. Europe by far seems mostly burdened by it. Her troubled relationship with patent morality ranging from the Oncomouse (Harvard/Oncomouse) to Edinburgh (E.P. Patent No. 0695351) to WARF (E-P. Patent No. 0770125) to CalTech (E.P. Patent No. 0658194) and now to Oliver Brustle (Oliver Brüstle v. Greenpeace) has all but proven the extreme difficulties to reach consensus in relation to ethical issues and patenting biotech inventions.

The moral uniqueness found in patent law has placed the patent system at the crossroads of science and technology and at the centre of the patents on life debate. Intentionally or not, the patent system is directly implicated in scientific developments by offering incentives to creators and companies. Although it has been over a decade since the implementation of the Biotech Directive, not much has improved in the European struggle to appropriately work with ethical issues enveloping biotech patents; thereby indicating a persistence of policy of patent confusion and delays. This failure to provide a level of certainty and consistency in its approach to examining morally contentious inventions signals a European continuum of a 'mess of confusion, disputes, and uncertainty expense' (Suthers 2003). As a result, it may be that SynBio will not even take off on the European soil, but instead search for a patently more stable place for its investments.

8.5.1 Is the Patent System Morally Impune?

Few issues divide researchers, patent community and public more than patenting emerging biotech. Supporters of patentability of emerging biotech point to the therapies and medical advances, while critics point to the 'tinkering with nature'. Funnily enough, a German patent attorney commented on the situation by saying, 'I have studied biology and have been practicing this profession for more than 20 years, and I know more about patents and biotech than those who play with emotions to address ethical concerns. Most of those who campaign don't have any serious ethical concerns and do it for publicity and are hypocrites' (Clash over stem cell patents 2007).

In contrast, with respect to SC patents, the public and groups such as Greenpeace maintain that stricter laws are needed and equilibrium between patents' benefits and costs (re)established. That Greenpeace campaigned hard on this matter is evident in legal actions filed against morally controversial patents, no patents on life campaign and even the pending appeal of the German patent (the Brüstle patent). In furthering its view, Greenpeace has called on the German Parliament to introduce stricter laws on SC research. In particular that, 'stem cells used for commercial purposes should not be allowed at all' (Clash over stem cell patents 2007). Should SynBio patents expect a similar fate to that of SC patents makes one more than wonder.

On the other hand, the Europabio, the biotech industry group, believes the exact opposite and maintains that the current laws are appropriate and that the 'technical framework provided for in the EU Biotech Directive is sufficient'. Further, the group asserts that ethical questions should be decided separately by Member Governments if there are specific moral issues in their countries. The Groups has said that Article 6 of the Biotech Directive 'should be interpreted widely and not narrowly and that patents should regulate technology' (Clash over stem cell patents 2007).

In contrast, American precedents to allow patents on almost anything and everything as long as the standard patentability requirements are satisfied exhibit a perturbing trend of patent examiners arbitrarily handing down patents on certain biotech inventions; clearly gesturing that morality and ethics hold little value in any decision making process at patent offices (Amani and Coombe 2005, p. 162). To some the Chakrabarty decision was seen as a first step for Corporations to own a blueprint of life. Interesting, Chief Justice Burger said while some of the bigger issues were raised in Chakrabarty, overall this was a small issues. Needless, to say the next 30 years proved to the contrary. Such precedents exhibit a perturbing trend of patent examiners arbitrarily handing down patents on hESCs, including even human clones (U.S. Patent No. 6211429) signalling that morality and ethics hold little value in any decision making process at patent offices (Amani and Coombe 2005, p. 162).

Some suggest (Kevles 1998) that broadening the scope of patentable subject matter so as to include patents on life forms took place within the judiciary because the US Congress refused to engage on the issue. Declining to act on the matter, the legislators have cleared the path for patent offices to expand patentability to material of human origins. Many have stated that such approach is not participatory nor democratic in nature and it has continued a trend, at least in the US, toward 'less popular participation in social decision making about technology as it impacts society' (Warner 2001).

In any case, by issuing ethically controversial patents, the patent office indirectly legitimises morally controversial technologies and continues to broaden the scope of patentable subject matter with no limits in sight. For example, in the absence of clear guidelines regulating new technologies such as hESC research and SynBio, scientists and patent attorneys get to determine the limits of patent eligibility by describing the subject matter in their patent applications (Bagley 2003). In addition, accelerating number of patent applications both at the USPTO and the EPO continues to overwhelm the system. This carries a risk of total system failure primarily because of its inability to provide the necessary quality of the granting procedure (Bagley 2003). The American judicial system is too passive and the Parliamentarians too buried under the economy of influences in order to perceive and fix patenting problems arising with new technologies.

Moreover, claims that ethics are outside the scope of patent laws or that there is no place for ethics within the patent system insinuate that patent system is in some way amoral or unethical; outside of the society's common moral norms. As difficult as it is to understand perspectives of that nature, evidence examined in earlier chapters fails to show why patent law is a special area of law which allows it to be ostracized from moral standards. Taking the US as an example, in issuing patents deemed socially inappropriate or even unacceptable (human clones, material of human origins…), the USPTO, is still exercising ethics, albeit bad ethics. But bad ethics is still ethics of sort (Crane and Matten 2004, p. 8). To the contrary, the EPO's endeavours to incorporate public order and morality in its decision making process, leaves behind a trail of confusing and inconsistent precedents, thereby further fuelling the uncertainty and anxiety among the stakeholders.

Although, many of these problems may still be far-fetched and not yet translated to SynBio, they are likely to become much more serious once SynBio takes off and begins to generate substantial profits. In any case, the arrival of SynBio may indeed present the last chance for recovery of the relationship between the biotech industry and patent morality. How patent offices approach rising ethical frictions with respect to patenting SynBio inventions may just decide how and under what conditions this type of scientific research takes place.

8.5.2 *Emerging Technologies Require Patent Stability*

Emerging technologies have become hotbeds of change and 'a site of contention where competing groups pursued incompatible normative visions.' Questions concerning technological developments are 'nothing less than questions about the future shape of societies, science and technology' (Hilgartner 2009, pp. 205–6). In fact, when it comes to new technologies and patents, patent law plays a key part in encouraging the progress and the direction of such emerging biotechnologies. In addition, 'how the market responds to these characteristics will determine whether and how the law must step in and tailor the rules of patent law to the needs of this nascent industry. It will also give us broader insight into the role of patents in enabling technologies' (Lemley 2005, p.630).

If the policy makers and public are interested in promoting innovation of interest to the society at large, 'nothing could be more central than the way we regulate intellectual property' (Lemley 2005, p. 63). Although, the patent system does not instigate the controversy surrounding new and emerging biotech, it does act as a catalyst in promoting a particular form of technology whether or not deemed socially controversial. By issuing patents on a particular form of technology, the patent system also promotes the direction which that technology is likely to take. When governments issue patents, they are 'intervening in the market to give particular individuals or businesses a monopoly over the commercial exploitation of that idea for up to 20 years (Gittins 2012).'

The mere nature of the patent system makes it an extremely fascinating object of study and to some ethicists like Sterckx it presents 'an almost perfect example of what fair social institutions should look like' (Sterckx 2005). In theory to say the least. However, current system's status quo is far from ideal where its eagerness to shift towards more socially and ethically favourable direction at its lowest.

Precedents such as Oncomouse (E.P. Patent No. 0169672), Edinburgh (E.P. Patent No. 695351), WARF (Use of embryos/WARF) at the EPO and Oliver Brüstle (Oliver Brüstle v. Greenpeace) at the CJEU might create more harm than good both the European biotech innovation and the European public. These precedents are creating an unfavourable environment which is increasingly caused by an ethically and socially imbalanced patent system.

In 2006, American Council on Foreign Relations (the Council) called for a patent reform and lamented about 'numerous structural' problems founded in 'fundamental misconceptions' (Maskus 2006, p. 5). One such misconception is the 'virtually unchallenged view that more patent protection necessarily provides greater incentives for innovation and commercialisation of technologies (Maskus 2006, p. 5).' Furthermore, the Council suggested that stronger patent system risks endangering technological innovation in the US. The Council goes further to say that, 'the patent policy needs to be balanced … Failure to rein in the patent regime could have global repercussions. To hinder innovation is to hinder the dynamic competitiveness of US companies (Maskus 2006, p. 6).' Similarly, the Canadian Biotech Advisory Committee states the purpose of the patent system is to attain 'the public good.…

The patent system attains this goal by providing inventors with a sufficient incentive…to disclose their inventions and to make their inventions available to the public' (CBAC 2002, p. 8).

On the other hand, the Australian Law Reform Commission considered the patent law 'ambiguous and obscure'. At present, it is unclear whether the Australian type of a morality provision 'generally inconvenient' can be invoked to exclude inventions from patentability on public policy grounds in Australia. This lack of clear distinction between patentable and non-patentable subject matter has generated concern, especially in the field of biotech and material of human origin (Australian Government 2009).

New biotech industry requires strong and clear patent laws. SynBio and like technologies, while controversial are also extremely important. Without biotech and life sciences research, the public is deprived of 'the much needed solutions to dietary, health, environmental and other problems' that plague the society (Chiapetta 1994, p. 160). The implementation of the Biotech Directive endured an arduous ten (10) year long debate signalling the importance of patent protection being available to biotech inventions. However, it is clear that the EPO's approach to interpreting the morality clause has been all but consistent. As a result, harmonisation as intended by the Biotech Directive remains elusive with interpretations of the morality clause varying in many aspects, even when harmonisation is attempted by judges committed to achieving uniformity. The EPO rulings demonstrate inconsistent and ambiguous interpretations of the morality clause even when interpreted by a single adjudicatory body (Gitter 2001, p. 21).

Faced with morally contentious subject matter, the OD at the EPO stated that, '[T]here is at present no consensus in European society about the desirability [of the Stanford patent], and public opinion is still being formed on this and related matters. It would be presumptuous for the EPO to interfere in this public debate' (R v Leland, p. 23).

Henceforth, a recent report from the EU recognises that one advantage of the US' patent system is that the USPTO has 'guidelines [that provide] legal certainty by giving a clear definition of what can be considered a biotechnological invention and what is eligible for patent protection'(Common European Communities, [93]).

One of the alternatives in solving European ethical problems with patenting new technologies would be the EPO's utilisation of Article 7 of the Biotech Directive. Yet, this is the only article that has not been transposed to the EPC rules or any EU Member State's patent office. Article 7 grants the European Group on Ethics in Science and New Technologies (EGE) the power to 'evaluate all ethical aspects of biotech' but, the EPO is still to engage in a discussion on how to handle ethical issues arising out of patenting biotech inventions with the EGE.

Either way, due to a consistent lack of a clear and consistent strategy in regards to SC inventions, the EPO in a way imposes strain on the European biotech sector and risks putting Europe's growth in other biotech areas behind that of the US, Australia and Japan. On the other hand, by issuing highly controversial and overly broad patents, the USPTO risks creating an unprecedented imbalance within the patent system which, eventually may lead to the collapse of the entire system.

8.6 Concluding Remarks

SynBio has the potential to create an array of major new industries, ranging from 'innovative biofuels to enabling products from cheap, lifesaving new drugs'. However SynBio technology has been described as the 'genetic engineering on steroids' surpassing the present dangers and potential abuses of (conventional) biotech. Incredible progress for SynBio as a technology suggests up and coming higher level activity on the patentability frontier. This in itself brings about the decades old, yet still unresolved question of what to do with ethical controversies in respect of biotech inventions.

The biotech mantra of needing the patent protection to succeed in the industry has been heavily criticized. This extreme dependency by bio and emerging technologies on patent protection has exposed fundamental uncertainties that afflict the very nature of patent protection. The patent with its old definition of a contract between the inventor and the society is said to enhance the state of the art for which in return the inventor is granted a temporary monopoly right to exclude. This is predicated on equilibrium. Yet, this equilibrium is in jeopardy and has been for some time. If the patent system's chaos of the European limbo and overwhelming but historically unintended patent flexibility in the US continues, the system's present imbalance may eventually lead to the collapse of the patent institution.

In particular so as SynBio crosses technology barriers and is bound to impact the patent system as none before. How and what impact this makes on patent law, remains to be seen. But, if SynBio is to avoid the faith of hESC patents in Europe and to an extent in the US, there needs to be a pro-active discussion between public, legislature and scientists on the issue of general ethical concerns raised by patentability of SynBio inventions and a strong will to have them addressed properly and in time, in the patent allocation system.

More than anything, the patent system should aim to re-equilibrate itself so as to simultaneously benefit society and promote sustainable industry based on ethics and concern for the environment, biodiversity and quality of life. The mere nature of SynBio gives the patent system an ideal opportunity to prove itself for what it really is designed to do.

While it is immensely important for biotech companies to be able to engage in life saving bio-medical research and as a result be allowed to patent biological material; it is equally as clear that biotechnological innovation cannot be adequately handled in the same manner as the traditional mechanical subject matter. Since SynBio innovation is in its infancy, it will be interesting to see whether Europe and the US utilise on the opportunity of addressing patentability of SynBio innovation pro-actively or whether they head for the repeat of challenges, inconsistencies and legal/business uncertainty of hESC patents. Any, shifting of the responsibility of patenting emerging biotechnologies on other shoulders, whilst satisfying in short-term, is unfeasible and unhealthy patent policy in long-term. The patent system's failures to understand the morality clause and adequately deal with emerging biotechnologies can only be remedied by admitting the problems and finding a way to resolve them. The problems surrounding patentability of SC inventions are well known, but a lack of will to disturb the traditional approach to patenting emerging and rapidly changing biotechnologies and to do so in line with social and public norms renders meaningful progress impossible.

References

Abbott A (2011) Stem cells: the cell division. Nat News Feat (14 Dec 2011)- http://www.nature.com/news/stem-cells-the-cell-division-1.9634. Accessed 20 May 2012
Agreement on Trade-Related Aspects of Intellectual Property Rights (TRIPs) (entered into force 1 January 1996)
Amani B, Coombe R (2005) The human genome diversity project: the politics of patents at the intersection of race. Relig Res Ethic Law Policy 27(1):152–188
Australian Law Reform Commission Discussion Paper No 68 (2004).
Australian Government, Advisory Council on Intellectual Property (2009) Patentable Subject Matter – Options Paper 2. Commonwealth of Australia, ACT.
IP Australia (2005) Australian patents for: microorganisms; cell lines; hybridomas; related biological materials and their use; and genetically manipulated organisms
Australian Law Reform Commission (2003) Genes and ingenuity: gene patenting and human health, Issue Paper No 27. http://www.alrc.gov.au/publications/executive-summary/genes-and-ingenuity. Accessed Dec 2012
Bahadur G, Morrison M (2010) Patenting human pluripotent cells: balancing commercial, academic and ethical interests. Hum Reprod 25:14–21
Ball P (2008) Synthetic biology: starting from scratch. Nature 431:624–626
Bagley MA (2003) Patent first, ask questions later: morality and biotechnology in patent law. Wm Mary L Rev 45:469–547
Basu S, Gerchman Y, Collins CH, Arnold FH, Weiss R (2005) A synthetic multicellular system for programmed pattern formation. Nature 434:1130–1134
Bennerand SA, Sismour MA (2005) Synthetic biology. Nat Rev Genet 6:533–543
Bently L, Sherman B (2004) Intellectual property law, 2nd edn. Oxford University Press, Oxford
Blakeney M (1996) Trade related aspects of intellectual property rights: a concise guide to the TRIPs agreement. Sweet & Maxwell, London
Callaway E (2011) European ban on stem-cell patents has a silver lining. Nature 478:441
Canadian Biotechnology Advisory Committee (2002) Patenting of higher life forms and related issues. CBAC, Ottawa
Case C-34/10, Oliver Brüstle v. Greenpeace eV (Delivered 18 Oct 2011)
Case G-0002/06, Wisconsin Alumni Research Foundation, OJ EPO 2009 306
Case T-315/03, Harvard/Oncomouse, Transgenic animals/HARVARD, O J EPO 2005, 246
Case T-356/93, Plant Cells/Plant Genetic Systems, O J EPO 8/1995, 545
Chapman AR (2009) The ethics of patenting human embryonic stem cells. Kennedy Inst Ethics J 19(3):267
Chiapetta J (1994) Comment, of mice and machine: a paradigmatic challenge to interpretation of the patent statute. William Mitchell Law Rev 20:155–190
Comment (2009) Recent patent applications in synthetic biology. Nat Biotechnol 27, 141
Convention on the Grant of European Patents (European Patent Convention) (2000) http://www.epo.org/law-practice/legal-texts/html/epc/2010/e/index.html. Accessed 11 Nov 2012
Crane A, Matten D (2004) Business ethics. Oxford University Press, Oxford
Dent C, Lim K (2009) Intellectual Property Research Institute of Australia and Centre for Ideas and The Economy, Submission No 36 to Australian Senate, Standing Committee on Community Affairs, Inquiry into Gene Patents

Diamond, Commissioner of Patents and Trademarks v. Chakrabarty, 447 U.S. 303, 206 USPQ 193 (1980)
Edwards C (2010) Will IP choke synthetic biology work? The Biomachine Blog (6 Jun 2010, 5:28 PM). http://blog.thebiomachine.com/2010/06/james-boyle-synthetic-biology-patent-fears.html. Accessed 10 Oct 2012
English Statute of Monopolies 1623 (UK)
Etheridge J (2005). Europeans Claim Victory in BRCA1 Gene Patent Battle. Bioworld International 3
European Group on Ethics in Science and New Technologies (2009) Ethics of Synthetic Biology. European Commission, Brussels
Gallini N (2002) The economics of patents: lessons from recent U.S. patent reform. J Econ Perspect 16:131–154
Gibson D et al (2010) Creation of a bacterial cell controlled by a chemically synthesized genome. Science 329(5987):52–56
Gitter DM (2001) Led astray by the moral compass: incorporating morality into European Union biotechnology patent law. Berkeley J Int Law 19:21
Gittins R (2012) Economics Editor, Sydney Morning Herald, We risk letting lawyers stifle innovation, Blog (31 Mar 2012). http://www.rossgittins.com/2012/03/we-risk-letting-lawyers-stifle.html. Accessed 5 May 2012
Gowrishankar J (2010) Craig venter, and the claim for 'synthetic life'. Curr Sci 99(2):152
Heller M, Eisenberg R (1998) Can patents deter innovation? The anticommons in biomedical research. Science 280:698–701
Hilgartner S (2009) Intellectual property and the politics of emerging technology: inventors, citizens, and powers to shape the future. Chic-Kent Law Rev 84:197–224
Implementing Regulations to the Convention of the Grant of European Patents of 5 October 1973, (2001)
Kemp E (2011) European Court bans stem cell patents, EuroStemCell Blog (18 Oct 2011, 1:17 PM). http://www.eurostemcell.org/story/european-court-bans-stem-cell-patents. Accessed 10 Oct 2012
Kevles DJ (1998) Diamond v Chakrabarty and beyond: the political economy of patenting life. In: Thackray A (ed) Private science: biotechnology and the rise of the molecular sciences. University of Pennsylvania Press, Philadelphia
Levaskaya A et al (2005) Synthetic biology: engineering Escherichia coli to see light. Nature 438:441–442
Lemley M (2005) Patenting nanotechnology. Stanford Law Rev 58:601–630
Maskus K (2006) Reforming US patent policy. Council on Foreign Relations, New York
National Research Development Corporation v Commissioner of Patents (1959) 102 CLR 252 (Austl.)
O'Malley M et al (2008) Knowledge-making distinctions in synthetic biology. Bioessays 30:57–65
Organisation for Economic Co-operation and Development (2002) Genetic inventions, intellectual property rights and licensing practices: evidence and policies. OECD, Paris
Patents Act 1990 (Cth) (Austl.)
Pottage A, Sherman B (2011) Kinds, clones, and manufactures. In: Biagioli M, Jaszi P, Woodmansee M (eds) Making and unmaking intellectual property. University of Chicago Press, Chicago, pp 269–283
Press Release, European Patent Office, Technical Board of Appeal Maintains Further European Patent Relating to Breast and Ovarian Cancer Susceptibility Gene in Amended Form. Accessed 19 Nov 2008
Press Release, European Group on Ethics in Science and New Technologies, Ethics of synthetic biology. Accessed 17 Nov 2009
Rutz B (2009) Synthetic biology and patents: a European perspective. EMBO Rep 10:S14–S17
Scherer F (2002) The economics of human gene patents. Acad Med 77:1364–1367

Schmidt M et al (2009) A priority paper for the societal and ethical aspects of synthetic biology. Syst Synth Biol 3:3–7
Shulman S (2001) The morphing patent problem. Tech Rev 104(9):33
Thurow LC (1997) Needed: a new system of intellectual property rights. Harvard Business Review 75:94–103
U.S. Patent Application No. 20070264688
U.S. Patent No. 5843780 (Issued, 12 Jan 1998)
U.S. Patent No. 6200806 (Issued, 3 Mar 2001)
U.S. Patent No. 6280718 (Issued, 28 Aug 2001)
U.S. Patent Publication No. 2007/0122826A1 (filed, 12 Oct 2006)
UK Parliamentary Office of Science and Technology, Synthetic biology, 298 Postnote 1–4. Accessed Jan 2008
Verbeure B et al (2006) Patent pools and diagnostic testing. Trends Biotechnol 24(3):115–120
Warner KD (2001) Are life patents ethical? Conflict between Catholic social teaching and agricultural biotechnology's patent regime. J Agric Environ Ethics 14(3):301–319
Willison DJ, Macleod SM (2002) Patenting of genetic material: are the benefits to society being realized? Can Med Assoc J 167(3):259–262

Chapter 9
Synthetic Biology: Challenges and Legal Questions

Jürgen Robienski and Jürgen Simon

Abstract "Synthetic biology – birth of a new technology." Under this label, the discussion on synthetic biology is conducted. But what is really new about the synthetic biology? Not much! 95–98 % of what is declared as Synthetic Biology is just a direct continuation of modern molecular biology, genetic research or genetic engineering. For these technologies the existing laws, especially the Gene Technology Law is applicable. Irrespective of this, various ethical, social and legal fields of conflict are discussed with respect to Synthetic Biology, particularly with regard to its implementation orientation, the enormous scientific progress and the sizeable (concrete) application potential. This discussion is focused on aspects of safety, security and justice/fairness. Stronger security measures with regard to the potential misuse seem to be needed. Freedom of research could be restricted as the international debate on the H5N1 virus has shown recently. For example, a Global Health Security Policy Board is under discussion. On the other hand, several national and supranational organizations come to the result that a strict regulation of Synthetic Biology would do more harm than good. Their result is to observe the developments of Synthetic Biology and to react flexible. This paper provides an overview about the German debate in the international context.

Keywords Definition of synthetic biology • Biosafety • Biosecurity • Freedom of research and publication • Global panel on biosafety • Proceduralization of the law • Protection of intellectual property rights

J. Robienski (✉) • J. Simon
Centre for Ethics and Law in the Life Sciences (CELLS),
Medical University Hannover, Hannover, Germany
e-mail: robienski@aol.com; jwsimon@web.de

I. de Miguel Beriain and C.M. Romeo Casabona (eds.), *Synbio and Human Health: A Challenge to the Current IP Framework?*, DOI 10.1007/978-94-017-9196-0_9,

9.1 Introduction

Synthetic Biology is – at least among some members of the scientific community and by parts of the media – promoted as one of the most considerable scientific disciplines of the twenty first century. It is thought to influence our life in all areas. With the aid of Synthetic Biology, man is lifted up as engineer or even creator of life, for whom nature is nothing but a construction kit which he can use to design and create new organisms with specific traits from single biological components and modules.

As yet, this eminent meaning is only known to few people. Only 17 % of the EU 27 population (18 % in Germany) have ever heard about Synthetic Biology.[1] This is also true for lawyers. The enormous significance of Synthetic Biology has not yet been acknowledged by jurisprudence. While there are a number of scientific projects investigating jurisprudential aspects of Synthetic Biology and some results have already been published, which tackle the necessity of legal regulation of this subject, most of the publications are issued by ethicists, politologists, environmental activists or natural scientists. In Germany, the one and only essay by a lawyer on legal aspects of Synthetic Biology was published by Luttermann in 2011 (Luttermann 2011, pp. 195 f.). However, this essay – while it is quite entertaining and worth reading simply due to its poetic and philosophical quality – mostly tackles general questions like what is life and calls for holistic thinking in jurisprudence, but without going into great detail about specific legal problems.

What might be the reason for the reluctance of German as well as international jurisprudence to investigate and discuss legal problems of Synthetic Biology? Is the potential of Synthetic Biology simply not recognized? In fact, this subject is often put on a level with genetic engineering, and the opinion predominates that Synthetic Biology is not more than "old wine in new wineskins" (Schwille 2011, p. 5; Zelder 2011, p.15).

Indeed, chances, goals, promises and open questions related to Synthetic Biology are nothing new. They resemble those put up in the 1980s in the context of genetic engineering.[2] The question is, however, if Synthetic Biology leads to a qualitative and quantitative leap ("industrialization"), which forces us to come to a new legal evaluation.

---

[1] Eurobarometer 73.1 Biotechnologie (2010) – Bericht zur Befragung zur Biotechnologie, in: Eurobarometer Spezial 328, p. 142.

[2] Hohlfeld, R. (1988), Biologie als Ingenieurskunst. Zur Dialektik von Naturbeherrschung und synthetischer Biologie, in: Ästhetik und Kommunikation 69/1988, p. 61: "In fact today physicists, chemists and molecular biologists using gene technology, chemical and biochemical synthesis methods and highly advanced automation techniques can construct biological agents, genes, cell-like membrane vesicles and organisms with a completely new genetic map, which nature has never seen before."; Eberbach, Wolfram (2012), Gentechnik und Recht, in: Eberbach et al., "Recht der Gentechnik und Biomedizin", 79. Erg.Lieferung, Band 1, Teil A. I. p. 13 (12) refering to the historical discussion of the risks of gentechnologie.

9.2 Definition of Synthetic Biology

One of the main reasons for the reluctance of lawyers to tackle this area probably is the fact that there is no legal definition and not even a consistent natural scientific definition for it.

The need for a "legal", or a jurisprudentially manageable definition, however, is most relevant particularly when a novel technology is under discussion. Novel technologies always raise the question whether new laws are necessary. With regard to Synthetic Biology, the question is if this technology brings about completely new potential risks, which would urge the legislative authority to issue a special law for it (Dederer 2010, pp. 71 f). This, however, is only the case if these specific risks are not fully regulated by already existing legal regulations or if even an adaptation of existing regulations to the specific risks of Synthetic Biology will not allow for an adequate solution.

In this context, Schmidt (2011b, pp. 112 f.) notices that the following questions must be answered before further safety considerations are started:

1. Which are the new challenges and problems that Synthetic Biology brings about?
2. Which details make these topics differ from those emerging in other areas of "Life Sciences"?
3. Which approaches, applications and results make Synthetic Biology unique?

It is evident that, as a prerequisite for a legal definition, a clear and consistent natural scientific, at least a preliminary one, is needed. The legislative authorities are principally free to assign a legal concept to colloquial terms, which may deviate from general language use and even come close to fiction (Ronellenfitsch 2008, p. 17). However, the German legislative authority has not yet developed a legal definition of Synthetic Biology. Furthermore, legal definitions in the area of natural sciences are usually based on natural scientific definitions. While it is common to expand or narrow down these natural scientific definitions, e.g. in order to define the range of application of a law or to describe a specific state of being that is aimed at ("range of ought to be" in German: "Sollensbereich"), the natural scientific definition always remains the central part (Ronellenfitsch 2008). As mentioned before, there is no consistent definition of Synthetic Biology as yet. This makes the legal authorities practically unable to develop a legal definition. Natural Sciences are urged to deliver their duty first. Accordingly, the German Council for Ethics declared at its convention on Nov 23, 2011 (Title of the convention "Workshop Life. The significance of Synthetic Biology for Science and Society") that there is still no consistent definition of Synthetic Biology but that it is rather an area of research which is still being built up. Worldwide, great efforts are made to come to a consensus upon the question what makes up the core idea and the novelty of Synthetic Biology (Catenhusen 2011, p. 85; Sauter 2011a, b, p. 23).

It should be mentioned here that there is broad agreement about the fact that a lot of what is presented under the label "Synthetic Biology" is indeed nothing new. Ninety five to ninety eight percent of what is declared as Synthetic Biology is just a straight forward continuation of modern molecular biology, genetic research or genetic engineering (Müller-Röber 2011, p. 70).

While there is no consistent natural scientific definition, it is still possible to draw a broad frame around the field which is currently discussed as Synthetic Biology.

There is broad agreement that the term "Synthetic Biology" was first introduced by Szybalski in 1974 (Schultz 2009). In the German technical literature, the term appeared from the 1980s onwards related to the discussion about the regulation of genetic engineering. Even though already at that time, a number of characteristics which are thought to be specific for Synthetic Biology, such as mechanization of biology, the paradigm of engineering with modularization or the dogma of creation of new life, occurred, the term Synthetic Biology is mostly seen as synonymous with modern genetic engineering (Lengeler 1988, p. 17; Herdegen 2012; Hohlfeld 1986, pp. 550–560; Hohlfeld 1984, pp. 550–560; Hohlfeld 1990)..

Only at the beginning of this millennium, the term Synthetic Biology appeared more frequently in scientific discussions, now however with the aim of differentiation from classical genetic engineering and from other biotechnologies such as molecular biology or system biology. Since 2006/2007 efforts are made to find a consistent definition of the scientific area of Synthetic Biology (Boldt et al. 2009, p. 8).

As the most common definition in the scientific community, Schmidt (2011a, b, pp. 111 f.) cites the one to find under: http://syntheticbiology.org/Who_we_are.html: "Design and construction of new biological components, instruments and systems and re-design of already existing natural biological systems for beneficial aims".[3]

This definition, however, is not sufficiently specific as a basis for a legal definition. Therefore, Schmidt continues by defining the following sub-groups (Schmidt 2011a, b, 112 f.):

(a) DNA-synthesis: chemical construction of genetic codes based on the matrix of a genetic code of an existing organism (with known nucleic acids)
(b) DNA-based biological circuits: Transfer of complete biological systems made of biobricks
(c) Minimal genome or minimal life form (Top-Down-Process)
(d) Protocells: living cells which are constructed new from bottom up
(e) Xenobiology: Creation of orthogonal biological systems which do not occur in nature, based on biochemical principles which do not occur in nature (XNA).

These five sub-groups are the most important areas of application of Synthetic Biology. They may be reduced to the following three main elements: **modification, copying and new creation** of "life".

Is this definition of Synthetic Biology suitable to distinguish this technology from other known "technologies", in particular from gene technology or genetic engineering?

Gene technology deals with isolation, analysis, modification and new combination of carriers of genetic information. In contrast to gene technology, genetic engineering refers to the practical usage, i.e. the types of procedures, working strategies and

[3] http://syntheticbiology.org/Who_we_are.html

methods, such as experimental methods to produce DNA-molecules containing new genes or combinations of genes, and to characterize, isolate and re-combine genetic material.[4] As stated in the justification for the first draft of the German Genetic Engineering Law (GenTG), which is mainly based on European guidelines and therefore comparable to other European regulations, "the systematic new combination of genetic material from living being using technical methods (genetic engineering) …"

And further on: "This law shall apply for genetic engineering work in closed systems, (now: genetic engineering facilities), for release and marketing of genetically modified organisms".

The scope of the GenTG is thus mainly determined by the definition of a genetically modified organism. § 3 No. 3 defines a genetically modified organism as an "organism, except for a human one, whose genetic material has been modified in a way that would not occur under natural conditions by cross-breeding or natural recombination;…. a genetically modified organism is also an organism which has developed by cross-breeding or natural recombination between genetically modified organisms or with one or more genetically modified organisms or by other types of propagation of a genetically modified organism, given that the organism's genetic material displays characteristics which can be traced back to genetic engineering".

According to the first alternative, an organism is seen as genetically modified in case that its genetic material has been modified in a way that does not occur under natural conditions. Additionally, the term GMO includes organisms which have developed by some sort of propagation of genetically modified organisms, provided that their genetic material displays characteristics which can be traced back to genetic engineering. § 3 No. 3 a GenTG continues with a list of procedures which are considered "particularly" as procedures for the modification of genetic material and result in the creation of a GMO according to § 3 No. 3. The term "particularly" implies that this list only contains examples, but is not complete. Other procedures may also be included, provided they belong to the exemptions according to § 3 Nr. 3 b und c, otherwise they are to be evaluated by the criteria given in § 3 No. 3.

The definition of a genetically modified organism further relates to the legal definitions of an organism and of genetic engineering works. § 3 No. 1 defines an organism as

> any biological unit which is capable to propagate or to transfer genetic material, including microorganisms (Ronellenfitsch 2004, pp. 22 f.).

This legal term is more comprehensive than the biological concept of an organism. The legal definition for an organism in terms of the GenTG is a sort of generic term for all cellular, multicellular and non-cellular biological units which are capable to propagate or to transfer genetic material. There is no limitation to living beings with a complex mineral content, cellular organisation and metabolism (Ronellenfitsch 2004, p. 23).

---

[4] Dritter Bericht der Bundesregierung über Erfahrungen mit dem Gentechnikgesetz (2008): Bt-Drs 16/8155, printed in: Eberbach et al. (2012): Band 2, Teil I, B. I., p. 3.

At first sight, the legal definitions of the GenTG, particularly that for GMO, cover all sub-groups of Synthetic Biology named by Schmidt. With regard to sub-group s, d and e, this applies at least as long as it is impossible to create artificial cells which serve as "chassis" for synthetically produced information. Since the term organism is defined quite broadly in the legal definition, this might also apply once it will be possible to produce artificial cells. Even an artificial cell is, by all means, a "biological unit which is capable to propagate or to exchange genetic material".

It must be concluded that even this differentiated definition of Synthetic Biology is rather unsuitable to distinguish Synthetic Biology from the legal definition of gene technology and genetic engineering, respectively. There may be a difference from a natural scientific point of view. In terms of the legal definition of the GenTG, however, Synthetic Biology is – at first sight – nothing new.

The only gap of regulation that could be identified is the question whether a "de novo" synthetically created cell is also a "biological unit which is capable to propagate or to exchange genetic material" in terms of the GenTG (Engelhardt, Margret 2010, p. 23). The Central Commission for Biological Safety (ZKBS) in germany noted in the recent interim report from November 06, 2012 that the most scientific approaches in synthetic biology are within the scope of the GenTG. Only novel living systems such as artificial cells (bottom up approach) without precedent in nature are not covered by the GenTG (ZKBS 2012, P. 8). In so far, a small clarifying supplement to the legal definition for the term organism in the GenTG would suffice to close that gap. This supplement could be phrased as follows: "any biological unit which is capable to propagate or to transfer genetic material, including microorganism and **any biological units created by technical means which do not occur under natural conditions and which contain genetic material that does not occur naturally**."

This supplement would clarify that synthetically produced or modified organisms or biological units as well as the use of even naked synthetically produced DNA definitely fall within the scope and field of control of the GenTG.[5]

9.3 Fields of Conflict

Irrespective of the question of definition, it should be noted that various ethical, social and legal fields of conflict are discussed with respect to Synthetic Biology, particularly with regard to its implementation orientation, the enormous scientific progress and the seizable (concrete) application potential. The focus of this discussion is on aspects of safety and justice/fairness. Especially these two areas of conflict raise important legal questions.

[5] It seems possible to achieve this result by interpretation of the law or by a decision of the ZKBS, in the same way the ZKBS evaluates new GMO or new forms of genetic engeneering.

9.3.1 *Biosafety and Biosecurity*

Like in the early development of recombinant DNA a lot of concerns have been raised (Balmer and Martin 2008, p. 15). And in 2004 the magazine Nature called for a broad discussion of the risks: "This is not only genes to be replaced. Now life is molded like clay. (…) The scope of such instruments is much larger than that of genetic modification and it is certainly much harder to foresee the actual risks. "[6]

Philip Ball cited in the same issue of Nature a report of the CIA on new Bio weapons in which the organization warned that using synthetic biology completely new pathogens and other organisms could be made, "worse than any previously known human illness " (Then et al., p. 21). In this context two fields of conflicts have to be distinguished.

While the German language only offers the single term "Biosicherheit" to describe the conflict fields relevant from a security point of view, the English language area makes a distinction between biosecurity and biosafety. The concept of biosafety is understood in terms of product and environmental safety. Biosecurity, on the other hand, refers to the security against abuse of Synthetic Biology, such as military or terroristic activities aided by the production of biological weapons.

9.3.1.1 Conflict Field Biosafety

The risks of new forms of life are complex – regardless of how simple its components are themselves. It is not just interaction with the environment, and gene regulation in living things leaves room for effects that go far beyond additive effects of the individual components. Whether the "creations" of synthetic biology in fact comply with the rules of controllable machines, may be doubted. Complex machines are "only" error-prone, but complex organisms are at the last consequence replicable, interacting, and neither retrievable nor controllable.

Generally, the problem is that in a risk assessment of synthetic organisms a recourse to the experience with existing life forms is only limited or not at all possible (ZKBS 2012, p.8). Thus, for example, it is doubtful that synthetic organisms can survive, because their new properties are not adapted to the environment, which could make them impossible to survive under natural conditions. On the other hand and in contrary, it is discussed that the organisms just because of the environment can spread very quickly, as ecosystems are not prepared for their new properties (IGSC 2009).

Similar problems the European Group of Ethicists sees: "Synthetic microorganisms released into the environment could initiate processes of horizontal gene transfer and affect biotic balances, or evolve beyond their functionality and elicit unprecedented side-effects on the environment and other organisms" (EGE 2009, pp. 27 f.)

[6] Futures of artificial life, Nature, Editorial, 2004, Vol 431, p. 613.

So, the first one is about the accidental and uncontrolled release into the environment, "as by their very nature seeking biological machines could evolve, proliferate and produce unexpected interactions that might alter the ecosystem" (EGE 2009, p. 27). Therefore, adequate biological control must be developed, for example "engineering bacteria to be dependent on nutrients with limited availability, and integration of self-destruct mechanisms that are triggered should the population density become too great" (EGE 2009, p. 27). And that is necessary before synthetic biology experiments start.

9.3.1.2 Conflict Field Biosecurity

The ethics experts from the European Commission explicitly warn against the risks of abuse of synthetic biology for the production of chemical weapons or for terrorist attacks.

Similar fears have thus been formulated by the German Research Association (DFG). "There is concern that individuals, terrorist organizations or states have the option to reconstruct pathogenic organisms or toxins and use them for hostile or warlike acts. A similar approach could be of concern and prosecuted by persons who such as computer hackers and computer viruses designers, or as interested lay people receive access to individual synthetic elements or the necessary substances and produce synthetic systems in an uncontrolled environment, including microorganisms" (Schultz 2009).

Even by the operators of synthetic biology, the possible misuse of gene synthesis to create new biological weapons is openly discussed (Garfinkel et al. 2007, pp. 38 ff.). In a report of the Craig Venter Institute measures are proposed to prevent through which it seems to be possible to prevent that gene segments are synthesized from dangerous microorganisms and sold: labs should be protected (for example through certification), gene synthesis engines be registered, and the order of gene sequences be controlled. Nouri and Chyba propose to equip the machines with synthetic synthesis blocking mechanisms that make the synthesis of certain genes impossible (Nouri and Christopher 2009, pp. 234–236). These proposals came from representatives of the two largest gene-synthesis companies. (DNA2.0)

Overall, the image of an applied technology risk has grown up before the public was sufficiently informed about possible risks and has discussed these risks. The legislature has so far not dealt with sufficiently necessary measures. How the actual subject is has been shown for example by the fact that the governments of Germany and the United States Involving intelligence services (FBI, BKA) have met with companies in February 2009 for discussion of further developments and their consequences.

"Life as Lego" or the "Do-it-yourself DNA" in the U.S. is now very successful: Thus, it was possible to order from more than 30 gene synthesis companies different genetic DNA. Production and mailing of DNA parts were completely legal, which could then later be combined to Marburg virus, or smallpox. And therefore, we have one of the biggest risks of synthetic biology named, the bio security problem.

Pat Mooney, for example, argues that responsible scientists could trigger together with civil society a movement for slowly growth. This movement needs to agree in particular on an "International Convention on the Evaluation of New Technologies" (ICENT) (Mooney 2010, p. 118). Therefore a code of ethics and standards should emerge for biological engineering as it has done for other engineering disciplines (Mooney 2010, p. 118).

According to the theory paper of DECHEMA (2011, p. 11) Synthetic Biology operates a use of genetic engineering methods, as it has been so far not been there. Therefore, internationally stronger security measures with regard to the potential misuse seem to be needed. The question here is how a sufficient safeguard against abuse is possible.

This question has recently become very explosive, without that synthetic biology just has directly to do with it.

9.3.2 Freedom of Research and Publication

The explosive issue at the end of the year 2011 arose, if the blueprint for a deadly and highly contagious virus should be published. For several months, scientists and security experts debated the issue, and finally even the World Health Organization (WHO) intervened in the discussion. As the first official body calling for the full publication of all details of two studies by Yoshihiro Kawaoka and Ron Fouchier about H5N1 virus – but only at a later date.[7] Meanwhile, both studies have been published (Kawaoka et al. 2012; Fouchier 2012).

Generally, it comes to biosecurity, therefore, research at and with potentially threatening organisms, but especially to the "fear" in the way of a future production of synthetic biology and the subsequent publication of research results.

In February this year a larger group of experts has agreed in discussions with the WHO that the moratorium on experiments with highly dangerous artificial bird flu virus as they were made in the high-security laboratories in Rotterdam, should be extended until further notice. The final document stated that it should be achieved in more public debates that security should be strengthened even more, just as the sense of security of the population (Cohen 2012).

Some researchers have claimed that it is now going on the occasion of genetically engineered avian influenza virus to a "biosecurity policy Marshall Plan". Here, the question is asked how much responsibility researchers can and should bear. How far can the freedom of research reach? Does it apply basically unlimited in the sense of the German Constitution, or do the newest developments lead to limitations when it is possible that terrorists can get to the blueprints of highly dangerous viruses. And how resp. to what extent should or can they be restricted by the authorities?

[7] World Health Organization, Statement 30. 11.2011: "WHO concerned that new H5N1 influenza research could undermine the 2011 Pandemic Influenza Preparedness Framework", www.who.int/entity/…/news/…/index.html

For the first time in the history of biological science, the U.S. National Advisory Board for Biosecurity (NSABB)[8] has recommended secrecy to protect mankind – also against bioterrorists. A blueprint for the super pathogens would be a monstrous weapon, thus the NSABB. If at all, only a censored version of the research should be published.

The NSABB was also considering a moratorium on similar cases. So far it has been asked in some cases by scientists or journals about to appraise studies that could involve potential conflicts of interest.

Researchers resist any approach that they perceive as limiting the freedom of research. "Such censorship is a clear breach of the rules of good scientific practice and leads to unnecessary dramatization", says a statement by the German Society for Virology. And also the influenza expert Hans-Dieter Klenk from Marburg University criticized the decision: "I would argue that research should be published in detail," he says. A sensational conclusion cannot be easily set in the world. "Research results will be published so, that other researchers can repeat it and check. This is science" (Kupferschmidt 2011).

The ultimate aim is to weigh the risks and benefits of a research field, which in the sense of "dual-use" has what it takes to save lives – or putting them at risk. In the Fink Report[9] from 2004, a U.S. study on dual-use problems, which also led to the establishment of the NSABB, the most critical experiments are listed. Among them are those that facilitate the transferability of a pathogen, or to increase its virulence or change it which hosts it infects. The modified H5N1 virus hits all three.

That the requirement of the U.S. health authorities to suppress technical information at least is right and certainly consistent with the U.S. Constitution, two lawyers from Georgetown University in Washington have made clear in an issue of "Science" earlier this year. Instead of discussing the abuse of power and attempted censorship, researchers and authorities should consider, how the high-risk research could be better organized and coordinated so that the dangerous experiments within the research community will carefully be examined and minimize the risks of abuse the same time.[10]

---

[8] Statement of NSABB (2012), Meeting of the National Science Advisory Board for Biosecurity to Review Revised Manuscripts on Transmissibility of A/H5N1 Influenza Virus, oba.od.nih.gov/.../biosecurity/.../NSABB_Statem...(access 27.12.2012)

[9] Biotechnology Research in the Age of Terrorism (Fink Report, 2004), Committee on Research Standards and Practices to Prevent the Destructive Application of Biotechnology, National Research Council, Washington D.C., www.nap.edu/openbook.php?isbn=0309089778 – (access 27.12.2012).

[10] *Kraemer, John D/Gostin, Lawrence O.* (2012), *georgetown Public Law and Legal Theory Research Paper No. 12-020* papers.ssrn.com/sol3/papers.cfm?abstract_id... – (*access28.12.2012*); *The Limits of Government Regulation of Science, Georgetown Medical Center, Office of Communication (2012), Balancing Scientific Freedom and National Security*, Two Georgetown professors explore a process needed to avoid the current dilemma faced by two scientific journals recently asked by the U.S. government to redact parts of scientific publications, January 19, explore.georgetown.edu/news/?ID = 61756...(access 23.12.2012).

After all, we have in Germany the anchor of freedom of research in the Constitution. Thus, according to Article 5, paragraph 3, sentence 1 GG is:

> Art and science, research and teaching are free.

The academic freedom is guaranteed as unconditional basic right. But the legislature can allow the intervention of research in constitutional goods such as life, health or property. Conversely, it may also restrict the research to protect such resources.

What are the barriers? The renowned German Max Planck Society has given guidelines and rules concerning the responsible use of freedom of research and research risks in March 2010. The regulations have been developed by the Working Group "Security and Defense Research" with the assistance of the Ethics Council.[11] Here, the Max Planck Society is very aware of the problem of "dual-use" and emphasizes it also.

Limitations of the research are first determined by legal norms that can limit the freedom of research to protect important constitutionally protected goods in the context of proportionality. Thus, for example research objectives such as the development of nuclear and biological weapons can be excluded or certain methods be regulated, such as experiments on humans.[12]

The Max Planck Society has also given principles for responsible ethical research, which shall be binding on the people in this society.[13] These principles, or similar from other organizations could be applied in principle to many organizations. They could also be made internationally binding. Nevertheless, the question arises whether they would actually solve such a problem as the research on the virus and the publication of research results. Ultimately, that remains a matter of balancing, as it becomes clear from the example of the guidelines and regulations of the Max Planck Society.

Another issue is whether all these internal commitments for researchers by their organizations actually lead to a sustainable legal obligation. This situation is not yet clear and would probably ultimately require a judicial decision.

9.3.3 Global Panel on Biosafety

In addition, also aspects of biosecurity should be rethought now. For the last the WHO is not responsible. But an appropriate staff of experts should be created who should be busy internationally, interdisciplinary and intellectually. Such Global

---

[11] "Security and Defense Research" Working Group (2010), Guidelines and Rules of the Max Planck Society On A Responsible Approach To Freedom Of Research And Research Risks, 19. 3., www.mpg.de/232129/researchFreedomRisks.pdf – (access 17.11.2012).

[12] "Security and Defense Research" Working Group (2010), pp. 3 f.

[13] "Security and Defense Research" Working Group (2010), pp. 6 f.

Health Security Policy Board[14] should "not be influenced by the interests of enforcing national security agendas, but open rather to look to find new answers to global issues" (biosafety expert Petra Dieckmann, virologists Christian Drosten and Stephan Becker). In any case, the problem has not even begun to be solved, and it requires many other considerations.

According to the DECHEMA and other companies as well as government agencies, the synthetic biologists themselves are required to work out good practices and standards together with the society. For example, German companies producing synthetic genes have committed on their own initiative to investigate the incoming orders first towards possible dangers of pathogenicity. With the help of modern database that is basically very efficiently.

Then, motivated by the goal of a global harmonization of these screening methods, on the initiative of a German company, the five largest commercial Gen synthesis companies have merged to the International Gene Synthesis Consortium[15] (IGSC)). They develop common standards for secure and fair global shipping synthetic DNA. Remained open, however, is whether also orders of so called "Doityourselfers" for the composition of pathogenic organisms with other companies than those that produce synthetic genes could be possible. So, are really all potential hazards covered by the formation of such consortia? If that happened around the world, as advocated already, it would surely result in a significant risk reduction, particularly as the underlying and basic "Harmonized Screening Protocol" sounds very ambitious.

9.3.4 Position of the U.S.A

In the international area, the position of the U.S. is of particular importance in science and in the field of economic realization of synthetic biology. And here the Presidential Commission for the Study of Bioethical Issues (PCSBI) has a prominent role. In consequence of the announcement of Craig Venter in May 2010, that he had made a synthetic cell, the Presidential Commission worked its first five months on the potential benefits and risks of this breakthrough, as well as on the study of the so-called Do-It-Yourself Biology.

The result is the demand for so-called "prudent vigilance" .in a "responsible stewardship".[16] Demanded is the right balance between completely uncontrolled research and the application of the restrictive "precautionary principle". This principle, applied rigorously, would require a complete and thorough understanding of all potential risks before applying the methods of Synthetic Biology. But the Report

[14] Global Health and Security in Question (ed. Andrew Lakoff/Stephen J. Collier), (2008), New York;

[15] International Gene Synthesis Consortium (IGSC), www.genesynthesisconsortium.org.

[16] Presidential Commission for the Study of Bioethical Issues (2010), New Directions. The Ethics of Synthetic Biology and Emerging Technologies, Washington, pp. 140 ff.

of the Presidential Commission of December 2010 believes that in a developing area such as Synthetic Biology a strict regulation would do more harm than good. Therefore, it is recommended that the development of regulations should be carefully handled.... subject to re-evaluation. Just because the development of Synthetic Biology is constantly dynamic, it is essential to set up regulatory bodies that deal with it continuously. In the specific case a group should do it which preliminary works for the White House Office of Science and Technology Policy and periodically reviews funding and regulation.[17] The proposal is to have more flexibility or proceduralization of the law, as we have it on the German and European level. That specifically means to observe the development of Synthetic Biology and then to respond quickly, sometimes immediately with laws or administrative regulations. These will be kept under constant observation and evaluated continuously.

The report of the Presidential Commission includes some specific suggestions. One is to mark new synthetic organisms, so they leave its marks in the case they should get out of the lab. Another is to construct consciously organisms so weak that they most likely cannot exist in another environment.

Other concerns were ignored by the proposals of the Presidential Commission, among others, how to deal with the in the U.S. around 2000 members strong "Do-it-yourself-community". These include, for example, the proposal for a compulsory registration of Doityourselfers. In this regard, concerns were raised that this could be counterproductive because a compulsory registration could encourage underground operations, which could even lead to a smaller overview of this community.

Whether the proposals of this Presidential Commission are implemented, must still be awaited. Therefore, the proposal part of the report contains 18 proposals designed to promote the ethical principles of Synthetic Biology, including the public welfare, the responsible management, intellectual freedom and responsibility, democratic deliberation, justice and fairness.[18] Some of these proposals, which should be published in the middle of this year, including certain concretization, will show whether the actors are willing to act seriously and with prudent vigilance in the field of synthetic biology.

9.3.5 Justice/Fairness

The conflict about justice is to be understood in terms of economic fairness. The focus is on the danger of monopolization due to patenting and limitation of access to important research results. In contrast to this, there is the concept of "open source". On the other hand it cannot be denied that the protection of intellectual property in the form of intellectual and technical inventory achievements by researchers and developers is a principle acknowledged e.g. by patent law, which generally also applies to Synthetic Biology.

---

[17] Ibid., pp. 147 ff.

[18] Ibid., pp. 115 ff.

Another important aspect of the debate about justice is the discrimination of poor (3rd world) countries, who get competition for their agricultural production.

9.3.6 New Life

Since the goal of Synthetic Biology is the creation of new living organisms, specific ethical questions arise, e.g. what is life? When does life start? Is man entitled to create new life? Are there changes in or concepts of man and life resulting from the possibility of creating completely new life? (Luttermann 2011, pp. 195 f.)

9.4 Legal Questions

9.4.1 General Questions

From a legal point of view, the main question is if and how law may contribute to solve the conflicts outlined here. Are existing regulations/ laws sufficient to comprise and solve all conflict fields of Synthetic Biology, or is there a need for the legislative authorities to take action? In case there is a need to take action, is it acute/ urgent, or does it allow to wait for further development in this area? Can and must the legislative authority act in a precautionary manner right now? Is the need for action a challenge for the national legislative authority, or do regulations on a European or international level take precedence to be effective? As far as the national legislative authority shall act, it must be sorted out to which extent he may become active without violating the preceding European law.

9.4.2 Legal discussion in Germany

While Synthetic Biology is not a completely new area of research, there are still only very few publications dealing explicitly and intensively with legal questions of Synthetic Biology. This is particularly true for Germany. In general, legal aspects are tackled (shortly) in the context of general expert reports, statements or policy documents in the context of ethical and social aspects. There are usually no thorough examinations, particularly not regarding individual facts of a case. Rather, it is demonstrated that the legal questions related to Synthetic Biology are not generally new, but more like well known problems with a new quality or intensity. In this context, the applicability of existing legal regulations as a whole is debated and potential need to take action identified. Exemplary contributions for the national German law are: The Perspectives of the Council of Ethics from 23.04.2009, the Joint Policy Paper for Synthetic Biology by DFG, acatech, et al. from 2009, the expert report by Boldt, Müller and Maio "Synthetische Biologie – Eine ethisch-philosophische Analyse" (Synthetic Biology – an ethical and philosophical analysis) from 2008, the contribution by Schmidt in "Synthetische Biologie – Die Geburt einer neuen Technikwissenschaft" (Synthetic Biology – birth of a new technical science) from 2011, the paper from Then Christopher "Synthetische Biologie und künstliches Leben – Eine kritische Analyse" from 2010 the script of Schummer, Joachim "DasGotteshandwerk. Die künstliche Herstellung von Leben im Labor", the answer of the German government from March 23, 2011 (Bt-Ds 17/5165), .the Convention of the German Council of Ethics "Workshop Life. The significance of Synthetic Biology for Science and Society" in November 23, 2011 and the 1. Interim Report of The Central Commission for Biological Safety (ZKBS) from November 06, 2012 "Monitoring der Synthetischen Biologie in Deutschland",

The Joint Policy Paper by DFG et al. concludes that there is currently no or at least no essential need to take action since the conflict fields of Synthetic Biology are covered by existing law and therefore sufficiently regulated. To the same conclusion comes the German government.[19] The questions concerning biosecurity are, so the authors, covered on international level by the "Biological and Toxin Weapons Convention" (BWTC) as well as by further international and national regulations, among them the "Kriegswaffenkontrollgesetz" (law for the control of war weapons). With regard to biosafety, coverage is given in particular by the GenTG, the AMG, the IFSG and the ChemG. Finally, questions of patent law are regulated by the EU guideline for biopatents, which has meanwhile been transferred into the German patent law. According to DFG et al., these regulations are currently sufficient to the greatest possible extent, leaving no acute need to take immediate action. This is also the prevailing point of view shared by German authorities.[20] This position is also in agreement with the legal opinion in various other European countries. Accordingly, the European Group on Ethics in Science and New Technologies (EGE) states:

> At the moment virtually all approaches to synthetic biology involve the use of genetic modification techniques. Therefore, within the EU they are regulated through the Directives and Regulations for genetic modification introduced initially in 1990 and substantially modified during the ensuing years.

Boldt et al. mainly present the current state of discussion and report international proposals for the improvement of biosecurity, biosafety and questions of patent law. In contrast to the Joint Policy Paper they still see the need for legal investigation and action. Similarly, the German Council of Ethics acknowledges the fact that the development of Synthetic Biology will not only revive the discussions which

---

[19] Bt-Ds 17/5165, p. 5; the same position has the scientific service of the German Parliament, Donner, Susanne et al., Statement of the scientific service of the German Parliament (2009) Nr. 60/09.

[20] Antwort der Bundesregierung v. 22.03.2011 (Bt-Drs: 17/5165); Luttermann, JZ 2011, p.195; Deutscher Ethikrat (Friedrich, Bärbel v. 24.01.2010); Wiss. Dienst d. BT r. 60/09 v. 15.07.2009; Parl. Ethikbeirat v. 01.07.2009, 16/13780; Sauter, Tab-Bericht 2011; Pühler, Alfred, Tagesspiegel v. 23.02.2011

already evolved around genetic engineering, but may create new problems and security risks which have not been discussed before. These problems ask for a reaction or rather, a debate about how to react. As a result of his latest convention in November 2001, the German Council of Ethics concludes that the demand for a consistent definition of Synthetic Biology, as well as its clear distinction to other technologies and an answer to the question what is the essential novelty of this technology and how to define its core element, life, are currently the most important tasks.

A further need for action is hardly seen, as Synthetic Biology in Germany falls completely within the range of application of the GenTG, so that questions of biosafety are mostly irrelevant. However, the importance of some sort of monitoring is emphasized, while it is noted that part of this is already existing in the form of a duty for evaluation and observation assigned to ZKBS (2012). In this respect, it is only reminded that this monitoring should be improved (Catenhusen 2011, pp. 85–86). However, with regard to the so called Do-it-yourself-biology and the biohacker community which is currently also developing in Germany (Charisius et al. 2012), at least the industry calls for action and regulation (Schmidt 2011a, b, 120; Engelhardt 2010, p. 22). This demand concurs with the demand by EGE to control and manage biohacking.

A much more critical position is represented by NGOs such as Testbiotech, with their leading protagonist Christopher Then, GeN[21] and the BUND.[22] They notice a need for legal action by legislative authorities particularly with regard to the risks of Synthetic Biology for the environment in the case of release (a lack of options for control and recovery, missing comparability of new organisms). The BUND proposes a moratorium for synthetic biology (Stagemann 2011, p.14). Testbiotech proposes a moratorium on research funding in the field of Synthetic Bioloy and also concrete changes of the GenTG (Then and Hamberger 2010). According to them, § 1 GenTG should be supplement as follows (Then 2010): "The aim of this law is .... the environment … and the protection from an uncontrolled proliferation of genetically modified or synthetically produced organism…".

The supplementation of the specific function defined in §1 GenTG seems not really necessary according to this opinion and has mainly declaratory character. In its most recent decision about the GenTG, the Federal Constitutional Court already clarified that the legal authorities hold a special obligation for care when evaluating long term consequences of the use of genetic engineering because the scientific state of knowledge has not yet been finalized (Then and Hamberger 2010). In this respect, the mandate of Art. 20a GG must be accounted for, which urges the legal authorities in their responsibility for future generations to protect natural resources. "This mandate demands for hazard control as well as for the prevention of risks. The environmental goods protected by Art. 20a GG include the preservation of biological variety as well as the protection of a species-appropriate life for

---

[21] Gen-ethisches Netzwerk e.V.

[22] Bund für Umwelt- und Naturschutz Deutschland e. V.

endangered animal and plant species."[23] In this context, the Federal Constitutional Court has made it quite clear that the aim of the regulations contained in the GenTG is particularly to guarantee protection from uncontrolled proliferation of genetically modified organisms.

In addition to this, Testbiotech demands to supplement § 16 GenTG as follows: "(2) A release of genetically modified or synthetically produced organisms must be prohibited if their proliferation cannot be controlled or their retrievability is not ascertained."

In general, such a regulation cannot be rejected from a constitutional point of view. As explained by the Federal Constitutional Court in the decision cited above, the evaluation of the risk of endangerment falls within the prerogative of the legislative authority and does not require a scientific – empirical prove of the real potential of endangerment by genetically modified organisms and their progeny. In a situation which cannot be clarified scientifically, the legal authorities are entitled to evaluate dangers and risks, even more so since the protected legal goods are fixed in the constitution and have a high value, and since the existing risk of unwanted or harmful, maybe even irreversible effects should be controlled in terms of the greatest possible precaution. The Federal Constitutional Court further refers to the explanatory statement No. 4 and 5 for guideline 2001/18/EG.[24]

The supplementation of § 16 GenTG postulated by Testbiotech, however, would in fact result in a prohibition of release, since it will be almost impossible to give conclusive evidence that unwanted proliferation of genetically modified or synthetically produced organisms can be controlled and recovery/ retrievability is guaranteed in all cases. This regulation would not only affect Synthetic Biology. It would in fact set up a prohibition of release for all areas of genetic engineering, i.e. for all genetically modified organisms. That way, a limitation would be put in place which has been postulated from the beginning of the discussion about genetic engineering. Even the long term investigation on environmental compatibility demanded by EGE would hardly be realizable, because as a last consequence, such a study would require the release of organisms. Only the controlled release can bring about "real" and comprehensive results about the environmental compatibility in natural surroundings.

Such a restrictive regulation on release will therefore hardly be accepted politically. The claim for it gives reason to speculate that the critics/opponents of genetic engineering are making use of the supposed novelty of Synthetic Biology in order to discuss and finally enforce their old demands for limitation of genetic engineering (Eberbach 2012, pp. 24 ff.).

Further legal questions are only starting to be discussed in Germany as yet. Particularly, the claims for registration of all DNA-synthesizers in a central database, registration of all researchers in the fields of biosafety and biodefense and the determination of criteria for the publication of data on highly pathogenic viruses or toxic substances, coming along with the limitation of freedom of

---

[23] BVerfG (2011), ibid.

[24] BVerfG (2011), ibid.

publication and freedom of science, which have been formulated at European level, have not yet found entry into the German discussion. Such postulations are hardly compatible with the German understanding of scientific freedom, which is protected by the German constitution. They would definitely interfere with the scope of protection defined for scientific freedom. It should be noted, however, that like all other basic rights which are guaranteed without reservation, scientific freedom may be limited due to conflicting constitutional law.[25] Generally, a legal basis is needed for this.[26] A conflict between basic rights protected by the constitution shall be solved by referring back to further corresponding regulations and principles as well as to the concept of practical concordance by interpretation of the constitution.[27] The protection of life and health of man, the freedom of profession and property of potentially concerned persons (Art. 2 Abs. 2 Satz 1, Art. 12Abs. 1, Art. 14 Abs. 1 GG) and the protection of natural resources (Art. 20 a GG) are important goods of constitutional rank which do justify a limitation of scientific freedom. The – restrictive – determination of criteria for the publication of data on highly pathogenic viruses or toxic substances, however, does not seem proportionate, because before scientific freedom is limited by such a measure, a milder but evenly efficient means, such as the regulation of Synthetic Biology, and Biohacking in particular, could be used and access to pathogenic DNA-sequences and technical instruments (sequencing instruments etc.) could be regulated more restrictively.[28]

Similarly, the recommendation given by EGE to promote/support a responsible way of reporting about Synthetic Biology by journalists, editors (including scientific editors) and other actors will hardly be realizable in Germany with regard to the freedom of opinion and the press.

9.5 Summary

It can be concluded that a jurisprudential discussion of the conflict fields and legal questions of Synthetic Biology does in fact not take place as yet, mainly due to a consistent natural scientific definition of this subject. According to the prevailing opinion, there is currently no need to take action and set up regulations. This is also true for the question of biosecurity, even if many experts warn of dangers arising from Synthetic Biology particularly in this area. The only aspect acknowledged is the necessity of a broad observation and discussion of Synthetic Biology, which is postulated by many in Germany, Europe and United States of America. The discussion of conflict fields of Synthetic Biology is still in an early, orientating state. It is, however, urgently important that the interdisciplinary approach, which is typical for

[25] Com.. BVerfGE 47, 327 (369); 57, 70 (99).

[26] Com. BverfGE 83, 130 (142); 107, 104 (120); 122, 89 (107).

[27] Com. BverfGE 47, 327 (369); 122, 89 (107).

[28] Bt-Ds 17/5165, p. 5.

Synthetic Biology and comprises different technical and natural scientific disciplines, is enlarged to include the humanistic disciplines to aim a holistic discussion.

References

Balmer A, Martin P (2008) Synthetic biology: social and ethical challenges. Institute for Science and Society/University of Nottingham, Nottingham, p 15

Biotechnology Research in the Age of Terrorism (Fink Report, 2004) Committee on Research Standards and Practices to Prevent the Destructive Application of Biotechnology, National Research Council, Washington D.C., www.nap.edu/openbook.php?isbn=0309089778. Accessed 27 Dec 2012

Boldt J et al (2009) Synthetische Biologie – eine ethisch-philosophische Analyse. Bern, Bundesamt für Bauten und Logistik, p 8, mentis verlag Paderborn 2012

Catenhusen W-M (2011) In: Simultanmitschrift der Tagung des Deutschen Ethikrat vom 23.11.2011, p 85 Mannheim, www.ethikrat.org/dateien/pdf/tagung-23-11-2011-simultan-mitschrift.pdf

Charisius H et al (2012) Unser kleines Gen-Labor, http://www.spektrum.de/alias/biotechnologie/unser-kleines-gen-labor/1153300

Cohen J (2012) WHO Group: H5N1 papers should be published in full. Science 335(6071):899–900. doi:10.1126/science.335.6071.899, 24 February 2012

DECHEMA (2011) Biotechnologie Arbeitskreis systembiologische und synthetische Biologie, Thesenpapier zum Stand der Synthetischen Biologie in Deutschland, pp 11

Dederer HG (2010) Neuartige Technologien als Herausforderung an das Recht – dargestellt am Beispiel der Nanotechnologie. In: Spranger T (ed) Aktuelle Herausforderungen der Life Sciences. Münster, Berlin, LIT Verlag, p 71 f

Deutscher Ethikrat Friedrich, B (2010) cited in "Leben aus dem Baukasten" Pressebericht in Deutscher Ethikrat Infobrief 01/2010, 4-5, Deutscher Ethikrat, Berlin

Donner S et al (2009) Statement of the scientific service of the German Parliament. Wiss. Dienst d. BT r. 60/09 v. 15.07.2009, Berlin, https://www.bundestag.de/dokumente/analysen/umwelt4

Eberbach W (2012) Gentechnik und Recht. In: Eberbach et al. Recht der Gentechnik und Biomedizin, 79. Erg.Lieferung, Band 1, Ebersbach and Lange and Ronellenfitsch, C.F. Müller, Heidelberg, München, Landsberg, Frechen, Hamburg, Loose-leaf collection Teil A. I. pp 13 (12)

Engelhardt M (2010) Die Politische Meinung Nr. 493, pp 23 (17)

Fouchier RA (2012) Airborne transmission of influenza A/H5N1 virus between ferrets. Science 336(6088):1534–41

Futures of artificial life, Nature, Editorial, 2004, vol 431, pp 613. Nature publishing group, www.nature.com/nature/journal/v431/n7009/full/431613b.html

Garfinkel MS, Endy D, Epstein GL, Friedmann RM (2007) Synthetic genomics: options for governance. The J Craig Venter Insitute, Rockville, p 38, ff

Dritter Bericht der Bundesregierung über Erfahrungen mit dem Gentechnikgesetz (2008) Bt-Drs 16/8155, printed. F. Müller, Heidelberg, München Landsberg, Frechen, Hamburg, Loose-leaf collection also: http://www. dip21.bundestag.de/dip21/btd/16/0891/1608/1608155.pdf In: Eberbach et al. (2012): Band 2, Teil I, B. I., p 3

Herdegen M (5. Erg. Lfg. 1992) In: Eberbach et al. Recht der Gentechnik und Biomedizin (2012), Band 1, Teil I, Einl. GentG, p 11 m. w. Nw

Herdegen (2012) C.F. Müller, Heidelberg, München, Landsberg, Frechen, Hamburg, Loose-leaf collection

Hohlfeld R (1984) Der Mensch als Objekt von Biotechnologie und biomedizinischer Forschung. In: Gewerkschaftliche Monatshefte 35, Bund-Verlag, Frankfurt/M, pp 594–596

Hohlfeld R (1986) "Die zweite Schöpfung des Menschen". In: Gewerkschaftliche Monatshefte 9, Bund-Verlag, Frankfurt/M, pp 550–560

Hohlfeld R (1988) Biologie als Ingenieurskunst. Zur Dialektik von Naturbeherrschung und synthetischer Biologie. In: Ästhetik und Kommunikation e. V. 69/1988, Berlin, p 61
Hohlfeld R (1990) Synthetische Biologie – Biologie als Ingenieurskunst. In: Grosch K, Peter H Herstellung der Natur? – Stellungnahmen zum Bericht der Enquete-Kommission "Chancen und Risiken der Gentechnologie"), Campus-Verlag, Frankfurt/M and New York
International Gene Synthesis Consortium (IGSC) www.genesynthesisconsortium.org
Kawaoka Y et al (2012) Experimental adaptation of an influenza H5 HA confers respiratory droplet transmission to a reassortant H5 HA/H1N1 virus in ferrets. Nature 485:13–14, (02 May 2012), published online
Kraemer JD, Gostin LO (2012) Georgetown Public Law and Legal Theory Research Paper No. 12-020 papers.ssrn.com/sol3/papers.cfm?abstract_id… – (access28.12.2012); The Limits of Government Regulation of Science, Georgetown Medical Center, Office of Communication (2012), Balancing Scientific Freedom and National Security, Two Georgetown professors explore a process needed to avoid the current dilemma faced by two scientific journals recently asked by the U.S. government to redact parts of scientific publications, January 19, explore. georgetown.edu/news/?ID=61756…Accessed 23 Dec 2012
Kupferschmidt K (2011) Mit den Waffen der Wissenschaft Vogelgrippevirus NSABB Forschungsfreiheit, Der Tagespiegel, 31 Nov 2011. www.markusschmidt.eu/?page_id=20
Lengeler J (1988) Die methodischen Grundlagen der modernen Gentechniken. In: Gentechniken und Individum, C. Heymanns, pp 17
Luttermann C (2011) Synthetische Biologie: Bausteine für Leben und Jurisprudenz, JZ 2011, Mohr Siebeck, Tübingen, pp 195 f
Mooney P (2010) Next Bang! Wie das riskante Spiel mit Megatechnologien unsere Existenz bedroht. Oekom, München, p 118
Müller-Röber B (2011) In: Simultanmitschrift der Tagung des Deutschen Ethikrat vom 23 Nov 2011, pp 70 Mannheim, www.ethikrat.org/dateien/pdf/tagung-23-11-2011-simultanmitschrift.pdf
Nouri A, Chyba CF (2009) Proliferation-resistant biotechnology: an approach to improve biological security. Nat Biotechnol 27:234–236
Presidential Commission for the Study of Bioethical Issues (2010) New Directions. The Ethics of Synthetic Biology and Emerging Technologies. Washington, DC, pp 140 ff
Ronellenfitsch M (2004) In: Eberbach (2012) "Recht der Gentechnik und Biomedizin", Band 1, Teil I, B. I. § 3 GenTG, p 22 f. C.F.Müller, Heidelberg, München, Landsberg, Frechen, Hamburg, Loose-leaf collection
Ronellenfitsch M (2008) In: Eberbach et al Recht der Gentechnik und Biomedizin (2012), Band 1, Teil I, B.I., p 17
Sauter A (2011) Synthetische Biologie: Finale Technisierung des Lebens – oder Etikettenschwindel. In: TAB-Brief Nr. 39, edition-sigma, Berlin, pp 23
Sauter, Tab-Bericht (2011) Pühler, Alfred, Tagesspiegel v. 23 Feb 2011
Schmidt (2011) p. 120; Wagner. In: Simultanmitschrift der Tagung des Deutschen Ethikrat vom 23 Nov 2011, p 81; Engelhard (2010), p 22
Schmidt M (2011) Biosicherheit und Synthetische Biologie. In: Pühler A (ed) Synthetische Biologie – Die Geburt einer Technikwissenschaft, acatech, Springer-Verlag, Berlin Heidelberg, pp 112 f. (111)
Schmidt M, Giersch G (2011) DNA synthesis and security. In: Campbell MJ (ed) DNA microarrays, synthesis and synthetic DNA, Chapter 6, M Schmidt, G Giersch - markusschmidt.eu. Accessed 19 Dec 2012 Nova Publishers, www.markusschmidt.eu/?page_id=20
Schultz N (2009) Perspektivenpapier Synthetische Biologie, http://www.ethikrat.org/der_files/Perspektivenpapier_Synthetische_Biologie_2009-04-23.pdf; DFG Synthetische Biologie
Schummer J (2011) Das Gotteshandwerk. Die künstliche Herstellung von Leben im Labor. Suhrkamp, Berlin, p 111
Schwille P (2011) In: Simultanmitschrift der Tagung des Deutschen Ethikrat vom 23.11.2011 workshop life. The significance of synthetic biology for science and society, pp 5. Mannheim, www.ethikrat.org/dateien/pdf/tagung-23-11-2011-simultanmitschrift.pdf

"Security and Defense Research" Working Group (2010) Guidelines and rules of the Max Planck Society on a responsible approach to freedom of research and research risks, 19. 3. www.mpg.de/232129/researchFreedomRisks.pdf. Accessed 17 Nov 2012

Statement of NSABB (2012) Meeting of the National Science Advisory Board for Biosecurity to Review Revised Manuscripts on Transmissibility of A/H5N1 Influenza Virus, oba.od.nih.gov/.../biosecurity/.../NSABB_Statem...Accessed 27 Dec 2012

Stegemann R (2011) In: Simultanmitschrift der Tagung des Deutschen Ethikrat vom 23.11.2011, pp 14 Mannheim, www.ethikrat.org/dateien/pdf/tagung-23-11-2011-simultanmitschrift.pdf

The European Group on Ethics in Science and New Technologies to the European Commission (cit. EGE) (2009) Ethics of synthetic biology, Opinion no. 25, Brussels, 17 Nov, pp 27 f

Then C (2010) Pressemitteilung von TestBiotech e.V. vom 15 June 2010, http://www.testbiotech.de/pressearchiv?page=4

Then C, Hamberger S (2010) Synthetische Biologie, Teil 1: Synthetische Biologie und künstliches Leben –eine kritische Analyse, Testbiotech, München, testbiotech e. V., pp 21 https://www.testbiotech.org/synthetische-biologie

Wiss. Dienst d. BT r. 60/09 v. 15.07.2009; Parl. Ethikbeirat v. 01.07.2009, 16/13780

World Health Organization, Statement (2011) WHO concerned that new H5N1 influenza research could undermine the 2011 Pandemic Influenza Preparedness Framework. www.who.int/mediacentre/news/statements/2011/pip_framework_20111229/en/index.html

Zelder O (2011) In: Simultanmitschrift der Tagung des Deutschen Ethikrat vom 23 Nov 2011, pp 15

Zwischenbericht der Zentralen Kommission für die Biologische Sicherhei- (cit: ZKBS) (2012) Monitoring der Synthetischen Biologie in Deutschland, p 8, accessed at: http://www.bvl.bund.de/DE/06_Gentechnik/03_Antragsteller/06_Institutionen_fuer_biologische_Sicherheit/01_ZKBS/01_Allg_Stellungnahmen/01_allgemeineThemen/zkbs_allgemeineThemen_node.html

Chapter 10
Exclusions and Exceptions to Patent Eligibility Revisited: Examining the Political Functions of the "Discovery" and "Ordre Public" Clauses in the European Patent Convention and the Arenas of Negotiation

Ingrid Schneider

Abstract This chapter sheds light on the normative and political functions of the exclusions and exceptions within the European Patent Convention. In addition, it deals with arenas in which negotiations about patent eligibility are taking place, and with discursive forms of governing Intellectual Property Rights. This will be exemplified at the case of Synthetic Biology. To that end, the article explains the inherent rationales of two fundamental limits within European patent law: (1) the boundary between discovery and invention (Art. 52 EPC) as exclusion from patentability; (2) the ordre public and public policy clause (Art. 53 (a) EPC) as exception from patent eligibility. Both these exemptions in patent law bear a normative function, however, as is argued, they rely on opposing inherent logics, functions, and regulatory aims. For the former exclusion, the guiding principle and teleology is to "enable access for all". The latter exception implies a converse logics, namely that preferably no one should access and apply the technological knowledge in question. The second part of the article contends that decisions on whether and how to grant patents in a new technical area also depend on institutional frameworks: From a political science perspective, the administrative, legislative and judicial arena will be distinguished. The third part asserts that metaphoric framing of new scientific advancements is another crucial factor for the question of patent eligibility. Semantic framing does relate to the articulation and mobilization of consent or dissent, and thus to public acceptance. Proceeding in such a manner means that research is "upstreaming" ethics by anticipatory impact assessment. Policy analysis in the biosciences is also regarded as an element in the constitutionalisation of Intellectual Property Rights.

I. Schneider (✉)
Centre for Biotechnology, Society and the Environment – Medicine, University of Hamburg, FSP BIOGUM, Lottestr. 55, Hamburg, D- 22529, Germany
e-mail: Ingrid.Schneider@uni-hamburg.de

I. de Miguel Beriain and C.M. Romeo Casabona (eds.), *Synbio and Human Health: A Challenge to the Current IP Framework?*, DOI 10.1007/978-94-017-9196-0_10,

Keywords Law • Ethics • Intellectual property • Constitutionalization • Synthetic biology • Political science • Public policy • Metaphors • Framing • Patents

10.1 Introduction

For a long period of time, exclusions and exceptions to patent eligibility, as inherent in the European Patent Convention, did hardly play any practical role in patent matters[1]. They had almost fallen into oblivion. However, the contentions around the European Union's Biotechnology Patent Directive (98/44/EC) reinvigorated attention to as well as interest in the boundaries of patent eligibility. Parliaments and civil society pointed to the respective clauses of the European Patent Convention and provided a different reading of these articles (Schneider 2010). This chapter will elucidate some of the normative and political functions of the exclusions and exceptions within the European Patent Convention. It will exemplify their potential at the case of Synthetic Biology.

Synthetic biology, a specific blend of science and engineering aims at constructing novel biological entities and redesigning existing ones. Researchers claim that synthetic biology will have great potential for healthcare, from allowing a better understanding of complex diseases to speeding up the development of new drugs and vaccines. Synthetic biology also intends to redesign metabolic pathways, to find new strategies for screening tumours and other diseases and to monitor how individual patients or groups of patients respond to specific therapies (OECD and Royal 2010; CBE 2011; Murray 2011). Practical applications for synthetic biology in the area of human health, however, are still in an early stage of research and development. It is not very clear, which products and methods and in which fields may eventually result from these scientific endeavours in the biosciences. Therefore, speculation, forecast, and uncertainty is pertinent in any inquiry about synthetic biology. The preliminary conclusion taken by the Presidential Commission for the Study of Bioethics in its report delivered in December 2010 to US President Obama may still be valid:

> "With the exception of semi-synthetic artemisinin and potential, near-term improvements in vaccine design, most of the anticipated health benefits of synthetic biology remain in the preliminary research stage. We are unlikely to see commercial applications from much of the biomedically oriented synthetic biology research for many years, although the pace of discovery is unpredictable" (2010: 67). Therefore, waves of hope and hype will probably also pertain to this emerging field, in the same way as they have accompanied many other biomedical projects and innovations over the last decades. (Kahn 2011; van den Belt 2009; Martin and Balmer 2008)

Synthetic biology seems to cross the boundaries between discovery and invention, and between life and non-life (Calvert 2008; Pauwels 2011). The delineations

---

[1] An earlier version of this article was published in *Law and the Human Genome Review*, No. 37, July–December 2012. The present version was revised and updated for publication in this volume.

between systems biology and synthetic biology remain fuzzy as well. It remains to be seen whether systems biology is the theoretical approach aiming at the exploration of fundamental organizing principles of life "top-down", and synthetic biology the "bottom-up" approach trying to understand and modify basic matters of life by artificial construction of some more or less simple organisms, or modules called "biobricks", or whether both approaches will become more intertwined.

By and large, the challenges posed by synthetic biology both mirror and remake the debates and struggles about genetic engineering and biotechnology in the 1980s and about nanotechnology in the Noughties (Torgersen 2009). In that respect, the main problems identified would be adverse affects of synthetically engineered organisms and drugs to human health and the environment, once they are intentionally or inadvertently released (Murray 2011). Such risks have to be tackled by regulatory authorities as the European Medical Agency or FDA, environmental agencies, and REACH, to name but a few. Intellectual property rights will hardly be able to contribute to the governance of these risks. Nonetheless, whether patents will be filed and granted for synthetic biology will have an impact on technological trajectories.

Due to the scientific research being in such an embryonic stage, this article will focus in a more abstract way on exclusions and exceptions to patent eligibility within patent law, by explaining their inherent rationales and constitutional content. In the European Patent Convention, two pivotal rules must be discerned: (1) The boundary between discovery and invention (Art. 52 EPC) and (2) the ordre public and public policy clause (Art. 53 (a) EPC). Both exemptions from patent eligibility bear normative and political functions, but their inherent logics, functions, and regulatory aims contradict each other, as will be elaborated. It will then be explored which implications about patent eligibility for products and methods of synthetic biology these two normative rules may bear. As a next step, from a political science perspective, several arenas of decision-making will be considered, namely the administrative, legislative and judicial arena, to make the case that these arenas do matter. The paper is predicated on the hypothesis that the arena in which synthetic biology patenting will be dealt with will be decisive for whether and how boundaries will be deployed. Another crucial factor having an influence on patentability questions is the metaphoric framing of synthetic biology which will be considered in the third step of the present analysis. It is assumed that framing relates to the articulation and mobilisation of consent or dissent, and thus public acceptance of synthetic biology.

Proceeding in that manner may be regarded as an attempt at "upstreaming" ethics and policy analysis in the biosciences. Such a temporal shift towards an early stage of research is first a result of intellectual property protection having moved upstream. Secondly, scientific knowledge and regulatory experiences point to the fact that research and patent filing practices themselves are setting preferences and prejudging rules for later application. They may thus act as precedence which can hardly be overruled at a later point in time. Therefore, research must be accompanied and critically interrogated by prospective technology assessment. In addition, it is intended to apply some lessons from scholarly research on the public understanding of science, framing and communication theories. The article is based on the assumption that institutional designs as well as framings of synthetic biology will have an impact upon whether and how products and methods in synthetic biology will become patentable or not. It also contends that the application of these limiting rules must be understood as a form of politicizing and constitutionalizing intellectual property rights.

10.2 Patent Eligibility and Exemptions from Patentability: Rules, Norms and Principles

All patent laws contain boundaries between what is and what is not eligible for patenting. The corresponding rules are often formulated as general terms and clauses. Interpretation of these clauses is primarily performed by patent offices in their granting practices, and by courts in liability cases (case law). These limiting rules and their evolution as performed by case law must be regarded as regulatory instruments that determine the governance of patent law and have an influence upon technological developments.

In European patent law, as enshrined in the European Patent Convention (EPC), inclusions in and exclusions from patent eligibility have different venues, take different forms, and rely on diverging rationales. In general, two key rules must be discerned:

1. The boundary between discovery and invention;
2. The ordre public and public policy clause.

Concerning the rationales underpinning these rules, we can distinguish between normative principles and consequentialist argumentations. As will be argued in this paper, exemptions from patentability are based on two fundamental, but different rationales. Both exclusions from patent eligibility mentioned above bear a normative function as they are legal reminders about meaningful restrictions to patentability which serve the public interest and the common good. Despite of the fact that both these boundaries "outwards" imply non-eligibility for a patent, they do rely on opposing inherent logics, functions, and regulatory aims. While in the first type of logics, "enabling *access for all*" is the guiding principle, in the second, converse logics, *no one should have access* to the technological knowledge in question. Without directly inquiring the consequences of these different regulatory aims yet, at this point, it may be sufficient to note that tensions may arise from these opposing policy goals.

Arguments can be made both at the normative level of deontological principles as well as be derived from macro-economic and socio-political considerations. In this article, it is assumed that boundaries govern the steering capacity *within* patent law and thus contribute to regulative (self-)control. In a first step, the reasoning and meaning of those two regulatory boundaries will be reconstructed which according to the author's view constitute policy instruments for patent governance. To begin with, the boundary between discovery and invention will be explored.

10.2.1 Exclusion: The Boundary Between Discovery and Invention

The most important rule in substantive European patent law for patent eligibility and its limits is contained in Article 52 EPC, which reads:

Art. 52 Patentable inventions

(1) *European patents shall be granted for any inventions, in all fields of technology, provided that they are new, involve an inventive step and are susceptible of industrial application.*
(2) *The following in particular shall not be regarded as inventions within the meaning of paragraph 1:*

(a) *discoveries, scientific theories and mathematical methods;*
(b) *aesthetic creations;*
(c) *schemes, rules and methods for performing mental acts, playing games or doing business, and programs for computers;*
(d) *presentations of information.*

(3) *Paragraph 2 shall exclude the patentability of the subject-matter or activities referred to therein only to the extent to which a European patent application or European patent relates to such subject-matter or activities as such.*

While the first paragraph determines the rules and criteria for patentability, the second paragraph presents the *exclusions* of certain subject matters and activities from patentability, and the third makes the famous "as such" restriction in the scope of applying these rules.

What are the basic assumptions in drawing this line of exclusion?

The major reason for excluding discoveries, scientific theories and mathematical methods from patentability is the assumption, that there is a *core* of abstract scientific knowledge about the world which must be available to each and everyone, and therefore remain in the public domain. This refers mainly to fundamental theories, but also to basic causality mechanisms. Hence, only such a publicly accessible knowledge commons can give rise to further scientific developments. First and foremost, the semantic distinction between discoveries and inventions therefore bears a normative function: It is a reminder that there are meaningful restrictions to patentability, which are in the public interest and serve the common good.

The non-patent-eligibility for discoveries and scientific theories primarily serves the purpose to keep basic research free from patentability. Even though a discovery often requires a much greater mental effort than an invention and it is also often much more far-reaching with respect to its impact, it should not be patentable to enable others to built upon it. Following this course of reasoning, a separate, related rationale for exclusion from patentability points to the cumulative and sequential character of knowledge. This norm is captured in Newton's renowned aphorism that if he was "able to see farther it was because he was standing on the shoulders of giants". Any invention also incorporates prior insights and thus owes to the work and findings of more or less tall predecessors (Merton 1985; Scotchmer 1991).

In this respect, from the semantic distinction in itself no clear-cut knife to separate discovery from invention can be derived. However, considerations on the impact can provide some contours: The protection of discoveries would necessarily be very broad and unspecific, since those are not directed to a clear-cut application or a defined single product. Therefore, by applying the principle of proportionality, to render a small inventive performance would not be proportional to potential high rewards, and thus an overly strong gain achieved by the patent holder could be the consequence (Hashimoto and Aida 2008). Another reasoning relates to the fact that the temporary monopoly provided by the patent would create a bottleneck. It would oblige others to ask the patent holder for a license and thus raise transaction costs (Nelson 1959, 2004). Patenting of basic research could thus create barriers for further research and development and finally rather inhibit than promote technological progress (Godt 2007: 140). At least, these considerations can be conceived as the unwritten credo which is inscribed in the EPC's article 52. Within the patent community, these exclusions are often summed up as being inventions which are "non-technical" in character.

To summarize, the exclusion of discoveries and scientific theories from patentability aims at "*enabling access for all*" to basic and important knowledge, laws of nature, and scientific as well as mathematical theories, in order to achieve the greatest scientific and societal gains.

The major reason for excluding discoveries from patentability is the assumption, that there is a core of more or less abstract scientific knowledge which must stay immediately in the public domain. As all inventors are "standing on the shoulders of giants", patenting of research in cumulative and sequential inventions could stifle technical progress.

At this point, I won't dwell and dig neither into the utilitarian foundations nor the practical difficulties or even aporia in taking and making such a clear-cut distinction between invention and discovery, and maybe as well between theory and application. Suffice is to say, that in the practical evolution of patent law, the distinction between discovery and invention has been largely fallen into oblivion and became almost irrelevant (Nack 2002).

10.2.2 Exception: The Ordre Public and Public Policy Clause

In contrast to the patent laws of countries such as the United States, the EPC includes a provision that relates specifically to the morality of the claimed invention. The so-called ordre public clause is codified in Article 53(a) of the EPC. It states:

Article 53

Exceptions to patentability

European patents shall not be granted in respect of:

(a) *inventions the publication or exploitation of which would be contrary to "ordre public" or morality, provided that the exploitation shall not be deemed to be so contrary merely because it is prohibited by law or regulation in some or all of the Contracting States.*

In the EPO's examination guidelines, the classic example given for an invention which would not be patentable under this provision is a letter bomb or a landmine.

Thus, it is about an invention which, although technical in character, can only be used in a manner which the majority of the public conceives as abhorrent or from which the public needs protection.[2] To reject patentability, an invention must not be capable of being used in a socially fruitful manner, thus a distinction between "good use and abuse" is conceived as impossible. The invention thus must, according to this concept, be used in a way which may violate human dignity and/or basic, constitutional norms and values, and thus undermine the foundations of the moral and institutional order.

The term "ordre public" expresses concerns about subject matters that threaten the social structures which tie a society together. "Morality" refers to the degree of conformity to moral principles. The concept of morality is tied to the values prevailing in a society. Such values are not the same in different cultures and countries, and may change over time. Therefore, the ordre public and morality clause bears a fluid notion. It is tied to concepts of public security and public safety, to the physical integrity of individual human subjects, but to the protection of the environment as well. Hence, it is interrelated with norms of the political system and collective codes of ethics. Some important decisions relating to patentability may depend upon the judgement about morality. According to this concept, it would be inadmissible that patent offices grant patents to any kind of invention, without giving any consideration of morality.[3]

In a similar manner, there is a public policy exception in the TRIPS agreement which states:

> *Article 27.2 Patentable Subject Matter*
>
> *Members may exclude from patentability inventions, the prevention within their territory of the commercial exploitation of which is necessary to protect ordre public or morality, including to protect human, animal or plant life or health or to avoid serious prejudice to the environment, provided that such exclusion is not made merely because the exploitation is prohibited by their law.*

The application of these exceptions, which need to be provided for under national law in order to be effective, means that a state may, in certain cases, refuse to grant a patent when it deems it necessary to protect higher public interests. However, the scope and application of these ordre public and public policy clauses has been subject of long and strong contestations. For decades, article 53(a) EPC had hardly ever been used, and the implementation of article 27(2) TRIPS, in particular in relation to article 27(1) TRIPS, is more than unclear (Porter 2009a). Patent lawyers, scholars, examiners, and judges have long warned against broader application of the ordre public clause. They argue that patent offices should and could not be moral arbiters, as they neither have competences nor the mandate to make judgements on morality. Another argument refers to the fact that moral rules often change quickly over time. Therefore, so the argument goes, patenting of an invention should not

---

[2] See EPO's Examination Guidelines, Part C, IV at http://legis.obi.gr/espacedvd/legal_texts/gui_lines/e/c_iv_3_1.htmlegis.obi.gr/espacedvd/legal.../c_iv_3_1.htm

[3] See UNCTAD, November 29, 2004 at http://www.iprsonline.org/unctadictsd/docs/RB2.5_Patents_2.5.3_update.pdf (last accessed 12 June 2012).

pre-empt political judgements and regulations. The main argument is that patent law was deemed to be "value-neutral"; regulation of new technologies should thus be left to other domains of law, such as criminal law, environmental law, special medical acts or self-regulation by professional disciplines such as medical associations. The patent community has considered the ordre public clause as a "narrow gateway" and has tried to keep this gate as much closed as possible (Thambisetty 2002; Schneider 2010: 236).

Until the incorporation of the provisions of the Biotech Patent Directive (98/44/EC) into the EPC, there was no specific guidance in the EPC on what inventions fell within Article 53(a) EPC. However, the biopatent directive implemented in its article 6 (2) a non-exhaustive list of exceptions. Therefore, the new Rule 28 of the EPC's implementation regulations states:

Rule 28 EPC:

Under Article 53(a), European patents shall not be granted in respect of biotechnological inventions which, in particular, concern the following:

(a) *processes for cloning human beings*;
(b) *processes for modifying the germ line genetic identity of human beings*;
(c) *uses of human embryos for industrial or commercial purposes*;
(d) *processes for modifying the genetic identity of animals which are likely to cause them suffering without any substantial medical benefit to man or animal, and also animals resulting from such processes.*

Thus inventions which concern the above are deemed to be immoral and hence unpatentable under the EPC.

Also of relevance is Rule 29 EPC, which as well is derived from article 5 of the EU's biopatent directive, which states:

Rule 29 EPC:

(1) *The human body, at the various stages of its formation and development, and the simple discovery of one of its elements, including the sequence or partial sequence of a gene, cannot constitute patentable inventions.*
(2) *An element isolated from the human body or otherwise produced by means of a technical process, including the sequence or partial sequence of a gene, may constitute a patentable invention, even if the structure of that element is identical to that of a natural element.*
(3) *The industrial application of a sequence or a partial sequence of a gene must be disclosed in the patent application.*

However, the relationship between paragraph 1 and 2 of Rule 29 EPC remains far from clear and has left ample space for diverging interpretations. So far, the first paragraph has hardly ever been used as a practical guidance for purposes of examination and patent grant. In contrast, the "purification and isolation" doctrine enshrined in paragraph 2 of Rule 29 EPC has been applied for genes, biomarkers and many other natural substances to treat them as patentable subject matter, just like any other chemical compound, provided that the biological material is isolated from its natural environment or technicall produced even if present in nature, and its industrial application is described in the patent application (Rutz 2009: S15).

In the following, I will try to give a reading of the ordre public clause which tries to uncover its underlying concept and principles. The ordre public and public policy objections (Art. 53 (a) EPC) are general ethical clauses, which must, according to the legal scholar Jan Kersten, be understood as "a lock which mediates constitutional standards for integrating patent law into the order of norms and values" (Kersten 2004: 129, translation I.S.). In this context, Kersten claims the need for a "horizontal and vertical constitutionalization of patent law" (2004: 125–146). The relationship between constitutional law and ordinary law in a hierarchically graded order thus unfolds dialectically: On the one hand, the constitutional law impacts upon the interpretation of the simple law, including patent law. On the other hand, the "abstract" constitutional norms require concrete embodiment in practical contexts (Kersten 2004: 129–130).

Furthermore, the concept of "public order and morality" can also be understood as a "public policy clause" which may become designed and refined by the legislator as a means in order to provide for innovation policies which are responsible and promote public welfare (Lausmann-Murr 2000: 181). According to this understanding, exemptions from patentability can also be introduced with respect to consequentialist considerations. When the (probable) impact of patents is concerned, implications for public health, nutrition, biodiversity, and other issues of general interest are taken into the equation. In this line of thought, possible detrimental effects of patents with regards to promoting monopolies, oligopolies, or anti-competitive cartels, or more general processes of economic concentration, for instance in the food, plant, or pharmaceutical industry, are focused. So far, such concerns, despite from becoming more articulated in the last two decades, have not yet entered the field of legal doctrines and the realm of interpretation of the public policy clauses in intellectual property rights. However, it should be reminded that until the end of the second world war, and in a number of countries even for several decades after 1945, many jurisdictions had exclusions for patents on food and also on drugs (or, to be precise, on chemical products in general, as opposed to patents on methods) (Dutfield 2009).

The EPC also contains provisions exempting "plant or animal varieties" from patent protection (article 53(b) EPC) and "methods for treatment of the human or animal body by surgery or therapy and diagnostic methods practised on the human or animal body" (article 53(c) EPC). However, in practice, these provisions have largely been curtailed by applying other related clauses that allow for the patentability of "products, in particular substances or compositions, for use in any of these methods" (article 53 (c) EPC). Therefore, it is not the law itself which has rendered limitations to patentability almost irrelevant but the interpretation and use of the law. This points to the administration of patent law by a specialized community of patent attorneys patent offices, and specialized patent courts.[4]

Critical voices insist upon the necessity to maintain boundaries within patent law in order to achieve coherence of the legal system and to provide for cross-compliance between legal norms in different areas (Eifert and Hoffmann-Riem 2008). However, whether and to what extent patent law itself could and should be

[4] For these correlations to be captured, an institutional analysis would be necessary, which cannot be provided in the context of this paper (see Thambisetty 2006; Schneider 2009a; Drahos 2010). I will, however, give some hints to this question below, in the next section.

considered a means of socio-political regulation of technological trajectories is a subject which is utmost contested.

For the purposes of this paper, another issue must be highlighted: The pivotal rationale for exclusion under the ordre public and public policy clause lies in the idea of an ex-ante control of the social desirability of an invention. The ban on patent eligibility serves to express the social disapproval of an invention. The patent ban in this case strives for restricting the dissemination and application of an invention. It is assumed that non-patentability serves as a dis-incentive for research and development. The purpose of the prohibition on patent grant therefore aims at making the non-patentable invention inaccessible for anyone: Nobody should access the knowledge and use it. Hence, in this case, technical knowledge is conceived as maleficent, dangerous, even "abhorrent". Thus, the effect assigned to the ordre public exemption is the exact opposite to the exclusion for discoveries which strives at "access for all" to be secured by non-patentability. Therefore, the ordre public exemption rather wants to suppress certain knowledge, whereas the exception for discoveries wants to spread broad dissemination of the technical knowledge in question.

But the ban on patent eligibility not only disapproves of a certain technique. Moreover, it can be seen as an instrument which aims at dis-incentivizing even the generation of such technological knowledge by removing a legal incentive (Grimm 2002).

That's why these two teleologies for exclusions from patentability rely on opposite inherent logics. They also point to the fact that both patent protection and a ban on patent eligibility can unleash quite contradictory effects: They can foster innovation as well as act as a disincentive for the further diffusion of technologies. Therefore, it is crucial to inquire patents as embedded in other social norms and rules, and within the socio-economic conditions for research and development, such as the funding of relevant research activities as well as the social acceptance of new technologies.

For the time being, this may draw attention to the limits of steering and controlling innovation through patent law and patent grant. However, it may also serve to raise awareness about the fact, that regulative principles have always been part and parcel of and within patent law itself, a fact which had almost been forgotten in the evolution of patent law after the Second World War (Robbins 2004). But the relentless expansion of Intellectual Property Rights from the 1980s on has also been countered more recently in political conflicts, and claims to recall boundaries within patent law as necessary governance mechanisms for the sake of public welfare have become more vocal (Schneider 2010; Haunss and Shadlen 2009; 'T hoen 2009; EPO 2007).

Without being able to go into the details, it must be stressed that patent law also includes other clauses which can be used as tools for curtailing and fine-tuning patent protection. The most important may be the inventive step clause which is determined by the (fictitious) person having ordinary skills in the art (EPC article 56; "non-obviousness" and PHOSITA in US patent law). This clause aims at preventing patents on trivial inventions. It may also serve as a way of tailoring patent law more specific to certain technologies (Gold and Durell 2005; Burk and Lemley 2003). Other scissors are the sufficiency of disclosure doctrine (EPC art. 83) and the provision that patent claims shall be clear, concise and be supported by the description (EPC art. 84). Instead of working as either-or principles, the latter provisions can serve to regulate the scope of protection conferred. They are thus more apt to fine-tune patent claims in the examination process. At present, it seems more likely that patent examination, grant, the Boards of Appeal of the EPO, and courts will refer to these aforementioned clauses of the EPC to tailor patent protection in synthetic biology and to deal with complexity and dependency issues of patent thickets and interoperability between synthetic parts of interconnected biological agents (Rutz 2009).

In the meantime, several thousand patent applications for synthetic biology have been filed. The database "Patent Lens" displays 6,252 results for a full-text search on the term "synthetic biology" in patent applications worldwide, including the same or similar applications in several jurisdictions and members of the same patent family.[5] Of these applications, several hundred patents may have got granted, probably often with substantial modification and narrowing down of what had been claimed for in the patent application and what had finally been granted by the patent offices. These numbers can only be regarded as a fairly rough estimation. So far, no detailed and in-depth analyses of patents on synthetic biology are available. To my knowledge, there is also no case law on synthetic biology patents as yet, and questions as to whether the creation of "synthetic life" could be considered immoral has not yet been addressed by any legislative authority or court to date.

The institutional machinery for handling the abovementioned restrictive clauses of the EPC as far as patent eligibility of subject matter as such is concerned, is discussed in the next section.

10.3 Who Decides Whether Exemptions from Patentability Apply?

Without being able to provide a full picture, this section addresses the question, *who* decides whether applications of synthetic biology in human health are treated and will be treated as patentable or unpatentable.

As has been stated previously, legislation can only provide broad general clauses. Given "the excessively long gestation period for any legal changes", some legal scholars have argued that "legislative action will hardly ever catch up with technological development" (Ullrich 2002: 27). Thus, patent offices must deal with incoming patent applications and process them. Therefore, judgements about the patentability of new technological developments and new subject matter are inherent and unavoidable for patent offices. Up to a certain point, the EPO and other

[5] Search performed at http://www.patentlens.net on 12 June 2012. Thanks to Cambia for having set up this excellent publicly accessible patent search platform.

patent offices must certainly have discretion to decide, and thus in fact act as a 'law maker', in the sense that interpretations of patentability must, at least to a certain extent, be conceived as policy-making-processes (Schneider 2007).

On the other hand, there are good reasons for stating that decisions about patent eligibility are political acts which should be reserved to the legislator. Hence, the dilemma can be framed as follows: Specific legislation, detailing exemptions to patent eligibility or at least its outer limits, would provide greater guidance to the EPO and the courts in making determinations about patent eligibility. Such legislation, however, might quickly be rendered obsolete by unanticipated advances in technology. Therefore, general clauses allowing for more interpretative flexibility, are unavoidable. More general legislation may retain relevance with shifts and changes in society's moral judgements and advances in technology. It will, however, grant the examination departments, the Boards of Appeal, and the Courts considerable leeway in creating or eliminating limits driven by moral or socio-economic considerations (Bagley 2003: 469). As a result, patent offices and judges act as law-makers in ultimately determining the interpretation of the content of legal clauses in treaty law.

At this point, it will be impossible to predict how synthetic biology will in the future be handled by the patent offices (Rutz 2007; Rai and Boyle 2007). However, we can point towards the fact, that it does matter in which arenas these questions are dealt with, and which actors will have an influence on the outcome (Eimer 2011). Therefore, it is suggested that institutional structures do matter. To this end, some lessons can be drawn from the past.

10.3.1 The Administrative Arena

First, I will address the administrative arena which seems to be the crucial arena where decisions are taken. The most important actors within this arena are the patent applicants, patent attorneys, patent examiners, and patent judges.

Many authors have pointed to the "epistemic community" of the patent system to explain its evolution in the last decades and the direction it has taken (Schneider 2010: 188–218; Yu 2011). According to Peter Drahos, it "is the patent community working with a set of assumptions, understandings, conventions and values that settles issues and problems of interpretation within the patent system. By doing so, the patent community probably exercises more influence on the direction and content of patent policy than legislatures, which in any case rely on committees of specialists to advise them on matters of patent policy" (Drahos 1999: 442).

This patent community, and particularly the specialised patent attorneys, are acting on behalf of their clients, the patent applicants. But their members are also trained in a special rationality which can be phrased as "pro-patent bias" (Boyle 2003). Both exert substantial impact on the interpretation of the law and the course of decisions taken.

Substantive patent law for new technological fields such as synthetic biology evolves in the interplay between the EPO's granting departments and its Boards of

Appeal which are a quasi-judiciary, and specialized patent courts. Patent examination, grant, and court decisions are thus tacit policy-making practices masked as mere administrative execution of law.

Concerning the structuration of the decisions, it must be borne in mind that the EPO is self-funded by the fees of the patentees. Furthermore, interests apart from the applicants' are not systematically represented within its system. Therefore, the EPO is at risk to conceive of itself as a service center rather than an organization working in the public interest, and to treat the applicants as customers to be served. It is thus susceptible to be captured by its clients (Hagel 2004). Over time, this has arguably resulted in an expansion of patent eligibility, in patents granted with a broad scope, and in boundaries within patent law being neglected. The EPO's "technocratic self-determination" (Ullrich 2004) has also raised questions about division of power, transparency, accountability, and democratic control (Schneider 2009a).

In the past, patent offices, pushed by patent attorneys representing the applicants, have tended to grant patents on biotechnological inventions. They were actively supported by the patent courts who often consciously worked towards overcoming barriers in the law. Case law was included into the examination guidelines, and thus the circle was closed. As a result, a broad tendency can be recognized to keep exemptions and restrictions on patent eligibility very low. The implicit ruling has been "in dubio pro patente" (in case of doubt: grant). At least from the 1980s on, or even for many more decades in the twentieth century (Kevles et al. 2009; Dutfield 2009), a worldwide erosion of restrictive boundaries in the patent offices' practices of patent granting can be observed. The horizontal self-governance of the patent community has led to the expansion of patent eligibility and has kept the application of restrictions, exceptions and flexibilities down. The patent community often perceived of the ordre public clause as a trojan horse for "extra-legal" considerations entering patent law which it has therefore combated and sought to contain strictly.

However, at least in Europe, the biotech patent directive marked a certain shift in this broad historic tendency. It transferred part of the decision-making process to the legislative arena. The rules within this arena will be analyzed in the next section.

10.3.2 The Legislative Arena

The legislative arena is a far more complex arena, in particular in the European Union. For law-making, the Commission, the Council, and the European Parliament have to interact.

If the co-decision procedure applies, the Parliament can become a major player. The legislative arena in Europe has proven to be more responsive to different stakeholders and lobby groups, both from industry sectors aiming at strengthening patents, and others, in particular SMEs and civil society organisations, aiming at reviving boundaries to patentability (Schneider 2009b; Eimer 2008).

In the past, the biotech and the software directive, both of them introduced by the European Commission striving for strengthening of patent protection, have resulted in strong contestations in the Council, where national governments are represented, as well as in the European Parliament. Both directives failed in their first round of law making and were rejected by the Parliament (biotech in 1995, software in 2005), but the biopatent directive (98/44/EC) finally was passed in 1998.

The rejection of the software directive can be regarded as a Phyrrus like victory, as it handed action over again to the patent community. In the biotech directive, however, the European Parliament resonated with concerns about ethical limits to patent eligibility, in particular with respect to the status of the human body and to gene patents. It also critically addressed the erosion of the public domain of open science. And it focussed on public health concerns such as access to and high costs for patented products (diagnostic tests, drugs), which put pressure on national health budgets. Finally, also the efficiency of patents which may stifle innovation if granted excessively due to the rise in transaction costs, patent thickets, and royalty stacking was questioned (Porter 2009b; Schneider 2010).

As a result, some precautions were taken, and exemptions from patentability, with specific regard to the ordre public clause, were codified in an non-exhaustive list of provisions, as already stated above (see Chap. 2.2., Rules 26–29 EPC).

The list of exemptions highlights the inalienability of human life. The provisions aim at preventing human embryos from being instrumentalized ("used") for industrial and commercial purposes. They thus try to separate the realm of the market from the sphere in which money cannot buy certain "things" (Walzer 1983). These provisions explicitly recognize and reaffirm the universal principle of non-commodification of the human body and try to inscribe it into patent law. By banning cloning and germ-line interventions from patent eligibility, they send the message that human life should not be manipulated, and that interventions in the genome should not be passed across to the next generation(s).

In their implementation of the biopatent directive, some national states even went further and banned natural genes as such (France, Switzerland) and "unmodified human embryonic stem cells" (Switzerland, Italy), as well as certain types of genetic screenings which may result in social discrimination (Italy) from patentability. Moreover, several states (Italy, France, Switzerland, Belgium) explicitly codified human dignity and human rights as moral norms into patent law. The Netherlands and Italy also made explicit reference to article 27(2) TRIPS in prohibiting methods which threaten life or health of humans, animals, plants or the environment from patent protection (Schneider 2010: 580–589).

In this respect, the ordre public exemption was broadened, and the "narrow gateway" within patent law became more open for morality considerations. Remarkably, several of these legal provisions were introduced before respective scientific success was ever achieved at the lab benches, and certainly not at the bedsides. So far, neither cloning of a human embryo nor germline intervention in humans have successfully been tried and become scientifically proven. Even more, some of these provisions had not been banned by criminal law, or at least not in all the member states of the Union (Casabona 2011). Therefore, the preventive and pre-emptive end of these provisions must be strongly emphasized.

To conclude, the biotech patent directive has marked a substantial shift towards more responsivity concerning the boundaries of patent law. Patent law was considered and used as a means to govern biomedical innovation – and even more so, to do this before the respective technologies had been fully developed. Thus, these provisions paradoxically aim at steering biomedical innovation prior to their occurrence. And they do so by using patent law as a steering tool. They could and should thus be understood as soft means of the governance of technology (Schneider 2008).

Much ink has been spilled ever since on whether this was a right move or a misconception of patent law. Legal scholars also have written lengthy articles on how narrow or broad these exemptions from patent eligibility should be interpreted and often tried to narrow down these provisions – contrary to the letter and the spirit of the exemptions, and to the intentions of the European Parliament (Plomer and Torremans 2009).

In the context of this article, suffice is to state that the "harmful knowledge" doctrine enshrined in the EPC's ordre public clause, as was outlined in the anticipating chapter above, has been implemented by the European legislator. In contrast, the discovery vs. invention boundary has found less articulation and responsivity in the biopatent directive. However, at least it was re-introduced in article 5 (1) of the directive 98/44/EC (see above Rule 29 (1) EPC). Some legal provisions and developments, however, have to bide their time until they are enforced, and as yet, at least to my knowledge, the latter paragraph lacks any active implementation by the patent offices.

Even though the results of the European biopatent directive may be regarded as ambiguous, and interpretation of these provisions has remained contested, it must be stressed that the directive did mark and make a difference. The legislative procedures gave impetus for a better balance of the patent system. They allowed for innovation to be qualified in terms of efficiency, sustainability and social desirability. Alternative models for effective and useful innovation (such as open source) were acknowledged – even if stronger legal implementation of such new social and juridical models is still some way off.[6]

[6] The perspective which was characterized above as "public policy concerns" of considering the implications of patent eligibility for broader social issues has not found strong repercussion in the directive's wording, even though it was strongly articulated in the legislative process. The exemption of patentability for plant and animal varieties was even weakened by the biotech directive (Baumgartner 2006). More recently, this exemption has become subject to renewed resolutions and claims in some European national states, as well as in the European Parliament. See the EP's Resolution adopted on 10 May 2012 "on the patenting of essential biological processes", available at: http://www.europarl.europa.eu/sides/getDoc.do?pubRef=-//EP//TEXT+TA+P7-TA-2012-0202+0+DOC+XML+V0//EN&language=EN (last accessed on 12 June 2012).

10.3.3 The Judicial Arena: Generalist Courts

Specialist patent courts in the respective nation states in Europe, the Boards of Appeal of the EPO, and the U.S. Court of Appeals for the Federal Circuit (CAFC) were blamed of having unduely expanded patentable subject matter in the past (Jaffe and Lerner 2005; Bessen and Meurer 2008). This paper cannot discuss the strengths and limitations of specialist patent courts. However, it is noteworthy that in the last decade in the US – contrary to the 1980s and in particular to the famous Chakrabarty case -, the Supreme Court seems to have been actively committed in becoming a counter-player to the CAFC in limiting the scope of patents and in introducing some mitigating effects.

Europe, due to institutional path dependencies and political constraints, so far does not have a specialist patent court at the EU level.[7] Whether and how the European Court of Justice could be capable and would and should ever take over a role similar to the US Supreme Court, remains to be debated.

In the context of this paper, it can only be pointed to the fact that specialist courts are inclined to have a "formal and tunnel vision" (Thambisetty 2006: 10) of the patent matters in question, as several commentators have noted. In contrast to their technically competent but often very technocratic gaze, generalist appellate courts with jurisdiction over patent matters may have a broader perspective on the issues at stake, and thus will possibly surprise the public with innovative interpretations of statutory law.

At least, the recent CJEU judgment of the Bruestle vs Greenpeace case (C-34/10, from 18.10.2011) seems to be an example for a different and unexpected sentence. In this ruling about the patentability of human embryonic stem cells, the Court has implemented a very broad and comprehensive definition of the legal term "human embryo" and a rather broad interpretation of the term "use", including purposes of scientific research and prior events on which an invention is based. Thus, it excluded any invention, which requires either the prior destruction of human embryos or their use as base material, from patentability (CJEU 2011; Schneider 2011).

The broad interpretation of the ordre public clause as given by the CJEU has been strongly criticized by the scientific and patent community, but also been welcomed by a number of politicians and ethicists. It is too early to speculate whether this case has set a precedent for future cases. It may suffice to say that the CJEU referred to the European Union as being not only an economic community but as well a "community of values". In its decision-making the CJEU followed the opinion of Advocate General Yves Bot who stated: "… the Union is not only a market to be regulated, but also has values to be expressed. Before it was even enshrined as

[7] On current debates about creating a European Patent Court in association with the controversial European Patent with Unitary Effect see (Ullrich 2012; Lamping 2011; Bakardjieva-Engelbrekt 2011), and the proceedings of the CEIPI Conference "What Patent Law for the European Union?", April 26–27, 2012 at the European Parliament of Strasbourg, presentations available at: http://130.79.201.195/index.php?id=12181&L=2 (last accessed on 12 June 2012).

a fundamental value in Article 2 of the EU Treaty, the principle of human dignity had been recognised by the Court as a general legal principle" (Bot 2011: No. 46).

The European Charta of Fundamental Rights which was adopted in the Lisbon treaty of the European Union, as well as the Oviedo Declaration of the Council of Europe can both be regarded as codifications of general norms and values, and may thus be seen as the foundations of a genuine European ordre public. Both institutional frameworks are expressions of broader constitutionalization processes at work. However, there is also moral pluralism within societies, and a broad range of differences in interpreting norms and values between the European nation states. Therefore, it remains contested whether European patent law should incorporate a strong and unified morality clause or whether such questions should be left to the principle of subsidiarity and to national discretion. Furthermore, some scholars advocate constitutionalizing Intellectual Property Law by incorporating human rights standards (Geiger 2006). However, there are competing conceptions as to whether intellectual property rights could and should be depicted as human rights or whether human rights are deemed restrictions to intellectual property rights (Grosheide 2010; Helfer 2003; Helfer and Austin 2011). Thus, human rights can both be regarded as norms which include intellectual property rights or as well as counter-norms to intellectual property claims, but elaborating on this debate would transcend the scope of this article.

At least, the CJEU judgment on the Bruestle case can be seen as a strong example of the constitutionalization of patent law which has finally ended the "extra-rationality" long time claimed for and by the patent community (Kersten 2004: 126). It has finally made patent law more receptive for ethical considerations. The Bruestle case made clear that the ordre public clause must not necessarily be a narrow gateway, and that a re-articulation of boundaries within patent law is possible. This move was endorsed by the European Parliament.[8]

However, the broad and coherent interpretation of the ordre public clause by the CJEU has become relativised and at least partly revised by a decision of the German Federal Court of Justice (Bundesgerichtshof BGH) in the German patent case Bruestle vs. Greenpeace in November 2012. The European Patent Office, in its examination and granting practices, also applies a very narrow reading of the CJEU decision, in contrast to the UK IP Office (Schlich 2012).

What needs to be emphasized in this paper is the institutional determination of patent decisions. As it seems, it does matter whether ethically difficult cases are dealt with by a specialist or a generalist court. Here again, the institutional design and machinery, not the law in itself, will have an impact on the outcome of patent decisions. Therefore, awareness and composition of generalist appellate courts with

---

[8] The Parliament "welcomes the recent decision of the European Patent Office in the WARF case and of the European Court of Justice in the Bruestle case, as they appropriately interpret Directive 98/44/EC and give important indications on the so-called whole content approach; calls on the European Commission to draw the appropriate consequences from these decisions also in other relevant policy areas in order to bring EU policy in line with these decisions" (N6 in the European Parliament's Resolution adopted on 10 May 2012 "on the patenting of essential biological processes").

jurisdiction over patent matters will likely be of increasing importance in the future, in Europe as well as internationally.

10.4 The Institutional Design for Patent Eligibility of Synthetic Biology Subjects Does Matter

As a preliminary conclusion, we can state that the respective institutional venues and arenas will have an impact on how synthetic biology will be treated in patent law.

10.4.1 Synthetic Biology in the Administrative Arena

If synthetic biology will be dealt with exclusively within the administrative arena, it will probably follow the same course as previous biotech patents. This may probably rather mean broad patentability, hardly any exemptions, and a narrow interpretation of the ordre public clause.

Concerning the administrative arena, it should be mentioned nonetheless, that the patent community is not as hermetic any more as it used to be in the past. Some economists and ethicists have gained access, and a younger generation of academic legal scholars has a more critical perspective on intellectual property matters, but it remains to be seen whether they will ever be able to enter the inner circle of decision-making. So far, an institutionalised mechanism within the EPO to regularly consult ethicists and members of other scientific disciplines on critical and sensitive cases does not exist, nor has an ethics and patent assessment advisory board been implemented, as proposed and requested several times by the European Parliament (Schneider 2009a).

Admittedly, opposition procedures, as initiated by citizens, professional organisations of scientists, civil society associations or even governments (see the famous "Edinburgh case") may have an influence on the decisions of the EPO's Boards of Appeal, and finally also on its examination guidelines. However, as the example of several opposition procedures in the notorious Myriad BRCA cases have shown, most of these decisions were taken on novelty and specific details of the patent claims in question. Therefore, they did not have a broader impact on the EPO's granting practice and the jurisdiction of its Boards of Appeal, as some initiators of the opposition procedures had hoped for (Murray and Zimmeren 2011: 313; Schneider 2010: 609–621).

Even though some technical and administrative measures have been taken by the EPO to improve the quality of patent grant ("Raising the bar" initiative), those are aimed primarily at increasing the efficiency of patent grant. Whether they may have a substantial impact on the design and decision-making of the examination and grant processes still needs to be seen and evaluated. The EPO – with respect to its presidency, its examiners, and its Boards of Appeal – is and remains highly reluctant to open up the gate of ordre public exemptions. (One of the few exemptions is the WARF case and the Decision G2/06 of the EPO's Enlarged Board of Appeal.) This attitude became also apparent in the EPO president's reaction to the CJEU decision on the Bruestle case: As EPO President Benoît Battistelli stated in his blog, the EPO

> is well aware of the sensitivity of the issues involved, and although biotech accounted for under 5 % of all European patent applications received in 2010 has set up a dedicated specialist taskforce and applies the rules very strictly (the grant rate in biotech is 28 %, compared with 42 % overall). Even so, every so often one of these cases becomes a cause célèbre. (...) If the judges rule in favour of a restrictive interpretation of biotech patentability provisions, the EPO will immediately implement it. The European legislator may also decide that further changes to the law are needed. Whatever is decided, I welcome evidence-based debate and invite all interested parties, especially associations active on these issues, to discuss them with us on the basis of objective data. It should also be kept in mind that changes to our legal framework are likely to have economic consequences, including possible deterrent effects for the siting of research centres in Europe.[9]

The latter refers to supposed detrimental economic and research effects of broad ordre public exemptions. The statement demonstrates that more stringent and rigorous controls with respect to patentability criteria, and a serious attempt at addressing ethically sensitive cases, not least for reasons of the reputation of the EPO, is pursued. But despite a more open attitude, the EPO also still seems to hold on to the mantra that more patents are better for research.[10]

Daring to provide a prediction on synthetic biology, it is expected that the ordre public exception of Article 53(a) EPC will be reserved for rare and openly "abhorrent" cases, such as "biological letter bombs". This may refer to synthetic viruses or biological weapons redesigned by synthetic biology methods which may provide threats to public health and to public safety as well as to public security. The reconstruction and modification of deadly viruses and bacteria, to enhance their virulence or to add pathological properties, and the danger of purposefully or accidentally transmitting highly infectious diseases has recently sparked broad debates within the scientific community itself with reference to whether the results of such research should be published or not and how policy-makers could and should regulate such biosecurity issues (Maurer 2011).[11]

Sensitivity to biosafety issues on the one hand, and to bioterrorism on the other hand, may preclude some of these subject matters from patent grant. It must be questioned, however, whether bioterrorists aiming at intentionally creating harmful

[9] http://blog.epo.org/uncategorized/patents-and-biotechnology-%E2%80%93-latest-developments/

[10] The EPO does apply a very narrow reading of the CJEU judgement, but does not handle this in a transparent way, for instance by clear indications in its examination guidelines. Cf. Schlich 2012, and several statements at the 23rd Annual Forum on Biotech & Pharmaceutical Patenting in October 2012 in London which ran under the title "Utilising Successful Strategies to Protect Your Global Biotech & Pharma Patent Portfolio and Maximise Revenues". See the presentation by Aliki Nichogiannopoulou, Director, DG1, European Patent Office, at http://www.econtext.ca/c5/2012/BiotechPharma/

[11] See also: http://news.sciencemag.org/scienceinsider/2011/11/scientists-brace-for-media-storm.html

organisms would file respective patent applications. The more pressing problem relates to the fact that research on harmful viruses, biochemicals and other agents is often not intrinsically malicious. Most often, research is of "dual use" for both protection from, control of and accountability for biological agents and toxins (Presidential Commission 2010: 71). Therefore, it is doubtful whether and to what extent barring such inventions from patentability would actually act as a dis-incentive and have a real impact on research and investment. Moreover, as the military forces itself will probably be the main investigators in such applications of synthetic biology, it is doubtful whether such lab creations will become disclosed in patent applications.

Nonetheless, the joint report by the Spanish Bioethics Committee and the Portuguese National Ethics Council for the Life Sciences (2011) has emphasized that synthetic biology could be a new source of risk to biosecurity and the release of new organisms may pose risks to the biosafety of life forms and ecosystems.[12] It is noteworthy that in their recommendations the two Councils advocate the principle of precaution, risk management, prior authorisation as well as periodic monitoring and inspection, including monitoring and follow-up on dual use (p.16 and 28). Recommending a "step by step" and "case by case" approach (p. 18) for synthetic biology as such may furthermore also be advisable for the granting of patents on synthetic biological methods and products. Actively requesting from patent applicants to disclose potential biological risks in the technical descriptions of their inventions could also possibly serve as a mode of encouraging research on and disclosure of risks, and thus increase transparency as well as contribute to the prevention of undesired consequences and eventually increase citizens' protection (Schneider 2008). In addition, the two Ethics Councils also made another important but different point, in addressing the "potential economic impact" of patents on processes and products derived from synthetic biology, as "the patenting of these developments could violate the ethical principle of justice" (2011: 29, recommendation 8). Whether such a recommendation may be read as precluding patentability as such and opting instead for open source models in synthetic biology (Rai and Boyle 2007) or whether it should encourage strict and rigid interpretation of patentability criteria by patent offices as well as courts (Rutz 2009) will certainly remain subject to further debates.

10.4.2 Synthetic Biology in the Legislative and Judicial Arena

If synthetic biology will be negotiated within the legislative arena, the prospects for broader interpretation of exemptions and for introduction of new special provisions could be more promising than in the administrative arena. However, there is a major

[12] Concerns over biosecurity and biosafety should be distinguished: "Biosecurity includes both state-based biowarfare and nonstate sponsored bioterrorism. Biosafety concerns, which some call "bioerror," include laboratory accidents, inadvertent releases of modified organisms into the environment, horizontal gene transfer between modified and unmodified organisms, and the capacity of living organisms to evolve and adapt in ways we cannot anticipate' (Murray 2011: 1324).

hurdle for synthetic biology to ever reach the legislative arena: Agenda setting powers for initiating European legislation remains almost exclusively within the remit of the European Commission.[13] Today, it seems highly unlikely that the European Commission will introduce special legislation for synthetic biology. Thus, the legislative arena will most probably be barred from performing action.

Concerning the judicial arena, both with regard to specialist and to generalist courts, there is a major adverse effect: Court decisions have to be initiated by filing lawsuits. These are costly, and they take a long time. Therefore, they must rather be seen as corrective mechanisms in hindsight. We should therefore not expect courts to take a pro-active stance and to provide anticipatory rule-making for synthetic biology.

10.5 The Importance of Metaphoric Framing for Discourse and Actor Coalitions

So far, a strong case was made for the institutional design as determining factor for synthetic biology's fate in patent law. However, another important variable which should not be neglected, is public discourse and the framing of what is at stake in synthetic biology. I might even go as far as to assert that the symbolic and metaphoric conceptions of synthetic biology will be at least as important as the technical intricacies.

According to social science research, framing is important in drawing attention to an issue, in highlighting and hiding several aspects, and it can be crucial for mobilising public support or dissent to policy questions (Rein and Schön 1996; Schön 1993; Schön and Rein 1994; Snow and Benford 1988; Snow et al. 1986).

Apparently, in publications about synthetic biology, the metaphoric use of language is pervasive. This has not gone unnoticed by linguists and scholars of communication studies and media analysts (see Hellsten and Nerlich 2011; Doering 2011, 2012; Brueninghaus 2011), as well as by legal historians (Dutfield 2010, 2012; van den Belt 2009).

One might even go as far as to ask whether the term synthetic biology itself is merely a metaphor which serves to create attention and to bind a most heterogeneous field of scientific activities together under a single umbrella term. Related to this somewhat heretical question is the query, whether synthetic biology is indeed new and a qualitative leap or just a new label for genetically "engineered" products and processes. Following this question means to inquire whether scientists stress the continuity or the novelty of what they are doing in their labs. And are synthetic biology's risks similar to those posed by genetically modified organisms (GMOs)? Those are to be tackled by adequate containment strategies which aim at inhibiting

[13] Even though some novel provisions have recently been introduced for a legislative initiative by the European citizens, neither the European Parliament nor the Council have gained full agenda setting powers within the EU.

growth, release and reproduction of synthetically manipulated organisms. Can we rely on established laws, regulations and procedures to deal with GMOs or does synthetic biology require new and more specific regulation? Which potential harms should be taken into account, for which potential benefits? And what is the role patent law could and should take within these regulations?

As analyses both of media reporting and scientific discourses of synthetic biology have demonstrated, cutting edge science on synthetic biology has been framed along metaphors which suggest analogies to different technical systems and domains. Most often, they are related to ideas of (complete) control and to analogies between biology and technical as well as digital domains. Life has been depicted as a machinery, a force, a network, a system or an interaction among system components (Doering 2012). The most common, "master" metaphors identified by linguists were the computer, the journey, the book, and the building. "Biobricks" are most often represented as "lego bricks", and scientists are portrayed as architects, engineers or computer programmers. Not rarely, the message is conveyed that synthetic biology would be about the transition from "reading" DNA to "writing" the genetic code. Concerning the verbs used, a lot of crafting and bricolage metaphoric is involved in the talk about tinkering, stitching, tailoring and playing – not least when science journals as well as the popular press asks, whether Craig Venter can stitch together a genome from scratch (Hellsten and Nerlich 2011).

The semantic framing of synthetic biology will definitely have an impact upon people's acceptance of synthetic biology as well as upon political expectations (Haunss 2011). Thus, metaphors and frames not only have a descriptive but also a prescriptive dimension (Schneider 2010: 75–102). They can serve to legitimize research and mobilise public support, or conversely, to delegitimize and contest synthetic biology. Metaphors depicting synthetic biology may even have an influence on whether the public will be alerted at all to synthetic biology or not. Whether and how ethical questions will be raised is also strongly associated to naming and framing strategies as well as to practices. How synthetic biology will be conceptualized within semantic oppositions will also possibly play a decisive role.

As has occurred in the biotech patent debate, it can be assumed that there will be an overlap between public acceptance of the technology as such, and of its patenting – even if, as has already pointed out in the first chapter, the relationship between patent eligibility, use and diffusion of a certain technology is far more complex and contradictory.

In which semantic oppositions synthetic biology will be phrased can even become decisive for whether a certain application will be eligible for patenting or not. Whether synthetic biology is conceived as "natural" or "synthetic" DNA may for instance have an influence on whether patenting might become contested as "patenting life" or accepted as novel and demonstrating true inventive spirit, thus also passing the inventive step and industrial application test. In the US, the "natural substances doctrine" as an exception from patenting may become revived, if "real" synthetic DNA or "real" synthetic life would become "unmasked" as impossible. Such a perspective is expressed in the following quote: "Putting it in its bluntest terms, genetic engineers are really just free-riders who tinker half-knowingly with what they have got and actually create nothing that was not there before" (Dutfield 2010: 533). According to this view, evolution is the greatest inventor and designer of life, and synthetic engineers are reckless pirates who can only bunglingly copy it. In the same line of reasoning, the "discovery" versus "invention" divide in European patent law could possibly be re-opened to public debate.

Hence, whether products and processes from synthetic biology are man-made, manufactured, and thus more or less completely artificial, will also possibly be subject to popular debates about patentability. The famous sentence from the US Supreme Court's "Chakrabarty" case deemed "everything under the sun made by man" eligible for patenting – being it machines or oil-eating bacteria.[14] This sentence was often cited by opponents as an expression of human hubris.

Canada's Supreme Court, however, in rejecting the patent on the Harvard Oncomouse in 2002, has put forward another distinction, namely between (patentable) lower and (unpatentable) higher forms of life. It did not specify, regrettably, how to draw the line.[15] But in transmitting the decision to the legislature, the Supreme Court of Canada has at least recognized the limits of its own law-making power and rightfully transferred it to the arena of representative democracy.

One of the terms most often associated with overzealous Craig Venter but less so with the synthetic biology project in general is the metaphor "Playing God".[16] This strong metaphor seems to capture all the morality claims in a nutshell. It frames synthetic biology as conflicting with essential concepts on the limits of human agency. Here again, human hubris is focussed as a temptation and a moral problem. Another critique refers to the reductionist view of life which is depicted as "nothing more than the sum of its parts" (Presidential Commission 2010: 135). Degraded to a toolbox, it is raising ethical concerns "related to the status of the organism, the motives of the scientists and the role of technology in our society" (Deplazes-Zemp 2011).

Possible counter-frames to this techno-materialist perspective on life seem to be inherent in metaphorical conceptions of life as a riddle, and of life as a secret (Doering 2012). The "riddle" metaphor still relates to the concept of a brainteaser – and may assign scientists the role of solving the puzzle, and explaining life to the benefit of humankind. Life as a "secret", in contrast, may more strongly put emphasis not only on the unexplored but also what's (ontologically) inexplicable about life. Life as a "secret" may also send out a message of warning against too much uncovering of what is deemed to be sacred, and hence call for "humility and awe" (Murray 2011: 1342).

Thus, "nature's subtlety and recalcitrance" (Calvert 2008: 395), the complexity of life – and its features such as growth, (self)-replication, and permanent variation –

[14] Diamond v. Chakrabarty, 447 US 303 (1980).

[15] http://www.lexum.umontreal.ca/

[16] On European, Asian, and Latin American editions of US magazine Newsweek in May 2007, the cover title stated "Playing God" (without question mark) and was printed in large letters besides a portrait of Craig Venter looking upwards, possibly demonstrating his thoughtfulness about the potential awesomeness of synthetic biology. Interestingly, neither the cover nor the article appeared in the US edition.

are stressed which marks a strong distinction to mechanic or technical devices, and should therefore beware from (too much) "tinkering" and "playing".

However, the overwhelming metaphor of the "game" in "playing" and exploring life may also have another ring to it. Here, synthetic biology is not about "playing god" but about "just playing", like children are playing with lego-bricks. The connotation associated to the metaphor "game" means that synthetic biology is not harmful but benignant and harmless. Nonetheless, as scientists are eager to emphasize, it is not a meaningless game they play with taxpayers' money, which must be belittled, but a serious game of adults which purpose is to benefit humanity. In this respect, synthetic biology promises to solve serious health problems and to provide solutions for grand and global challenges ranging from climate change to demographic shifts. The latter can be seen as an attempt at justifying generous research grants and downplaying and black-boxing possible risks, both to the environment and to human health. Or, following Hellsten and Nerlich (2011), such metaphoric can also be used to "whitewash and greenwash" synthetic biology, and thus serve ideological and strategic purposes.

In as much as "Playing God" and "Frankenstein" metaphorics demonize synthetic biology they do at the same time highlight its potentials, and thus add to its allure and power of appeal. Therefore, using such metaphors may carry the risk to be taken in by the enthusiasm and the promissory attitude of some scientists. Hence, such critique may become just a reversed mirror image of the hype about synthetic biology. At the end of the day, at least for academic scholars, it would be preferable to deflate the hype and to soberly deconstruct overly optimistic promises and overrated socio-economic expectations.[17]

For some readers, the previous excurse may deviate too far from the topic of this article, namely the limits within patent law and the ordre public and public policy clause in particular. These considerations should, however, serve as a reminder: In the decades-long controversies and contestations of the EU's biotechnology patent directive, similar questions were raised which were of utmost importance for moralizing and politicizing intellectual property rights. The rallying call "No to patents on life" provided a common language for oppositional voices, created collective identities, and was instrumental for forming advocacy coalitions of unusual and new actors within the patent domain. Depicting genes as "common heritage of humankind" was a strong – if hard to understand – metaphor to reject private appropriation by temporary legal monopolies.

[17] Jonathan Kahn therefore suggests "skeptical vigilance" and states: "Time and time again over the past two decades, new advances in biotechnology have rolled out to great fanfare and great promises. As time horizons are met and promised results repeatedly fail to materialize, new promises are made for new technologies, each time pushing back the ever receding time horizon for concrete results. To be clear, these advances are not failures. Each and every one has made significant contributions to scientific knowledge and produced some limited concrete results. But they have uniformly failed to live up to the hype initially put forward to promote them." (Kahn 2011: 1351) Eleonore Pauwels deplores that "fundamental questions about what applications of synthetic biology would advance societal goals and be considered sustainable are ignored" (Pauwels 2011: 1465). See similarly also (Martin and Balmer 2008; Torgersen 2009).

It remains to be seen whether a similar wave of contestation will arise and whether synthetic biology will provoke persistent disputes like GMOs, embryonic stem cells, and biotechnology patents. If so, it will rather be the parliaments' role to resonate with such frames and claims, whereas the patent community will probably be much less responsive, if not even outright hostile to such supposedly "wrong" framings of the matters in question.

However, as I have tried to lay out in this section, metaphorical framing is part and parcel of synthetic biology. It is neither restricted to certain camps nor to opponents, but at least deployed in almost the same manner by synthetic biology protagonists themselves.

10.6 Conclusion

It was demonstrated that European patent law provides two crucial outwards boundaries to patent eligibility. First, the exclusion of discoveries from patentability, and second the ordre public and morality exception. Even though both, if applied, have the same result, namely non-patentability, their teleologies are fundamentally opposed: In the first case, the provision aims at broad and unrestricted access to the technical knowledge in question, in the second case, what's aimed for is rather disapproval and suppression of such knowledge, and even prevention of such knowledge being generated at all.

Whether products and methods resulting from research in synthetic biology will fall under one of these provisions cannot yet be determined, as research is in an early stage of development. As yet, it can be expected that the ordre public exception of Article 53(a) EPC will be reserved for rare and openly "abhorrent" cases of applications in synthetic biology, such as harmful synthetic viruses or biological weapons redesigned by synthetic biology methods which may provide threats to public health and to public security. Sensitivity to biosafety issues and to bioterrorism may preclude some of these subjects from patent application and grant. However, as research is often of "dual use" for both protection from, control of and accountability for biological agents and toxins, it will be difficult to discern "good use " from "abuse", as research on harmful viruses, biochemicals and other agents must not be intrinsically malicious. Therefore, it is doubtful whether and to what extent barring such inventions from patentability would actually have an impact on such research and investment.

The other boundary, the "discovery" clause as exemption from patentability, will also most likely not be applied upon patent applications for synthetic biology, because in most European countries a well as in the US, there is a long tradition of patents on chemical matter and other substances derived from nature, if isolated, purified, and modified, and even higher life forms got patented in Europe by the EPO. Therefore, at present it seems more likely that patent examination and grant in synthetic biology will refer to other clauses and articles (namely articles 56, 83 and 84 of the EPC) to tailor patent protection. Instead of working as dichotomic "either-or" principles, the latter provisions can serve to regulate the scope of protection conferred. They are thus more apt to fine-tune patent claims in the examination process.

It was further argued, that predictions on whether the exclusion for discoveries on the one hand, and the ordre public and public policy exception on the other hand will be deployed in the case of synthetic biology will strongly depend on the arena in which synthetic biology patents will be negotiated. Should synthetic biology invariably be dealt with almost exclusively in the administrative arena, both provisions will probably hardly ever be employed. Should synthetic biology patents, however, enter the legislative arena, then there could be more leeway for innovative interpretations of the statutory legal boundaries. The same could become true for the judicial arena, should generalist courts get a say over patentability decisions. However, both arenas will, for the time being, probably be barred from decision-making. Whatever arena comes into play, it was argued that the framing of synthetic biology will have a decisive impact on social and political attention devoted to these matters, on whether conflicts will arise, and finally on patentability questions. In sum, the interaction of legal and constitutional boundaries, political arenas, and social framing has to be taken into account for explaining the governance and direction of intellectual property in synthetic biology. Proceeding in such a manner is an attempt at "upstreaming" ethics, anticipatory impact assessment, and policy analysis in the biosciences and also a tool for constitutionalizing intellectual property rights.

References

Bagley M (2003) Patent first, ask questions later: morality and biotechnology in patent law. William Mary Law Rev 45(2):469–547

Bakardjieva-Engelbrekt A (2011) Dilemmas of governance in a multilevel European patent system. In: Lidgard HH (ed) National developments at the intersection of intellectual property and competition law, Swedish studies in European law 3. Hart, Stockholm

Baumgartner C (2006) Exclusion by inclusion? On difficulties with regard to an effective ethical assessment of patenting in the field of agricultural bio-technology. J Agric Environ Ethics 19:522

Bessen J, Meurer MJ (2008) Patent failure. How judges, bureaucrats, and lawyers put innovators at risk. Princeton University Press, Princeton

Bot (2011) Opinion of advocate general Bot, delivered on 10 March 2011, Case C-34/10, Oliver Brüstle v. Greenpeace eV

Boyle J (2003) Enclosing the genome: what squabbles over genetic patents could teach us. In: Kieff SF (ed) Perspectives on properties of the human genome project. Elsevier/Academic Press, Amsterdam, pp 97–122

Brueninghaus, A (2011) Framing cutting edge science: media representations of systems biology. Presentation at workshop "different forms of life? Comparative perspectives on systems and synthetic biology. 19–20.01.2012, at BIOGUM, University of Hamburg

Burk DL, Lemley MA (2003) Biotechnology's uncertainty principle. In: Kieff SF (ed) Perspectives on properties of the human genome project. Elsevier/Academic Press, Amsterdam u.a, pp 305–154

Calvert J (2008) The commodification of emergence: systems biology, synthetic biology and intellectual property. BioSocieties 3(4):385–400

Casabona RMC (2011) Criminal policy and legislative techniques in criminal law on biotechnology. Int Rev Penal Law 82:83–108

CBE (2011) Synthetic biology. A joint report by the Spanish Bioethics Committee (CBE) and the Portuguese National Ethics Council for the Life Sciences. Lisbon-Barcelona. http://www.comitedebioetica.es/documentacion/docs/en/Synthetic_Biology_CBE-CNECV.pdf.. Accessed 24 Oct 2011
CJEU (Court of Justice of the European Union) (2011) C 34/10 – Bruestle v Greenpeace
Deplazes-Zemp A (2011) The conception of life in synthetic biology in: science and engineering ethics. http://philpapers.org/rec/DEPTCO-3
Doering M (2011) The metaphorical 'ethicisation' of technology: the case of synthetic biology. Presentation at workshop "taking stock of figurative language and thought". Mulheim, 21 May 2011
Doering M (2012) The conceptual framing of 'life' in systems biology: the metaphorical forging of a concept in scientific discourse. Presentation at workshop "different forms of life? Comparative perspectives on systems and synthetic biology, 19–20.01.2012, at BIOGUM Research Centre for Biotechnology, Society and the Environment, University of Hamburg
Drahos P (1999) Biotechnology patents, markets and morality. Eur Intellect Prop Rev 9:441–449
Drahos P (2010) The global governance of knowledge. Patent offices and their clients. Cambridge University Press, Cambridge
Dutfield G (2009) Intellectual property rights & the life science industries: past, present & future, 2nd edn. World Scientific, New Jersey
Dutfield G (2010) Who invents life – blind watchmakers, intelligent designers or genetic engineers? J Intellect Prop Law Pract 5(7):2010, 531
Dutfield G (2012) The genetic code is 3.6 billion years old: it's time for a rewrite. In: Lever A (ed) New frontiers in the philosophy of intellectual property. Cambridge University Press, Cambridge
Eifert M, Hoffmann-Riem W (2008) Geistiges Eigentum und Innovation. Duncker & Humblot, Berlin
Eimer T (2008) Decoding divergence in software regulation: paradigms, power structures, and institutions in the U.S. and the EU. Governance 21(2):275–296
Eimer T (2011) Arenen und Monopole. Softwarepatente in den USA und in Europa. VS, Wiesbaden
European Parliament (2012) Resolution adopted on 10 May 2012 "on the patenting of essential biological processes". http://www.europarl.europa.eu/sides/getDoc.do?pubRef=-//EP//TEXT+TA+P7-TA-2012-0202+0+DOC+XML+V0//EN&language=EN. Accessed 12 June 2012
EPO (European Patent Office) (2007) Scenarios for the future. Munich
Geiger C (2006) Constitutionalizing intellectual property law? The influence of fundamental rights on intellectual property in Europe. In: 37 International Review of Intellectual Property and Competition Law, pp 371–406
Godt CH (2007) Eigentum an Information. Tübingen: Mohr Siebeck.
Gold ER, Durell K (2005) "Innovating the Skilled Reader: Tailoring Patents to New Technologies" 19(1) Intellect Prop J 189, http://www.cipp.mcgill.ca/data/publications/00000055.pdf. Accessed 18 June 2014
Grimm D (2002) Die Wissenschaft setzt ihre Autonomie aufs Spiel, Interview in der FAZ vom 11 Feb 2002, 48
Grosheide W (2010) Intellectual property and human rights: a paradox. Edward Elgar, Northampton
Hagel F (2004) Serving two masters: the balance between the applicant and the public«. Patent World 161:22–24
Hashimoto K, Aida T (2008) Antibody patenting without antibodies: a global trend. Nat Biotechnol 26(12):1341–1343
Haunss S (2011) The politicisation of intellectual property: IP conflicts and social change. WIPO J 3(1):129–138
Haunss S, Shadlen KC (eds) (2009) Politics of intellectual property. Contestation over the ownership, use, and control of knowledge and information. Edward Elgar, Cheltenham
Helfer LR (2003) Human rights and intellectual property: conflict or coexistence? Minn J Law Sci Technol 5:47
Helfer L, Austin GW (2011) Human rights and intellectual property: mapping the global interface. Cambridge University Press, Cambridge/New York

Hellsten I, Nerlich B (2011) Synthetic biology: building the language of a new science brick by metaphorical brick. New Genet Soc 30(4):375–397
Jaffe AB, Lerner J (2005) Innovation and its discontents: how our broken patent system is endangering innovation and progress, and what to do about it. Princeton Univ. Press, Princeton, NJ
Kahn J (2011) Synthetic hype: a skeptical view of the promise of synthetic biology. Valparaiso Univ Law Rev 45(4):29–46
Kersten J (2004) Das Klonen von Menschen. Eine verfassungs-, europa- und völkerrechtliche Kritik. Mohr Siebeck, Tübingen
Kevles D, Gaudillière J-P, Rheinberger H-J (eds) (2009) Living properties: making knowledge and controlling ownership in the history of biology. Max Planck Institute for History of Science, Berlin, Preprint No. 382
Lamping M (2011) Enhanced cooperation – a proper approach to market integration in the field of unitary patent protection? In: 8 International Review of Intellectual Property and Competition Law 2011, pp 879–925
Lausmann-Murr D (2000) Schranken für die Patentierung der Gene des Menschen: "öffentliche Ordnung" und "gute Sitten" im Europäischen Patentübereinkommen. Nomos, Baden-Baden
Martin PA, BALMER A (2008) Synthetic biology: social and ethical challenges. http://www.bbsrc.ac.uk/organisation/policies/reviews/scientific-areas/0806-synthetic-biology.aspx
Maurer SM (2011) End of the beginning or beginning of the end? Synthetic biology's stalled security agenda and the prospects for restarting it. Valparaiso Univ Law Rev 45(4):73–132
Merton RK (1985) On the shoulders of giants: a shandean postscript. Harcourt Brace Jovanovich, San Diego
Murray TH (2011) What synthetic genomes mean for our future: technology, ethics, and law, interests and identities. Valparaiso Univ Law Rev 45(4):1–28
Murray K, Van Zimmeren E (2011) Dynamic patent governance in Europe and the United States: the Myriad example. Cardozo J Int Comp 19:287–342
Nack R (2002) Die patentierbare Erfindung unter den sich wandelnden Bedingungen von Wissenschaft und Technologie. Heymann, Köln
Nelson RR (1959) The simple economics of basic scientific research. J Polit Econ 67:297–306
Nelson RR (2004) The market economy, and the scientific commons. Res Policy 33:445–471
OECD, Royal Society (2010) Symposium on opportunities and challenges in the emerging field of synthetic biology – synthesis report. www.oecd.org/sti/biotechnology/synbio
Pauwels E (2011) Who let the humanists into the lab? Valparaiso Univ Law Rev 45(4):133–157
Plomer A, Torremans P (2009) Embryonic stem cell patents: European patent law and ethics. Oxford University Press, Oxford
Porter G (2009a) Human embryos, patents and global trade: assessing the scope and contents of the TRIPS morality exception. In: Plomer A, Torremans P (eds) Embryonic stem cell patents: European patent law and ethics. Oxford University Press, Oxford, pp 343–367
Porter G (2009b) The drafting history of the European biotechnology directive. In: Plomer A, Torremans P (eds) Embryonic stem cell patents: European patent law and ethics. Oxford University Press, Oxford, pp 3–26
Rai AK, Boyle J (2007) Synthetic biology: caught between property rights, the public domain, and the commons. PLoS Biol 5(3):e58
Rein M, Schön DA (1996) Frame-critical policy analysis and frame-reflective policy practice. Knowl Policy 9:85–104
Robbins J (2004) Patenting life: historical justifications and objections. Paper given at 4S/EASST Annual Meeting. Paris. 26 Aug 2004
Rutz B (2007) Synthetic biology through the prism of scenarios. Biotechnol J 2(9):1072–1075
Rutz B (2009) Synthetic biology and patents. A European perspective. EMBO reports. 10: 514–517
Schlich GW (2012) Examination of human embryonic stem cell inventions in Europe: the first glimmers after the doom of the Brüstle decision. In: CIPA Journal, 2012. http://www.schlich.co.uk/CIPA_October2012.html
Schneider I (2007) Governance of the European patent system. In: European Patent Office (ed) Scenarios for the future, interviews. Munich 2007, 579–609. http://documents.epo.org/projects/babylon/eponet.nsf/0/F172DE5BB2B9B15BC12572DC0031A3CB/$File/Interview_Schneider.pdf

Schneider I (2008) Geistiges Eigentum und öffentliche Ziele. In: Hoffmann-Riem W, Eifert M (eds) Geistiges Eigentum und Innovation. Duncker & Humblot, Berlin, pp 309–362
Schneider I (2009a) Governing the patent system in Europe: the EPO's supranational autonomy in need for a regulatory perspective. Sci Public Policy 36(8):619–628
Schneider I (2009b) Can patent legislation make a difference? Bringing parliaments and civil society into patent governance. In: Haunss S, Shadlen KC (eds) The politics of intellectual property: contestation over the ownership, use, and control of knowledge and information. Edward Elgar, Cheltenham/Northampon, pp 129–157
Schneider I (2010) Das Europäische patent system. Wandel von Governance durch Parlamente und Zivilgesellschaft. Campus, Frankfurt am Main
Schneider I (2011) Das EuGH-Urteil "Brüstle versus Greenpeace"(Rs. C-34/10): Bedeutung und Implikationen für Europa. Zeitschrift für geistiges Eigentum/Intellect Prop J 3(4):475–510
Schön D (1993) Generative metaphor: a perspective on problem-setting in social policy. In: Ortony A (ed) Metaphor and thought. Cambridge, Cambridge University Press, pp 137–163
Schön D, Rein M (1994) Frame reflection: toward the resolution of intractable policy controversies. Basic Books, New York
Scotchmer S (1991) Standing on the shoulders of giants: cumulative research and the patent law. J Econ Perspect 5(1):29–41
Snow DA, Benford RD (1988) Ideology, frame resonance and participant mobilization. Int Soc Mov Res 1:197–219
Snow DA, Rochford EB, Worden SK, Benford RD (1986) Frame alignment processes, micromobilization and movement participation. Am Sociol Rev 51:456–481
Thambisetty S (2002) Understanding Morality as a Ground for Exclusion From Patentability Under European Law. Eubios Journal of Asian and International Bioethics 12(2002):48–53.
Thambisetty S (2006) The institutional nature of the patent system: implications for bioethical decision-making. In: Lenk C, Hoppe N, Andorno R (eds) Ethics and law of intellectual property: current problems in politics, science and technology. Ashgate, Aldershot, pp 247–268
'T hoen E (2009) The global politics of pharmaceutical monopoly power: drug patents, access, innovation and the application of the WTO Doha Declaration on TRIPS and Public Health. AMB, Diemen
Torgersen H (2009) Synthetic biology in society: learning from past experience? Syst Synth Biol 3(1–4):9–17
Ullrich H (2002): Patent Protection in Europe: Integrating Europe into the Community or the Community into Europe? In: EUI (European University Institute Florence) Working Paper Law 2002/5.
Ullrich H (2004) Harmony and unity of European intellectual property protection. In: Vaver D, Bently L (eds) Intellectual property in the New Millennium. Cambridge University Press, Cambridge, pp 20–46
Ullrich H (2012) Harmonizing patent law: the untamable union patent. In: Janssens VO (ed) From European rules to Belgian law and practice (Essays in honour of F. Gotzen), Brussels (Bruylant), pp 244–294 (pre-publication as Max Planck Institute for Intellectual Property and Competition Law Research Paper No.12-03, http://ssrn.com/abstract=2027920)
US Presidential Commission for the Study of Bioethics (2010) New directions. The ethics of synthetic biology and emerging technologies. http://www.bioethics.gov/documents/synthetic-biology/PCSBI-Synthetic-Biology-Report-12-16-10.pdf
Van Den Belt H (2009) Playing God in Frankenstein's footsteps: synthetic biology and the meaning of life. Nanoethics 3(3):257–268
Walzer M (1983) Spheres of justice: a defense of pluralism and equality. Basic Books, New York
Yu PK (ed) (2011) Analysis of intellectual property issues. WIPO J 3(1). Available at http://www.wipo.int/export/sites/www/about-wipo/en/wipo_journal/pdf/wipo_journal_3_1.pdf

Chapter 11
Patentability, Synthetic Biology and Human Genome

Carlos María Romeo Casabona

Abstract For centuries the mechanism of the patent has been extremely useful to adequately reconcile the interests of the inventor with the society in which the task is developed. The result of its existence has been the creation of a favorable scenario for the exploitation of human ingenuity, spurred by the possibility of obtaining individual benefit, which is compatible with the collective management of the benefits of their innovation. However, current developments in science question the validity of this framework. Hence, the realisation of a thorough analysis of the paradigm of intellectual property protection currently in force is of particular importance. This text aims to shed some light in this regard. In order to maximize its clarity, it has been structured into several sections. Its first section is devoted to the analysis of current regulations regarding synthetic biology, emphasizing its essential characteristics. Subsequently, some considerations will be included on one of its most controversial aspects, which refers to the "moral clause". Finally, it introduces some considerations on the issue of synthetic biology and its place in the patent legal system.

Keywords Synthetic biology • Intellectual property rights • Gene patents • BRCA patents • European directive biotechnology

---

This paper has been partially published in: Romeo Casabona, C. M., "*La promoción de las innovaciones tecnológicas, un desafío económico y jurídicos para las Biopatentes*", Teoría y Derecho. Revista de Pensamiento Jurídico. Número titulado Biotecnología y Derecho. Encuentros y Desencuentros. Junio 11/2012, pp. 95–111, and in: "*Synthetic Biology. A joint report by the Spanish Bioethics Committee and the Portuguese National Ethics Council for the Life Sciences*", at: http://www.comitedebioetica.es/documentacion/docs/en/Synthetic_Biology_CBE-CNECV.pdf

C.M. Romeo Casabona
Inter-University Chair in Law and the Human Genome, University of Deusto and University of the Basque Country, Avda. de las Universidades 24, 48007 Bilbao, Spain
e-mail: carlosmaria.romeo@ehu.es

I. de Miguel Beriain and C.M. Romeo Casabona (eds.), *Synbio and Human Health: A Challenge to the Current IP Framework?*, DOI 10.1007/978-94-017-9196-0_11,

11.1 Introduction

Nowadays, it is almost a common assertion that the acceleration taking place in the development of new products and procedures relating to biotechnology, as well as the complexity that already some composite products reveal, especially those derived from emerging biotechnologies such as synthetic biology, are giving rise to critical positions in relation to the capacity of current patent laws for appropriate legal responses to new emerging situations. This situation is cause for concern as it is also being considered in other sectors, such as information and communication technologies.

Hence, the realisation of a thorough analysis of the paradigm of intellectual property protection currently in force is of particular importance. This analysis should, on the one hand, bear in mind the existing European legislation, which is the embodiment of an entire historical tradition, as well as the rationale for justifying it; on the other, the challenges and new requirements to which our intellectual property rights configuration faces, among other reasons, by one of particular importance: the emergence of new biotechnologies. In this paper, both sides of the analysis will be considered, so as to bring a holistic view of the issues involved in the case of synthetic biology and patent system.

11.2 The Patent as a Means of Legal Protection from Biotechnological Innovations: The European Regulatory Framework

11.2.1 Fundamental Regulatory Principles

When properly focusing on the issue of patentability of synthetic biology products related to human health and, moreover, the possible alternatives to this procedure, one should always bear in mind a fundamental idea: European regulation assumes the general principle that biotechnologies are legally protected, primarily or exclusively through a patent.

It is also important to recognize that state regulations, that is, the rules of each of the Member States, remain the legal reference framework in intellectual property. This is undoubtedly due to an unwillingness replace the existing general regime of each country regarding patents for a common regulation, as stated in the Recitals no. 8 of the Preamble of the Directive 98/44/EC notwithstanding the necessary adaptations to the conditions provided in the Directive (art. 1).

With regard to the admission of the patent application, it is worth noting the emphasis of the same document in the case of Biotechnology by pointing out that it should always show the alleged novelty or biotechnological innovation complying with each and every one of the traditionally recognized requirements of the patent, a requirement that is present in the recitals of the Preamble (recitals no. 22), as in its articles (arts. 3.1 and 5.3). Moreover, it should be taken into account that while it is true that the Directive offer a flexible understanding of the requirements of the patent (new and non obvious inventions), it is also true that in the third case, the industrial application has been chosen to maintain, apparently at least, a high level of requirements.

Thus, it is remarkable how the directive stresses that the person submitting the patent application must sufficiently demonstrate the industrial application of biotechnology product, that is, its usefulness must be clearly defined and fully stated. Obviously, this point will be crucial for determining the patentability or otherwise of some of the most primitive synthetic biology, whose real value is sometimes far from being demonstrable, which is a commendable barrier for the existence of "trivial patents", a dysfunction that could result in a general blockage of the entire sector.

Finally, it is important to note that within the sphere of European legislation, it has also been traditionally important to clarify what may be patentable or not, according to the nature of the subject matter of the patent. This is particularly true in cases in which biotechnological material is involved, especially if they are human biological elements or the human body itself (section 5). In this regard, it is stated as a general principle that products considered patentable are those that are compounds or contain biological material or the procedures by which they are produced, processed or use biological material, provided that they comply with the traditional requirements of the patent: new inventions, which involve an inventive step and are susceptible to industrial application (art. 3.1). In consequence, the biological material isolated from its natural environment is patentable, or that has been produced by means of a technical procedure, even if it already exists in its natural state (art.3. 2).

11.2.2 The Specific Legal Framework in the Case of Parts of the Human Body

It should be noted that with regard to biological material (bearing in mind that the fundamental point of attention of this paper focuses on synthetic biology applicable to humans), we highlight that the Directive expressly states that it could constitute a patentable invention "An element isolated from the human body or otherwise produced by means of a technical process, including the sequence or partial sequence of a gene, may constitute a patentable invention, even if the structure of that element is identical to that of a natural element" (art. 5.2). It requires that the industrial application of a sequence or a partial sequence of a gene should be disclosed in the patent application By contrast, the human body, at the various stages of its formation and development, and the simple discovery of one of its elements, including the sequence or partial sequence of a gene, cannot constitute patentable inventions (art. 5.1)[1].

As for the stated conditions for patentability, debate continues on whether the sequencing of a gene or part of it, isolated in the laboratory or obtained by other

[1] The EPO accepted, even prior to the approval of the Directive 98/44/CE, the patentability of some human proteins (i. e., relaxin). OEP, resolution, 18 January 1995.

technical process is really inventive. Indeed, the emphasis in this regard that a gene or DNA functional fraction can be identified with a chemical molecule, but an essential difference persists, which lies in that what really matters in that molecule is the genetic information, which it is the carrier and not its support as such; if the structure of that information "is identical to that of a natural element, we have a discovery and not before an invention." Therefore, contrary to the position of the Directive, a doctrinal trend maintains that reproduction by a technical procedure or isolation of that information does not constitute an inventive step, essential presupposition for recognizing the patent, notwithstanding that the procedure itself could be the technical procedure of reproduction or isolation of the human body element (the DNA sequence).

This discussion still remains, even if different courts have provided some legal criteria to face it. In fact, in 1998 the United States Patents and Trade Marks Office accepted the patenting of two human genes responsible for breast and ovarian cancer in women (BRCA1 and BRCA2) the early detection of which is highly effective in preventing these cancers. However, subsequently in 2010 a North American district judge annulled the patent of both genes, because it was considered that the mere purification of these genes does not on its own modify an essential characteristic of the DNA, namely, its nucleotide sequence, or more precisely the capacity to detect mutations in these genes (US District Court ruling of 29 March 2010 (Association for Molecular Pathology *v.* UPSTO)). The susceptibility of these patients to develop a cancer depends on whether the essential characteristics of the genes remain unaltered. Consequently, the purified genes are not something different from that which exists in nature. But in July 2011, an appeal to the Supreme Court of New York (Judgement 31 July 2011) partly overturned the decision, partly reverting to the previous situation, by recognising the patent under discussion in its ruling. However, warning was given that this would not extend to analyses of genetic sequences to determine the predisposition of patients to these illnesses.

Afterwards, the American Civil Liberties Union and the Public Patent Foundation filed a petition for certiorari with the Supreme Court with respect to the second Federal Circuit Decision. On November 30, 2012, the Supreme Court agreed to hear the plaintiffs' appeal of the Federal Circuit's ruling. Finally, on 13 June 2013, the Supreme Court of the United States ruled that "A naturally occurring DNA segment is a product of nature and not patent eligible merely because it has been isolated, but cDNA is patent eligible because it is not naturally occurring" (Association for molecular pathology et al. vs. Myriad Genetics, Inc, et al.). From that moment on, the discussion has resumed and nobody fails to recognise the major importance it can have from many different points of view (clinical, ethical, legal, economic).

11.3 The Limit of Public Order and Morality

The morality clause (Moral clause) enjoys special importance in everything that refers to synthetic biology, inasmuch as that in some sectors it has been argued that such an instrument could be used to curb seemingly immoral developments of this technology. Thus it is worthwhile bearing in mind some key points about this tool.

Chief among these is that, regardless of whether or not they can attend or not to the requirements of the patent, the European legal framework excludes the same inventions whose commercial exploitation would be contrary to public order or morality (art. 6.1). It is an exclusionary clause that already appeared in earlier European conventional legislation (CPE of 1973) and has been renewed in accordance with legislation introduced by the Directive. However, in reality it has never been applied, nor by EPO, or any other national court on EU territory, except as indicated below. This lack of application responds both to pragmatic reasons consistent with flexibilization development regarding the patent concession, as well as to the difficulty of its application, in the case of indeterminate legal concepts, whose content is always hard to unravel.

11.3.1 Explicit Cases of Patent Exclusion

The patent exclusion explicitly stated in the Directive are not a closed list of the patent limits on the grounds of public order or morality, but only state a few assumptions, for example, those assumptions that are an apparent contravention of those limiting principles.

11.3.1.1 Exclusions Relating to Animals

With regard to animals, the patent shall not be granted with respect to processes for modifying the genetic identity of animals that would mean, for the animals themselves, suffering or physical handicaps without substantial benefit to man or animal, nor animals resulting from such processes (art. 6.2, d).

11.3.1.2 Exclusions Concerning Human Beings

As a projection or realization of this general exclusion clause, some exclusion cases are expressly stated below. Thus, with regard to human biological material, the reproductive cloning procedures for human beings, processes for modifying the germ line genetic identity of human beings and the methods in which human embryos are used are excluded (art. 6.2, A, b and c).

In this regard, in all probability the case that has generated the most controversy concerning the exclusion or otherwise of the patent in virtue of the applicability of some of the possible grounds for exclusion, refers to patent human embryonic stem cells. Indeed, to the lack of Directive's precision on this possibility, other elements are added that have not helped clarify the situation, as some ill-considered decision of the EPO, -which had to be subsequently rectified- or the pressure exerted by powerful research groups dedicated to the development of new therapies with these cells (the transfer of these cells once differentiated in the laboratory) that expect to find in the protection granted by the patent the best way to ensure millionaire returns. Recently, a judgement of the EU Court of Justice (Great Hall) has cleared the issue momentarily (see Sect. 11.3.1.2.2), but only partially because although it has established a binding interpretation on the definition of embryo, it has left the question open as to whether or not it can be considered an embryo to the embryonic stem cells.

The Previous Discussion of the Scope of the Exclusion of the Patent Regarding Human Embryos

The key question at this point is whether the exclusion of the patent on methods in which human embryos are used, include the use of embryonic stem cells, because although it is clear that the origin of these cells are found in extracted human embryos, their subsequent processing in the laboratory does not involve the use of these embryos as such, but only the separated cells of the same. However, according to another interpretative criterion of this clause, in this case relevant to having originated in the EPO (EPO, Decision of the Enlarged Board of Appeal dated 25 November 2008 G 2/06), the fact that generally the obtention of stem cells involves the destruction of the corresponding embryo also means that it would be using embryos, which would be reason to exclude the patent. Finally, specifically as to whether the mere use of embryonic cells falls under the exclusion clause, in light of its origin, it is argued that only the use of totipotent stem cells would fall under the rule of exclusion, given its ability to give rise to a complete being, therefore, also a human embryo; this would not happen with multipotent and pluripotent cells, which do not enjoy that capacity.

The trend, which is spreading, moreover without sound legal basis (but the same is true for other interpretive positions mentioned), is to consider that this case is not included in the exclusion cause of the mentioned patent and therefore should recognise the patent to the derived stem cells as well as those modified in the laboratory.

On the other hand, within the EU Member States framework it is open to diverse trends. Thus, the German Federal Patent Court (2006) has stated that there is no patentable product obtained from human tissue, restriction that seems to go even beyond the European regulation.

Finally, there is the "Edinburgh patent" case, according to which the patent was granted with respect to the genetic modification of mammalian stem cells in order to provide them with a survival advantage compared to other unwanted differentiated cells (1999); by not specifying that they were non-human mammals, because mammals in English is a generic sense, which also covers humans if not otherwise specified, it might be assumed that the patent could also be extended to humans, which was contrary to the public order clause and caused contestation of the patent before the EPO. After a long process, the EPO has maintained this patent with amendments, in order to restrict its indicated scope.

The discussion of the criminal aspects at this point revolves around whether it should be prohibited and, where necessary, constitute a crime, the creation of human embryos for research purposes, as well as whether it is permissible to use stem cells from supernumerary embryos leftover from assisted reproductive techniques. The European Convention on Human Rights and Biomedicine prohibits the first (art. 18.2) And leaves to the discretion of the States the second, provided that, in the latter case, is formally authorized by law (art. 18.1). It has also raised the possibility of cloning for the creation of clones to obtain from them stem cell for research. There are very different positions in the internal laws of the EU Member States. In Spain the PC considers the fertilization of human eggs with different procreation purposes, a crime (art. 161.2); non-criminal legislation allows the technique of ovocyte activation using nuclear transfer for research purposes, provided certain conditions are met (V. Law 14/2007, of July 3 of Biomedical Research (art. 33.2).

The Binding Interpretation of Embryo of the European Court of Justice (Brüstle v. Greenpeace Case)

As already anticipated, the EU Court of Justice (ECJ) has recently established a binding interpretation for all Member States on the patent exclusion clause in the procedures in which human embryos are used (Judgement 18 October 2011 (case Brüstle v. Greenpeace)). This interpretation has been detailed by the court in the following terms:

1. *Article 6(2)(c) of Directive 98/44/EC of the European Parliament and of the Council of 6 July 1998 on the legal protection of biotechnological inventions must be interpreted as meaning that*:

- *any human ovum after fertilisation, any non-fertilised human ovum into which the cell nucleus from a mature human cell has been transplanted, and any non-fertilised human ovum whose division and further development have been stimulated by parthenogenesis constitute a 'human embryo'*;
- *it is for the referring court to ascertain, in the light of scientific developments, whether a stem cell obtained from a human embryo at the blastocyst stage constitutes a 'human embryo' within the meaning of Article 6(2)(c) of Directive 98/44.*

2. *The exclusion from patentability concerning the use of human embryos for industrial or commercial purposes set out in Article 6(2)(c) of Directive 98/44 also covers the use of human embryos for purposes of scientific research, only use for therapeutic or diagnostic purposes which is applied to the human embryo and is useful to it being patentable.*
3. *Article 6(2)(c) of Directive 98/44 excludes an invention from patentability where the technical teaching which is the subject-matter of the patent application requires the prior destruction of human embryos or their use as base material, whatever the stage at which that takes place and even if the description of the technical teaching claimed does not refer to the use of human embryos.*

Understandably, it is likely that this ruling has a direct impact on emerging biotechnologies, and is open to a predictable and intense debate in the sector, which could be particularly important if they tried using their own synthetic biology tools to create some pseudo-embryonic human life form.

There are, however, some aspects of the judgement that are questionable. For the moment, the broad concept of the human embryo used can be the object of debate, that is, decisions as well as also including in this category the unfertilised human egg, which has been applied nuclear transfer techniques or parthenogenesis without waiting to see if the egg initiates the cell division process and is stabilized in the early stages (which is how it has been done generally, in light of the importance that is indicate by scientists that have the assurance that the cell division process has effectively begun, as it is not expected to be a physiological process, like a human egg fertilized by a human sperm).

Second, it takes no position on whether a human stem cell obtained from a human blastocyst stage embryo is already a human embryo or otherwise. It is therefore debatable whether it was wise to leave in the hands of national judges the decision at issue, "in the light of the advancement of science", by a diversity of approaches that can lead to the implementation of the same European legal norm (Directive 98/44/EC). Moreover, the determination of what is the status of science does not seem that it should be conditioned by the peculiarities of internal laws, but it is true that sometimes these have already settled this issue by adopting a restrictive or extensive legal definition on the human embryo. It must be recognized that it is a very complex task, both from a legal point of view as well as from the cultural traditions of member States, to establish a uniform concept of the embryo in relation with stem cells, without forgetting that, in contrast, the ECJ has not renounced the realisation of other controversial issues, such as cloning and parthenogenesis, which involve all researchers within the EU. At the very least, and perhaps for practical reasons, the ECJ could have explicitly reserved the possibility of resolving this issue in the future if so required, as it has done now with other aspects of the provision in consideration.

Finally, it should be noted that the ECJ considers the patent excluded when the prior destruction of human embryos is required or their use as raw material, or it has been stated or is not carried out as described. This position is consistent with the legal exclusion of the Directive of the methods designed for using human embryos, since the destruction of the embryo involves its use. This assertion, along with the fact that the use for diagnostic or therapeutic purposes applied to the embryo and that are useful for the same, strengthens the indirect protective legal framework of the human embryo which was already included in the Directive, and that the judgement emphasizes without a benefit of doubt.

11.3.2 Effects of the Patent Exclusion Clauses

It is very important to keep in mind that the granting of the patent is actually only the right to prevent third parties from exploiting the invention for commercial purposes without the consent or authorization of the patent holder. It probably has some relationship with these issues and the public policy clause that indicates the provision of the directive that the Commission should report every 5 years to the European Parliament and the Council on possible problems that this Directive has presented in relation to international agreements for the protection of human rights to which Member States have adhered to (Article 16, a).

Therefore, the admission of the patent should not be confused with the activity itself, the use of the product or procedure obtained, is permitted or prohibited in another legal system, for example, criminal law That is, to use an example, the patent does not recognize human cloning techniques, as they are considered contrary to public order or morality, as we have seen, but there could be, however, a state law that would allow - or to the contrary, prohibit it. For example, human reproductive cloning is a crime in some European legal systems (See e.g. art. 160.3 of the PC), which is an indication that commercial exploitation may be contrary to public order and reason to reject the patent, as ultimately the ECJ has held in its judgement as discussed earlier (Brüstle case). In the opposite case, the exclusion of the patent by specific legislation does not mean it should be understood as a prohibited activity (e.g., Commercial exploitation); only that it does not enjoy the protection afforded by a patent. Therefore, it should be emphasized that one thing is that it is permitted or not, the use of the product, and quite another to recognize or not, the patent of the product or process in which this activity rests. But it is clear that the exclusion of the patent introduces indirect mechanisms of protection against the product or process involved.

11.4 Towards New Aspects of the Patent or Alternative Solutions?

The crucial question to be addressed in any event, in the specific case of synthetic biology is whether its appearance is not a challenge or incomprehensible for the current patent system or, on the contrary, it will provide an appropriate legal framework appropriate within the same system. In this respect, it is noted that some solutions have been pointed out to satisfactorily adjust the current legal framework for this new technology. Thus, it seems clear that obtaining material without replication capacity, products, and procedures obtained, are subject to the general rules of the patent, outside the specific field of biotechnology. In view of the legal requirements for such a system, to start with they would not be excluded from the patent. Being more precise, we would indeed have to distinguish three cases:

- If material not capable of replication is involved, the products and procedures obtained will be subject to the general rules on patenting i.e. will lie outside the area of law relating to biotechnologies. From the point of view of the legal requirements of such a regulatory system, material capable of replicating itself will be excluded from patenting.
- If, on the contrary, material capable of replicating itself and which constitutes some new, simple life form (artificial life) is involved, the invention would be subject to the specific rules intended for this type of living organism. That is to say, as has been discussed above, currently the patenting of micro-organisms is allowed, from the legal point of view, understanding these to be not only unicellular organisms but also other simple multicellular forms that could be created in the laboratory.

- The laboratory creation of more or less complex multicellular living organisms seems to be an aim of synthetic biology that is only achievable in the medium to long term. And it is unthinkable, at least based on current scientific knowledge and technology, that it would be possible to "create" or "recreate" higher animals, specifically mammals. Consequently it seems unnecessary to evaluate this possibility, taking current axiological parameters as a starting reference point. Therefore it seems advisable at the moment to leave their evaluation for some time in the future. Nevertheless, according to current European legislation, the patenting of such hypothetical, substantially "recreated" mammals would be acceptable. However, the hypothetical future creation of human beings would probably come under the limiting clause on morality and public order, particularly during the initial embryonic phase.

Having said this, in strict observance with the current patent system, it is not however necessary to stress the existing uncertainties about the patent system being agile enough for investors when it comes to complex products that can be tributaries of a variety of partial patents of its respective components. Hence the scepticism, more or less justified, of some specialists and scientists who have come to propose a thorough review of the current patent system (see e.g., The Manchester Manifesto 2009) and even explore other alternative routes, capable of stimulating innovative activities and also provide a benefit of the same for the entire society.

Outside of the patent system, it is necessary to situate the open source and the business agreement pathways that undertake various forms of cooperation between enterprises in the same sector. In the first case it would involve the voluntary grouping of a number of companies in the same sector, undertaking to provide information resulting from their research, in exchange for an agreed price, leaving out of the group other players in the sector, that is, access to industrial information shared by the members of the same. This system, which has obvious advantages, deserves several objections, as complex structures will be needed, but which will be vulnerable from having to engage in good faith and in strict confidence with the participants, so that if any of them is breached, it will be necessary to resort to other legal instruments to support those previously known, such as business confidentiality (as an extended concept, depending on the case) and the patent itself, on which its resignation does not seem reasonable, but, additionally it can also promote practices contrary to competition, such as the establishment of domino positions and even cartels. The intervention of the courts of competition may be necessary when there are situations in which the abuse of a dominant position by a certain company can lead to serious dysfunctions for the smooth running of an entire biotechnology sector such as this.

Thus, the patent remains the required legal reference, although it is true that it needs a thorough revision that combines flexibility and efficiency of the patent with an adequate protection for biotechnological inventions. The use of alternative and complementary tools to the patent, subject to the conditions already set forth may be, in certain cases, a more than healthy initiative.

11.5 Conclusions

Throughout this study we have seen how the patent has been providing legal cover to modern biotechnology, a sector with a great innovative and productive potential. It is true that this solution has been through the flexibilization of some "classic" requirements of the patent, namely inventive activity, as opposed to discovery, which has given rise to conflicting judgements. Also the patents related to human embryonic material have been a subject of dispute.

More recently another pathway was proposed, even as an alternative to the patent, which is more flexible and dynamic, given the complexity that some biotechnological products or processes and in view also of the long and expensive resolution process for vindication by patent offices.

This study supports the validity of the patent as the most effective legal instrument to protect the results of the investigation, subject to the modifications required by the system before the present and future needs and also without prejudice of the possibility of using other complementary pathways.

References

Byk C (2009) La patente sobre células madre humanas. In: Romeo Casabona CM (ed) Retos de la investigación y comercialización de nuevos fármacos. Cátedra Interuniversitaria Fundación BBVA – Diputación Foral de Bizkaia de Derecho y Genoma Humano & Ed. Comares, Bilbao/ Granada

Comité de Bioética de España/Conselho Nacional de Ética para as Ciências da Vida (2011) Biología sintética. Opinión conjunta. Lisboa - Barcelona. 24 de octubre de 2011

Comité National Consultatif D'éthique Pour les sciences de la vie et la Santé. Avis nº 64 (2000) on L'Avant-Projet de loi portant la transposition. Dans le code de la propriété intellectuelle de la Directive 98/44/CE du Parlement Européen et du Conseil. en date du 6 juillet 1998. relative à la protection juridique des inventions biotechnologiques

De Miguel Beriain I Synthetic biology and IP rights: in defence of the patents system in J. Boldt (ed.), "Synthetic biology, Ethics and Society", Springer VS (under printing).

Kesselheim AS, Mello MM (2010) Gene patenting – is the pendulum swinging back? N Engl J Med 10(1056):1–4

Knoepffler N, Robienski J, Romeo Casabona CM (2011) Konfliktmanagement am Beispiel humaner Gentechnik und verbundener Techniken (IVF). Friedrich-Schiller-Universität Jena

Lobato García-Luján M (1995) Oficina Europea de Patentes: Decisión de 18 de enero de 1995 (Asunto Relaxina). Law Hum Genome Rev 3:177–192

Martín Uranga A (2011) Biopatentes biotecnológicas. Enciclopedia de Bioderecho y Bioética. Romeo Casabona CM (Dir.). Cátedra Interuniversitaria Fundación BBVA – Diputación Foral de Bizkaia de Derecho y Genoma Humano & Ed. Comares. Granada, pp 1225–1233

Martín Uranga A (2003) La protección jurídica de las innovaciones biotecnológicas. Especial consideración de su protección penal. Cátedra Interuniversitaria de Derecho y Genoma Humano. Ed. Comares, Bilbao

Mcmanis C (ed) (2007) Biodiversity and the law. Intellectual property. Biotechnology and traditional knowledge. Earthscan, London

Paredes Castañón JM (2001) La protección penal de las patentes e innovaciones tecnológicas. Mc Graw Hill, Madrid

Presidential Commission for the Study of Bioethical Issues (2010) The ethics of synthetic biology and emerging technologies Washington D.C.

Romeo Casabona CM (2001) La protección jurídica de las innovaciones biotecnológicas: la cuestión de su patentabilidad. IDEI, Madrid. Diez conferencias magistrales sobre nuevas tecnologías y propiedad industrial. nº extraordinario

Romeo Casabona CM (2010) Why patenting life is a controversial economical activity: European legal implementation and penal related issues. In: Romeo Casabona CM (ed) Global food security: ethical and legal challenges. Wageningen Academic Publ, Wageningen, pp 37–45

Schneider I (2010) Das Europäische Patentsystem. Wandel von Governance durch Parlamente und Zivilgesellschaft. Campus Verlag, Frankfurt am Main/New York

Schneider I (2011) Das EuGH-Urteil ‚Brüstle versus Greenpeace'(Rs. C-34/10): Bedutung und Implikationen für Europa. ZGE/IPJ: 475–510

Supreme Court of the United States, Association for molecutal pathology et al vs. Myriad Genetics, Inc, et al, Certiorari ot the United States Court of Appeals for the Federal Circuit

Chapter 12
Patentability of Synthetic Biology Under the European Patent Convention (EPC)

Francisco J. Fernandez y Brañas

Abstract In the biomedical field the developments of recent years in cloning, transgenic animals and plants, genome sequencing, stem cell research, pharmacogenomics and many other technologies have required important changes in the legislation and law interpretation of the Boards of Appeal of the European Patent Office. Although the extent of further developments is difficult to predict, the present law and jurisprudence provide a far more solid foundation to accommodate new developments than they have in the past.

It is foreseen that the new field of synthetic biology will not raise questions that cannot be answered by present legislation and interpretation of the law by the Boards of Appeal. The more "synthetic" biology becomes, the closer to classical chemical areas and the further away from the controversy raised by the patenting of products which exist in nature it becomes. The more "standardized" genetic and molecular engineering is, the more "predictable" and reliable it becomes for industrial and medical application.

Keywords Synthetic biology • European patent office • Moral clause • Intelectual property

12.1 Introduction

Synthetic biology is often defined as the "designing and engineering of biological parts, novel devices and systems as well as the redesigning of existing, natural

F.J. Fernandez y Brañas
Department of Biotechnology, European Patent Office, The Hague, The Netherlands
e-mail: ffernandez@epo.org

I. de Miguel Beriain and C.M. Romeo Casabona (eds.), *Synbio and Human Health: A Challenge to the Current IP Framework?*, DOI 10.1007/978-94-017-9196-0_12,

biological systems".[1] The technologies included in this definition are very diverse and build on existing metabolic engineering and genetic engineering techniques. Synthetic biology can be characterised by (a) the scaling up of classical metabolic engineering techniques on the basis of a deeper knowledge of the genetic background and metabolic pathways of microorganisms, (b) the chemical synthesis of tailored-made DNA and (c) the application of engineering principles to genetic technologies for the production of standardised building blocks which can be used in the design of new parts, devices and systems.

Numerous patent applications have been filed and granted in recent years for "engineered biological parts" or "redesigned biological systems". Patents in this area usually claim the production of chemical compounds by fermentation of engineered microorganisms, e.g. bacteria transformed with foreign genes or manipulated to over- or under-express some others. Furthermore, the use of bacterial strains with useful metabolic properties, mutated or transformed for production of chemicals, water treatment or bio-remediation is one of the oldest fields in biotechnology.[2] The production of artemisinic acid in yeast which can be transformed by chemical means into artemisinin and derivatives for the preparation of anti-malarial drugs (Balmer and Martin 2008)[3] is usually regarded as an example of synthetic biology. Although the concept of transferring genes from one species, genus or even kingdom to another (in the artemisinin case genes encoding enzymes are transferred from Artemisia annua to Saccharomyces) is at present being applied to bacteria, viruses, mammalian cells, GMOs (plant and animals) and others, these techniques have not always been categorized as "synthetic biology".

Similarly, many patent applications have been filed and granted for polynucleotides, oligonucleotides and proteins which do not exist in nature. These include fusion proteins, vectors, engineered antibodies, interfering RNA, engineered enzymes and a long list of other constructs, some of them approved for therapy and with many undergoing clinical trials. All these products are synthetic, in the sense that the natural wild type counterpart has been manipulated and modified, or has been created from scratch. Although many would consider these products the result of advanced genetic engineering and not synthetic biology, the borderline between the two remains blurred, and consensus as to the meaning of "synthetic biology" lies some way of.[4] Synthetic Biology is a cutting edge (bio) technology with deep

---

[1] The Royal Academy of Engineering, Synthetic Biology: scope, applications and implications, May 2009, ISBN 1-903496-44-6

[2] "Diamond vs Chakrabarty" decision regarding a US patent filed in 1972 in the US relates to a "a bacterium from the genus Pseudomons containing therein at least two stable energy-generating plasmids, each of said plasmids providing a separate hydrocarbon degradative pathway" This human-made, genetically engineered bacterium is capable of breaking down multiple components of crude oil. Because of this property, which is possessed by no naturally occurring bacteria, Chakrabarty's invention was believed to have significant value for the treatment of oil spills (http://supreme.justia.com/us/447/303/case.html#308)

[3] See also: *Nature*, Vol 440, 04-2006, 940–943.

[4] *Nature*, 27(12), December 2009, 1071–1073

roots in current molecular biology techniques albeit with unclear boundaries delimiting it from its close relatives genetic and metabolic engineering.

The application of engineering principles to biotechnology and the complete redesign of biological parts and systems make this field very attractive and at the same time create concerns and fears. It is attractive because it can lead to the development of future predictable biological systems such as synthetic microorganisms capable of producing chemical compounds, or medicaments tailored to the patient and capable of being delivered upon response to a specific physiological or pathological status. However it also creates anxiety and alarm in relation to potential environmental risks and ethical concerns. One of the points of public discussion is industrial property and the patenting of products derived from synthetic biology. The thesis of the present article is that the present European Patent Convention and the case law issued in the last 30 years by the European Patent Office in the biomedical field constitute a solid legal foundation able to accommodate the new developments of Synthetic Biology and provides for the granting of patents with a high presumption of validity and which are ethically correct from the perspective of the European Patent Convention and the European Directive 44/98/EC of 1998. It emphasises the principles of patentability under the European Convention in areas of synthetic biology such as synthetic microorganisms, pharmaceutical products, diagnostic tests and screening processes.

12.2 Patentability Requirements and Provisions Under the EPC Specific to Biological Inventions

After the approval of the European Directive on the protection of biotechnological inventions 44/98/EC in 1998, the essential articles of the Directive were incorporated into the EPC (Rules 26–29 EPC).[5] Rule 26 EPC refers to the European Directive as a supplementary means of interpretation and defines the terms "biotechnological

[5] http://www.epo.org/about-us/epo/legal-foundations.html. The European Patent Organization is an intergovernmental organization that was set up on 7 October 1977 on the basis of the European Patent Convention (EPC) signed in Munich in 1973. The Organization currently has 38 member States, comprising all the member states of the European Union together with Albania, Croatia, Serbia, the former Yugoslav Republic of Macedonia, Iceland, Liechtenstein, Monaco, Norway, San Marino, Switzerland and Turkey. Its mission to grant European patents in accordance with the EPC is carried out by the European Patent Office. The Organization has its seat in Munich (Art 6 EPC).

The European Patent Convention Act revising the EPC of 29 November 2000 entered into force on 13 December 2007. Upon entry into force of the revised text of the Convention, the text valid until that time (the "EPC 1973") ceased to apply (cf. Article 8(2) Revision Act).

After the grant of the European Patent and the publication in the European Patent Bulletin, the patent must be validated before the corresponding National Member State. The rights conferred by the European patent are, from that moment, the same as would be conferred by a national patent granted in that State. Infringements to the European Patent are dealt with by National law thereafter (Art 64 EPC)

invention" and "biological material". Biological material is, according to Rule 26, "any material containing genetic information and capable of reproducing itself or being reproduced in a biological system".

The European Directive (Art 3), the EPC (Art 52) and the TRIPS agreement (Art 27) consider patentable any invention, in any field of technology, provided that they meet the requirements of novelty, inventive step and industrial application. It follows that inventions relating in general to biological material and in particular to synthetic biology are prima facie patentable, provided that said inventions do not fall under the exceptions and exclusions to patentability (Art 52(2), Art 53(a)(b)(c) EPC, Art 27(2)(3) TRIPS).

Inventions concerning synthetic biology may relate to biological material according to the definition of Rule 26(3) EPC. It appears from this definition and the list of patentable inventions recited in Rule 27 EPC that the origin of the material is not relevant (biological material can be isolated from natural sources or be produced by means of a technical process, see Rule 27(a) EPC), as long it contains genetic information that reproduces itself or is reproducible in a biological system. Whether synthetic biology departs so much from natural biological systems so as to be considered "non-biological" is difficult to predict, and future case law may need to be established in this respect. Come what may, the European Patent Office has a long standing practice and a consistent case law in the assessment of the patentability of both biological and non biological material.

12.3 Patentability of "Synthetic" Microorganisms

According to current practice and case law of the EPO, the term "microorganism" is interpreted broadly and includes not only bacteria and yeasts but also fungi, algae, protozoa and human, animal and plant cells, plasmids and viruses.[6] In principle, synthetic "protocells", cells with a synthetic minimal genome or synthetic viruses (Balmer and Martin 2008)[7] are likely to be regarded as "microorganisms", though further interpretation from the Boards of Appeal of the EPO in this respect may be required. Under Article 53(b) EPC and Rule 27(c) microbiological processes and the products thereof are patentable. The concept of microbiological processes encompasses processes, microorganisms as such and the products made or modified through microbiological processes.[8]

From the above one can draw the conclusion that future processes to produce or modify chemical compounds using "synthetic" microorganisms as well as the synthetic microorganisms as such would in principle be regarded as patentable inventions. This is currently the case with engineered bacteria and the application of classic techniques of metabolic engineering. Typically, such patent applications

[6] See T356/93, OJ 1995, 545 ; See also: G1/98, OJ 2000, 111

[7] See also: *Syst Synth Biol*, Vol 3, 55–63, 2009.

[8] See T356/93, OJ 1995, 545.

may contain claims covering processes to produce or modify chemical compounds, chemical compounds as such and the microorganisms used in the processes. The microorganism may be claimed as a specific strain deposited with a depositary institution (Rule 31 EPC). Claims of broader scope are not excluded, provided there is sufficient technical support and the whole scope of the claim can be reproduced without undue burden by the skilled person.[9]

Concerns over the scope or the breadth of the claims of recent patent applications as filed have been voiced in the media.[10] However it should be born in mind that the filing of a patent application does not in itself impose any constraints on the applicants as to the nature and initial subject-matter for which protection is sought. Only formal requirements and payment of patent fees have to be met. When a patent application is published (18 months after the filing/priority date), it has not been fully scrutinized and examined by patent offices. Only a preliminary opinion on patentability is given to the applicant together with the search report (PCT and EP procedures), but this preliminary opinion, in the case of the PCT international procedure, is only made available to the public upon entry into the national or regional (for example European) phase. This entry may be delayed up to 31 months from the priority date (R 159 EPC). Therefore for PCT applications, only the search report containing the relevant prior art is available to the public until the application enters the regional phase or the applicant requests a preliminary examination (IPER). This fact introduces an element of uncertainty regarding the patentability of the claims contained in the patent application in the PCT international phase.

An example of a broadly drafted patent application[11] is EP06825527 stemming from WO2007047148, dealing with the production of microorganisms containing a minimal set of genes. After the international application entered the regional European phase, the Examining Division in charge of the application objected as to lack of novelty and lack of inventive step and considered that the application as filed did not sufficiently disclose the invention. The application has now been abandoned and no divisional application has been filed.

During examination of an application in the European phase under the EPC the breadth of a claim is examined in detail. Firstly, the broader the claim, the more likely it may be affected by the disclosure of prior art and be objected to for lack of novelty (Art 54 EPC). Secondly, the broader the claim, the more susceptible it is to prior art disclosures regarding inventive step (Art 56 EPC). Thirdly, and under the assumption that the subject-matter of the claims has been declared new and inventive, a full examination will be carried out regarding clarity of the claims, the presence in the claims of the essential technical features necessary to perform the invention (Art 84 EPC) and whether the whole scope of the claim can be carried out by the skilled person without undue burden or the application of inventive skill (sufficiency of disclosure, Art 83 EPC).

---

[9] See T409/91; T435/91.

[10] See: http://www.bbc.co.uk/news/10150685

[11] *Nature Biotechnology*, 25: 822 (2007) http://www.nature.com/nbt/journal/v25/n8/full/nbt0807-822.html

The mere fact that a claim is broad is not in itself a ground for considering the application as not complying with the requirements of sufficiency of disclosure of Art 83 EPC. Only if there are serious doubts, substantiated by verifiable facts, may the application be objected to in this respect.[12] It is not among the tasks of a patent office to carry out the invention claimed in order to examine if the invention has been described in a manner sufficiently complete for the skilled person to put it into practice. Therefore the examination of the requirements of Article 83 EPC may be based only on serious doubts supported by facts and evidence (e.g. published documents, experiments carried out by other parties or common general knowledge). In the absence of serious doubts Examining Divisions and Opposition Divisions must accept that the requirements of sufficiency of disclosure are met.

The procedure under the EPC comprises mechanisms by which third parties may submit comments or evidence relevant for the patentability of the invention, including sufficiency of disclosure. Comments may be filed by third parties at any stage of the procedure after the publication of the application (Art 115 EPC).Up to 9 months after the publication of the grant of the patent any person may oppose the patent (Art 99 EPC) on the grounds, among others, of lack of sufficiency of disclosure (Art 100(b) EPC), and provide arguments or evidence in this respect. Decisions of the Examining Division and the Opposition Division may be appealed by any party to the proceedings (Art 106 EPC).

The general guiding principle is that the scope of a granted patent should correspond to its technical contribution to the state of the art.[13] Although this requires a difficult balancing exercise between "scope" of the claims and "disclosure" in the description, it is believed that the current practice of the European Patent Office, the consistent case law of the Boards of Appeal and the procedural mechanisms for other parties to intervene result in a very reliable procedure and a granted patent with a high presumption of validity.

12.4 The Economic Effect of the Patent and Synthetic Microorganisms

It is known that the economic effect of a patent is determined among others, by the type of license agreement and other economic factors.[14] In relation to synthetic microorganisms the opinion has often been expressed in the media that broad patents should not be granted for synthetic microorganisms in order to prevent the creation of a monopoly which would place this new field of technology in the hands

[12] See: T19/90

[13] See: T409/91; T435/91

[14] *Genetics in Medicine*, Vol 12, Apr 2010, Suppl

of a few. The Boards of Appeal of the EPO have noted however that Art 52 EPC expresses the general principle of patentability for inventions which are industrially applicable, new and inventive, and that the EPO has not been vested with the task of taking into account the economic effects of the grant of patents in specific areas and of restricting the field of patentable subject-matter accordingly.[15] In a decision relating to the BRCA1 case,[16] the Board in question stated that the consequences for public health care of the exploitation of the patent are the result of the exclusionary nature of the rights granted by a patent, that is the right to stop competitors from using the invention. This right is the same in all technical fields, and there is no basis in the EPC to distinguish between inventions in different technical areas in this respect.

12.5 Ethical Issues

Article 53 EPC defines the exceptions to patentability. According to this article, European patents shall not be granted in respect of "*inventions the commercial exploitation of which would be contrary to "ordre public" or morality; such exploitation shall not be deemed to be so contrary merely because it is prohibited by law or regulation in some or all of the Contracting States*". How should this Article be interpreted in relation to issues such as uncontrolled release of artificial microorganisms in the environment, bioterrorism and patenting and the creation of monopolies (Balmer and Martin 2008)

With regard to patent monopolies, it has already been said above that the EPO cannot take into account the economic effect of the grant of the patent to restrict the field of patentable subject-matter, and that the exclusionary nature of the right conferred by the patent is inherent to the system and common to all technical fields.

With respect to bioterrorism, in the rare case that an application is directed to this type of criminal or other similar offensive behaviour, Art 53 is applied and the application excluded from patentability (similarly with a letter-bomb or anti-personnel mines). Nevertheless "*the mere possibility of abuse of an invention is not sufficient to deny patent protection pursuant to Art 53(a) EPC if the invention can also be exploited in a way which does not and would not infringe "ordre public" and morality*".[17]

A patent application for a synthetic microorganism will normally have an acceptable non-offensive use (e.g. bioremediation, biochemical transformations, diagnosis, therapy, use as an experimental reagent etc.). Nevertheless a possible or hypothetical offensive use could be envisaged by the reader (e.g. bioterrorism).

---

[15] See: G1/98, OJ 2000, 111, reasons, 3.9

[16] See: T1213/05

[17] See: T866/01, reasons 5.7–5.9, 9.8; Guidelines for examination in the European Patent Office, Part G, Chapter II, 4.

The refusal of an application under Art 53(a) on the basis of this possible offensive use would be unjustified, as long as there are acceptable purposes for which the invention can be used.[18] Classical examples typically given as illustration of the above are a process to break open lock safes or a copying machine with an improved precision of reproduction. Although both inventions could be misused by burglars to break safes or copy bank notes, the acceptable purposes prevail. In such cases, the deletion of references in the application to offensive uses is required (Rule 48(1) (a)).[19]

12.6 Environmental Issues

The risk of release of microorganisms to the environment, accidentally or intentionally, and the effect of the environment on the released microorganisms and the possibility of further mutations and contamination of the natural "gene pool" is a known concern in the media (Balmer and Martin 2008). According to T356/93[20] the concept of "ordre public" encompasses the protection of the environment and accordingly, inventions the exploitation of which is likely to seriously prejudice the environment are to be excluded from patentability as being contrary to "ordre public". The Boards of Appeal of the EPO have clarified that the questions relating to "ordre public" and "morality" of Art 53(a) EPC cannot be disregarded by the EPO when assessing patentability,[21] and have to be answered in each particular case depending on the merits thereof and the particular facts and evidence in question.[22] It should be born in mind that in most cases the environmental risk in relation to the exploitation of the invention cannot be anticipated from the disclosure of the patent application. It is only after comprehensive tests carried out by the competent bodies, not available to the patent offices during the prosecution of the case, that a realistic assessment is made by the authorities and a decision on the exploitation of the product taken.[23] This is one of the reasons why a patent does not give authorisation to exploit an invention, and later regulatory approval by the competent authorities must be obtained. The EPO is not vested with the authority to carry out tasks which are the duty of regulatory bodies.[24]

---

[18] See: G1/98, OJ 2000, 111; Guidelines for examination in the European Patent Office, Part G, Chapter II, 4.1.2

[19] Guidelines for examination in the European Patent Office, Part G, Chapter II, 4.1.2

[20] See: T356/93, OJ 1995, 545, reasons point 5.

[21] See: T19/90, reasons point 5.

[22] See: T356/93, OJ 1995, 545.

[23] See: T356/93, OJ 1995, 545, reasons 18.4.

[24] See: T356/93, OJ 1995, 545.

12.7 Synthetic Biology and Therapeutic Applications

The potential application of synthetic biology to the pharmaceutical and medical field has been extensively described in the literature[25] and there is the expectation that synthetic biology will bring dramatic advances in drug discovery, drug production, drug delivery and treatment of diseases such as cancer. Many of these developments are still to come and many will be filed as patent applications. However, the patentability issues likely to emerge in the future can already be answered with the present legal framework of the European Patent Convention and the case law of the Boards of Appeal.

12.8 Screening Processes and Biological Models

In vitro screening processes and synthetic biological systems to discover potential drugs or pathological behaviour[26] are normally patentable, provided the classical requirements of novelty, inventive step and industrial applicability are complied with. In vivo screening processes using animal models are objected to under Article 53(a) for moral reasons if humans are not explicitly excluded from the scope of the claims. According to Rule 28(d), "processes for modifying the genetic identity of animals which are likely to cause them suffering without any substantial medical benefit to man or animal, and also animals resulting from such processes" are not patentable. Consequently transgenic non-human animals and processes using them are only patentable when there is a positive weighting between the (likelihood of) medical benefit and the (likelihood of) animal suffering.[27] For environmental matters see above.

12.9 Drug Production

There are no particular problems associated with the patentability of processes for the production of drugs using advanced techniques of synthetic biology, the production of artemisinin in yeast being a typical example of a cost-effective alternative means of production of an anti-malarial drug.[28]

---

[25] *Nature Reviews Genetics*, Vol 11, May 2010, 367

[26] *Nature Reviews Genetics*, Vol 11, May 2010, 367

[27] See: T19/90; T315/03.

[28] See: *Nature*, Vol 440, 04-2006, 940–943; see also Balmer and Martin (2008).

12.10 Drug Delivery and Therapeutic Therapy

Under European legislation, Article 53(c) EPC, European patents shall not be granted in respect of "*methods for treatment of the human or animal body by surgery or therapy and diagnostic methods practiced on the human or animal body; this provision shall not apply to products, in particular substances or compositions, for use in any of these methods*". Therapy includes prophylaxis and treatment, as well as the relief of pain, discomfort, malfunction or incapacity.[29] The prohibition in relation to therapeutic and surgical methods is absolute, and no claim can be granted which includes at least one step falling within the methods of Article 53(c), see below with regard to diagnostic methods. The exclusions of Art 53(c) are based on public health considerations, and the fact that "*physicians should be free to take all actions they consider suitable to prevent or to cure a disease, and in this exercise they should remain uninhibited by patents*".[30]

However, Article 54(4) allows the patentability of any substance or composition, comprised in the state of the art, for use in the methods of Article 53(c), provided that its use for any such method is not comprised in the state of the art. This is what is commonly known as a "first medical use", which is granted to the first time that a substance or composition is shown to be useful in therapy. This use-related product claim takes the form of "compound X for use as a medicament" or similar drafting, which gives a broad generic protection for the product when used in any therapeutic method.

When a substance or composition is already known to have been used in a method of treatment referred to in Article 53 (c) EPC, it may still be patented under Article 54(5) for any second or further therapeutic use, provided said use is new and inventive. The claims are drafted in the form "compound X for use in the treatment of the specific disease Y". The use may not only be the treatment of a new disease, but also the treatment of the same disease by a different therapeutic method such as the dosage regime of the drug,[31] the route of administration of the drug[32] or the specific patient population to be treated.[33] In contrast with the general principle applied to product claims, the novelty (and non-obviousness, if any) of a use-related product claim under Art. 54(5) EPC is derived from the intended medical use. This exception to the novelty requirement applies only to substances and compositions and cannot be extended to other products, such as an apparatus, instrument or device.[34] A claim directed to a device for an intended medical use (e.g. an implantable biosensor, etc.) is to be construed as a claim directed to a device that is *suitable for* that medical use and would consequently lack novelty if the device is known in the prior art.

---

[29] See:T144/83; T19/86

[30] See: G2/08, OJ 28–10-2010, reasons, 5.3.

[31] See: G2/08, OJ 28–10-2010

[32] See: T51/93

[33] See: T19/86

[34] See: T 1172/03

The present legal framework offers sufficient scope for patenting the intended medical uses of products derived from synthetic biology techniques. Different genetic constructs (switches for controlled and tunable gene delivery, time delay genetic circuits, self-destruct systems, etc.) can be patented as such or in terms of first or subsequent use-related product protection offered by Article 54(4) (5) EPC. The same can be said for engineered viruses, bacteria and eukaryotic cells.

12.11 Diagnostic Methods

Article 53(c) EPC prohibits the patenting of diagnostic methods carried out on the human or animal body. According to the Enlarged Board of Appeal,[35] to be defined as a method of diagnosis excluded from patentability the claim should contain the following four phases: (i) an examination phase involving the collection of data, (ii) the comparison of the data with standard values, (iii) the finding of any significant deviation and (iv) the attribution of the deviation to a particular clinical picture. Only in the case where all the steps that have technical character are carried out on the human or animal body is the method excluded under Article 53(c). Typically, methods where the collection of data is done in vitro or in a sample are immediately accepted as patentable. Devices (for example, bio-sensors) are always patentable as such, provided they are new and inventive.

12.12 Conclusion

The topic of synthetic biology and patents is often analyzed within the same perspective and with the same arguments commonly used against the patenting of any other biological material. Detractors of the patent system often argue that if gene patenting, patents on diagnostic methods, patents on stem cells etc. pose a threat to society, then synthetic biology goes beyond that menace by granting monopolies for very dangerous and unreliable scientific developments to a few. The arguments disregard the contribution and support that patent protection has provided in past decades to innovation, particularly in the field of medicine and health.

There are numerous examples of developments which have been secured by patents, from the production of virus-free blood derivatives (immunoglobulins, anti-hemophilic factors and the like) to the production of mediators like interferon, erythropoietin or interleukin or hormones like insulin for human administration. Major advances in cancer diagnosis, and the administration of very successful anti-cancer drugs are today possible thanks to the knowledge of the molecular and genetic factors involved in cancer and the expression markers present on cancer cells. The humanization (making human or human-like) of antibodies has seen the

[35] See: G1/04

greatest advances in cancer treatment ever. The future of personalized medicine, a patient-tailored treatment based on genomic or proteomic characteristics, is already a reality and will become progressively more relevant in the future. The advances made in human and animal vaccination could not have been imagined a few decades ago.

Equally, through the establishment and genetic modification of microorganisms, the very clean and environmentally friendly production of chemical compounds (amino acids for animal feed, bio-polymers, bio-fuels, starch, ethanol, antibiotics etc.) has been achieved. Efficient cleaning of sewage and residual waters is now made possible with cultured bacteria.

It is doubtful that the above achievements could have been made without patents. The contribution of public funds to research and development is limited, and not only public, but also private investment is necessary to find better medicaments against cancer, to cure or palliate orphan diseases, to prevent and cure systemic infections and to provide safer and cleaner industrial processes. The difficulty of the bio-medical sector to finance the future development of new drugs is well known. Bio-medical innovation is becoming progressively complex, expensive, uncertain and heavily burdened.[36] The patent system palliates this situation and offers a safeguard to the investments made. Patents guarantee a financial return and make developments which require vast investments of very high risk sustainable. The exclusionary nature of the patent system is inherent to it and forms the basis for this reward to the innovation made.

The role of the European Patent Office is to support innovation by granting patents with a high presumption of validity. Only the Examining Divisions and Opposition Divisions of the European Patent Office are responsible for the examination of European patent applications and European Patents (Articles 18 and 19 EPC, a three examiner Division possibly enlarged with a legally qualified examiner). Their decisions can be appealed before the Boards of Appeal (Article 106 EPC), an independent second instance judicial body of the European Patent Office, and the granted patent can always be challenged before the National Courts. The examination of the patent application determines if the classical requirements of patentability are met and whether the commercial exploitation of the invention is not contrary to "ordre public" or morality and other exceptions defined in Art 53 EPC. However, it is not for the European Patent Office to decide which food should appear on the shelf of a supermarket or which drug may be administered to a patient. For this to happen, the national or supra-national regulatory bodies take responsibility and have the authority to decide. Neither the economic impact of the patent monopoly nor how this exclusionary right may affect the service offered by health providers has any role in the granting process. The public regulatory authorities are there to control and limit the general principle of market freedom.

It is worth reminding the reader that a patent application is not equivalent to a granted patent. Only when the application has been examined for patentability requirements in the European Patent Office is there some certainty about the breadth

[36] *Nature Biotechnology*, 30: 964–975, 2012

of the claims and the validity of the patent. The claims of the published patent application only reflect the wish of the applicant to obtain the maximum protection possible for the invention and the need to have a tactically broad position to fall back upon during examination. Only about 30–40 %[37] of published patent applications filed in biotechnology before the European Patent Office result in a granted patent. In almost all cases the granted claims differ notably (with narrower scope) from the claims of the patent application as published.

In the biomedical field the developments of recent years in cloning, transgenic animals and plants, genome sequencing, stem cell research, pharmacogenomics and many other technologies have required important changes in the legislation and law interpretation of the Boards of Appeal of the European Patent Office. Although the extent of further developments is difficult to predict, the present law and jurisprudence provide a far more solid foundation to accommodate new developments than they have in the past.[38]

It is foreseen that the new field of synthetic biology will not raise questions that cannot be answered by present legislation and interpretation of the law by the Boards of Appeal. The more "synthetic" biology becomes, the closer to classical chemical areas and the further away from the controversy raised by the patenting of products which exist in nature it becomes. The more "standardized" genetic and molecular engineering is, the more "predictable" and reliable it becomes for industrial and medical application.

Disclaimer: *The present article reflects the personal views of the author which may not necessarily be identical with the official position of the European Patent Office on the subject.*

References

Balmer A, Martin P (2008) Synthetic biology: social and ethical challenges. Institute for Science and Society/University of Nottingham, Nottingham

Genet Med (2010) Gold ER, Carbone J. Myriad Genetics: In the eye of the policy storm 12(Suppl)

Nature (2006) Ro DK. Production of the antimalarial drug precursor artemisinic acid in engineered yeast. 440:940–943

Nature Biotech (2009) 27(12):1071–1073

Nature Biotechnol (2012) Fernandez JM, Stein RM, Lo AW. Commercializing biomedical research through securitization techniques 30:964–975

Nature Rev Genet (2010) Khalil AS, Collins JJ, Synthetic biology: applications come of age. 11(5):367–379

Syst Synth Biol (2009) Deplazes A and Huppenbauer M, Synthetic Organisms and living machines: Positioning the products of synthetic biology at the borderline between living and non-living nature. 3:55–63

The Royal Academy of Engineering (2009) Synthetic biology: scope, applications and implications. Royal Academy of Engineering, London. ISBN 1-903496-44-6

---

[37] % of the total of EP, Euro-PCT and PCT (EPO as ISA) patent applications filed before the EPO.

[38] European Commission, Patenting DNA sequences (polynucleotides) and scope of protection in the European Union: an evaluation. S J R Bostyn, 2004, EUR21122, Dir Gen for Research food quality and safety. Paragraph 10.14.

Chapter 13
Synthetic Biology and IP Rights: In Defence of the Patent System

Iñigo de Miguel Beriain

Abstract The idea of intellectual property rights has been the subject of considerable debate in recent years. The raising of synthetic biology has contributed to enforce it. This paper defends the idea that, despite its doubtless defects, patent system continues to be the best way to encourage research in fields such as synthetic biology related to human health. The need for change that this sector seems to demand is not so much related to the instruments used to protect intellectual property as the way in which they are used.

If the companies that work in the field of synthetic biology reproduce the pharmaceutical industry models it will indeed be possible that this promising discipline will not be adequately developed. But this will not be due to patenting itself but rather to a wrongful mindset adopted by those who participate in the market. It is therefore necessary for public authorities to intervene actively to foster attitudes in favour of cooperation, as far as cooperation is more advantageous not only for society but also in order to develop this sector.

The policy maker's task will be to design instruments for stimulation where private initiative is incapable of generating cooperation mechanisms by its owns means. Conduct which tries to exploit the nature of patenting to obtain individual profit and contributes nothing to help synthetic biology advance must be carefully monitored according to public interest, while public stimulus must be used to promote the maximum opening up of the new discoveries to the public.

This paper is also related to the research project Synbio, Análisis de las implicaciones de la biología sintética en el ámbito de la propiedad intelectual (Código S-PE12UN013), SAIOTEK 2012 Departamento de Industria, Innovación, Comercio y Turismo del Gobierno Vasco.

I. de Miguel Beriain
Interuniversity Chair in Law and the Human Genome, University of the Basque Country, Universidad del País Vasco, Euskal Herriko Unibersitatea/Universidad de Deusto, Bilbao, San Sebastián, Spain
e-mail: idemiguelb@yahoo.es

I. de Miguel Beriain and C.M. Romeo Casabona (eds.), *Synbio and Human Health: A Challenge to the Current IP Framework?*, DOI 10.1007/978-94-017-9196-0_13,

Keywords Synthetic biology • Open source • Moral clause • Patent trolls • Patent sharks • Access to knowledge • Intellectual property rights • Anticommons

13.1 Introduction

On 26 November 2009 a group of leading intellectuals, including a number of Nobel Prize winners, such as Joseph Stiglitz and John Sulston, published The Manchester Manifesto.[1] This Manifesto advocated for a thorough review of the current intellectual property system. The changes proposed would establish a new legal model which they hoped would allow a more efficient and fair development of new technologies, such as synthetic biology. The manifesto aimed to combine the stimulation of innovation with an equitable distribution of the benefits from such activity to the whole society. The reaction to this declaration was not slow in coming. Just 1 day later, the Chartered Institute of Patent Attorneys (CIPA) published a note in which it criticised the authors' views on patents as 'ill-informed and misleading'.[2]

The discussion described above is just one example of how the idea of intellectual property rights in general and patents in particular has been the subject of considerable debate in recent years. The possibility of deciphering the human genome triggered a fierce argument between those who advocated allowing the patenting of our genes and those who, in contrast, considered that this would be an outrage against human dignity. Subsequent scientific development has only deepened the differences that separate the two points of view. The emergence of technologies such as synthetic biology is a good example of this, as far as its very nature presents substantial challenges to the current regulatory framework. The extreme complexity of a technology that combines such diverse disciplines as biology, chemistry, engineering and computing cannot be easily managed by means of a legal paradigm created in a world in which modern sciences, such as synthetic biology, did not yet exist.

However, the principal problem posed by synthetic biology is not so much its technical complexity, but rather its ability to question the fundamental principles of patent systems, posing questions such as: Is it possible to maintain that this system is efficient for the development of synthetic biology or does it, on the contrary, act as an obstacle which will impede future progress? Does patenting create the ideal regulatory framework for stimulating the emergence of efficient and competitive markets or, in contrast, does it tend to discourage investment in a fragmented market where monopolies ultimately emerge?

---

[1] See: http://www.isei.manchester.ac.uk/TheManchesterManifesto.pdf. Accesed at 12 February 2013

[2] See: http://www.cipa.org.uk/pages/press/article?D5C2CBED-894B-488B-ACD2-07B01E204A06. Accesed at 12 February 2013. The CIPA note was subsequently commented on by John Harris, Sarah Chan and John Sulston, on behalf of The Manchester Manifesto Group: http://www.isei.manchester.ac.uk/themanchestermanifesto/responses/ Accesed at 12 February 2013

The objective of this paper is to propose some responses to these questions based on the study of a specific conceptual framework, namely that of synthetic biology related to human health. This is the part of the market where the tendency to follow the patterns established by the pharmaceutical industry is more pronounced and therefore where questions such as those posed can best be studied.

13.2 Regulating Synthetic Biology: Basic Premises

As mentioned, my objective here is to discuss whether patent system is an efficient mean of optimising the development of synthetic biology in the field of human health. However, before starting that discussion, it is worth clarifying some ideas that are, in my opinion, fundamental for supporting my argument.

The first is purely conceptual. In my opinion, synthetic biology must not be conceived as a new discipline on the basis of its subject matter, which does not differ from that of genetic engineering, but rather on the basis of the mindset that is required to manage it. If synthetic biology is constructed on the same theoretical basis as genetic engineering, it will just be an extension of it. However, if it manages to detach itself from the mindset that accompanies genetic engineering, creating its own paradigm, it will be much easier to avoid some of the clichés that would otherwise hamper its development.

In this respect, it is thought that synthetic biology has emerged as the result of a mixture of different knowledge areas, amongst which are biology, engineering, chemistry, computing, etc. Each one of these different disciplines and the markets they create behaves in a completely different way. The question to clarify in the case of synthetic biology is which mindset will finally succeed. This will give us the first important clue about the usefulness of a patenting system applied to this technology. In my opinion, synthetic biology must be considered as a complex technology, such as electronics or software, as opposed to biotechnology in general, which is a discrete technology, i.e. a technology where the majority of the new products emerge as a consequence of occasional discoveries. It would therefore be a monumental error to think of synthetic biology as if it were a *biotechnology* applied to human health. As has been said, it must be conceived as a complex technology that will only be successful if it imitates the mindset of the technologies that share this characteristic. It will be much simpler to optimise its development if we are conscious of this issue when thinking about the best way of applying rules to synthetic biology, as we will immediately tend to copy the stimulation patterns for the electronic industry and not those for the pharmaceutical industry.

The second idea that I would like to underline is purely ethical and consists of the fact that the existence of patents is not a requirement of justice. It is not true that if patents did not exist we would be violating a fundamental human right to enjoy the benefits of our efforts. Given that this statement seems to contravene Article 27 of the Universal Declaration of Human Rights, which states that *"everyone has the right to the protection of the moral and material interests resulting from any scientific, literary or artistic production of which he is the author"*, it is worth making a brief comment about this. There are at least three reasons why this statement can be sustained without a human right being violated. First, as James Wilson has argued, it is possible that there are no real reasons for thinking that the right to intellectual property is a fundamental right. Second, to state that everyone has the right to enjoy the benefits of their efforts does not necessarily mean that the mechanism for satisfying this right has to be patenting. Without going further than the methods that already exist, copyright constitutes a widely accepted alternative to patents. It is used, for example, in the development of software. Third, even if this right did exist and had to be protected by patents, there would never be a situation where we could talk about an unlimited right. As the mechanism of public patent licences demonstrates, these can be limited when there are public interest reasons for doing so. Consequently, it can be concluded from the above that the right to patenting is not a basic human right but rather a legal right, as there are other forms of protection for intellectual property. Furthermore, and even if a right to patenting can be justified, we should always settle some limits on it according to public interest considerations.

However, concluding that an individual does not have a human right to a patent as the result of his/her creative effort, or that at the very least this patent will never be unlimited, does not in itself resolve the debate about the application of patents to synthetic biology related to human health. It simply shifts the argument to one of practicality. It may be that patents are not necessary for reasons of justice, but are essential for practical purposes. Consequently, the discussion turns towards the questions that I formulated in the introduction. Having established the necessary basis for the discussion, these questions can now be discussed below.

13.3 The Patenting System in Synthetic Biology Related to Human Health: A Constructive Analysis

In recent years, patent trolls have become a real problem for the development of all those technologies which rely on the production of complex items, composed of several parts and often protected by associated patents. Patent trolls or patent sharks could be defined as *"patent owners who do not intend to exploit a patent but who enforce their patent rights against purported infringers"* (Henkel and Reitzig 2008). The companies that could be characterized as patent trolls usually have hidden intellectual rights and appear, threatening to sue R&D companies, when their rights have been inadvertently infringed. In relation to this, it could be concluded that their business model consists on suing others or charging license or settlement fees without producing anything (Rutz 2009).

The main problem that these types of companies present is that they have sufficient capacity to slow down or even completely paralyse a specific research process. In a sector such as synthetic biology applied to health, where multiple parts often have to be used, it is not difficult for them to find a way of blocking a whole project where a substantial investment has already been made, through holding the patent of one of its essential parts.

The patent sharks, with all their influence, intentionally reach a position of power over many companies without the companies having sought directly to put themselves in such a position. In fact, the development of an artefact through synthetic biology can frequently infringe on a patent, through ignorance of the existence of that patent on one of the parts of which the artefact is composed. The very structure of the sector, as well as the difficulty involved in seeking detailed information about existing patents, result in this type of occurrence, no matter how much care is taken. And as Henkel and Maurer have stressed, in the case of synthetic biology, *"intellectual property rights will often be hard to identify, fragmented across many owners and sometimes overly abroad"* (Henkel and Maurer 2009).

This situation almost inevitably results in there being a significant risk in investing in fields such as synthetic biology applied to human health, since an investment which in principle is very profitable can see its dividends profoundly reduced through the need to make the payments demanded by those who hold a patent. Consequently, it can be stated that the system of patents can in the long term cause a reduction in interest in this technology by private initiative, due to the negative factors impeding its development.

Given this disturbing situation, it is clearly worth asking what we can do to prevent such counter-productive effects on the well-being of society. The problem is that it is not easy to find a way of preventing attacks by patent sharks or preventing companies active in this sector from blocking one another without at the same time eliminating the whole patenting system. In relation to this, I think that the patenting system is specifically based on the idea of blocking. What the patent gives the creator is not a right to exploit his or her invention, but rather the right to prevent others from doing so. However, this does not mean that it is not possible to adopt certain measures to make a system of patents compatible with efficient action in the market that one is trying to regulate. These measures can come from the strategy of the technological companies themselves or from intervention by public agencies. Regarding the former, in 2008 Henkel and Reitzig (Henkel and Reitzig 2008) proposed adopting various undoubtedly useful strategies:

1. *High-technology firms should move away from building huge patent portfolios for the purpose of cross-licensing with competitors.*
2. *Companies must simplify technical standards and create more modular designs.*
3. *Companies must begin cooperating with their competitors early in the R&D process.*
4. *Firms must foster interdepartmental and inter- company cooperation.*
5. *Companies must stop flooding patent offices with insignificant invention*

Regarding public institutions, there are various mechanisms which could contribute to improving the functioning of patents in relation to synthetic biology applied to human health. First, the length of time taken by patent applications related to this technology should be reduced. This would contribute substantially to the elimination of the blocking problem, above all when this is caused by patent sharks. However it would, without doubt, also produce dysfunctions. From a theoretical point of view it would represent a radical break from the general principle that patents do not discriminate with regard to the object to which they are applied. This would involve a drastic change in the paradigm. From the pragmatic point of view, it would lead to a considerable decrease in the profit/investment ratio in a sector which in itself already has a high level of risk associated with it. This would lead to a considerable decrease in the funding assigned to synthetic biology.

Second, there are the policies for raising the bar by the Patents Offices. These consist, basically, in reconsidering the criteria that are used for granting a patent, raising the level of the requirements to the point where it would be very complicated for "trivial" patents to be awarded. These trivial patents are the problem that, in the final analysis underlies the current issue of "patent sharking", together with the proliferation of patents on objects that are of little specific use. In this respect the position adopted by the European Patent Office is more adapted to the needs of this sector than the position adopted by other patent offices. The obvious problem of these measures is that they involve increasing the work load and the burden on the patent offices over and above that which they are currently experiencing. This is without taking into account the political obstacles that make adopting this line of action difficult.

The third of the options available is the use of the patent licence mechanism. This consists of the public bodies responsible for protecting the right to intellectual property being able, under specific circumstances, to temporarily or permanently suspend a company's right to a patent in the public interest. The obvious problem presented by this mechanism is that it represents a negation of the current intellectual property system and, if used too widely, could introduce a significant risk factor to the sector in which it occurred, frightening off the entry of private capital. Consequently, it should only be used as a last resort, i.e. in those cases where it was clear that in the field of synthetic biology applied to human health the patents system was not assisting the advancement of technological development, but rather was completely blocking it, and that this blocking was impeding the fulfilment of fundamental common interests. A more moderate alternative would be to use a system of compensation linked to the licence. This would constitute a form of full or partial expropriation of a property right in the public interest.

Finally, we must not forget that the public authorities have an undeniable ability to influence the way in which the market is organised. A policy of adequate subsidies or even the direct purchase of the patents on parts that are used in a standardised way can, in the final analysis, help the synthetic biology market applied to human health to function more like the electronics market than the pharmaceutical industry market. For this type of intervention to be carried out adequately, there would need to be an adequate identification of the needs of the market, or of the dynamics of the industry, which would make it possible to subsidise the development of the necessary parts, on condition that these would be subject to some form of semi-free use afterwards. Another way of achieving this would be to buy other parts able to be standardised in their first phases of use, so that we could benefit from the advantages of their standardisation. Similarly, linking the subsidies to the use of parts not protected by patents would contribute to making these the standard parts in the sector. This would result in a considerable increase in the efficiency of the system at a low cost.

13.4 Synthetic Biology, "Open Source" and Business Agreements

The problems presented by the patent system for the development of synthetic biology have led to various legal alternatives to this paradigm being proposed. The best known of these is the one that appeals for the use of "open source" in this sector, as synthetic biology contains all the elements necessary for this type of alternative to be productive.[3] There have been various attempts to put this alternative into practice. The best known are Cambia's Bioforge Initiative, started in 2005, and the work of The BioBricks Foundation (BBF), "*a not-for-profit organization which encourages the development and responsible use of technologies based on BioBrick™ standard DNA parts that encode basic biological functions*".[4] Up until now, however, the results of these projects have not been very satisfactory, which suggests that establishing an open source system in this sector will be complex.

Another type of formula that encourages cooperation between companies without renouncing the profits from individual ownership seems more promising. I refer to those situations where a group of companies that may even be competitors decide between themselves to create a library of common parts. These parts would be

[3] In relation to this, we cite a particularly interesting article by Joachim Henkel & Stephen Maurer, who wrote the following some years ago: "Synthetic biology contains almost all of the same ingredients that make embedded Linux successful. First, synthetic biology's parts approach emphasizes strong modularity. This allows the work of creating a parts library to be spread over many companies. It also makes it possible for companies to earn profits by patenting some parts while making others openly available. Second, we expect companies to have fairly idiosyncratic parts needs. This means that they cannot simply 'free ride' by waiting for others to make what they need. It also suggests that companies can often share parts without losing their technological 'edge' to competitors. Third, different companies will have different expertise. This suggests that community-based libraries will often outperform company ones. Finally, the synthetic biology market will probably include large numbers of small, idiosyncratic customers. This makes patent licensing less lucrative and, by comparison, openness more attractive"(Cf: Henkel and Maurer 2007).

[4] In the Draft Version of the BioBrick™ Public Agreement (2010), it is stated that" the BioBricks Foundation, Inc. (the "Foundation") was established to foster and advance innovation, research, standardization, and education in synthetic biology through the open design, construction, distribution, understanding, and use of BioBrick™ compatible parts, namely standardized genetic materials and associated functional information, in ways that benefit the world. The Foundation believes that a free and easy-to-use legal framework for sharing and making use of engineered genetic materials underlies and serves these goals. Some such genetic materials may be subject to patents; some will not be".

freely, exchanged subject to cooperation and confidentiality agreements. The devices obtained using these parts, however, would be the exclusive private property of the company that developed them, which would retain the profits from this activity. This type of initiative makes it possible for companies to make great savings in terms of research costs, but they are also not problem free. First of all, there is no doubt that there would be a cost to society as a whole, as it would be deprived of the knowledge of information that would remain exclusively reserved for the members of a "club" of companies with these characteristics. The risk of the emergence of some type of holding protected by strong entry barriers would be far from negligible. In addition, and from the perspective of the companies involved, it has to be recognised that this library would not, in principle, be protected from third parties. It would be perfectly possible for someone to patent one of these parts at any given time which would lead to serious difficulties for the participants. Obviously, this risk could be avoided if the participants in the initiative patented their parts before making them available to the other companies, but in that case the saving in costs would decrease dramatically.

13.5 A Final Thought: A System Based on a Revised Form of Patenting

Based on everything I have said here, we can reach a conclusion: that despite its doubtless defects the patents system continues to be the best way to encourage research in fields such as synthetic biology related to human health. The need for change that this sector seems to demand is not so much related to the instruments used to protect intellectual property as the way in which they are used. If the companies that work in the field of synthetic biology reproduce the pharmaceutical industry models it will indeed be possible that this promising discipline will not be adequately developed. But this will not be due to patenting itself but rather to the lack of vision of those who participate in the market. It is therefore necessary for the public authorities to intervene actively to foster attitudes in favour of cooperation rather than accepting the use of patents to block progress, when cooperation is more advantageous not only for society but also for industry in the sector. The policy maker's task will be to design instruments for stimulation where private initiative is incapable of generating cooperation mechanisms for itself. Conduct which tries to exploit the nature of patenting to obtain individual profit and that contributes nothing to help synthetic biology advance must be carefully monitored in the public interest, while public stimulus must be used to promote the maximum opening up of the new discoveries to the public. If we succeed in making these proposals achievable, I consider that it is perfectly plausible to carry on with synthetic biology associated with human health, even without substantially changing the current system for protecting intellectual property rights or, more precisely, even thanks to it.

References

Henkel J, Maurer SM (2007) The economics of synthetic biology. Mol Syst Biol 3:117

Henkel J, Maurer S (2009) Parts, property and sharing. Nat Biotechnol 27(12):1095–1098

Henkel J, Reitzig M (2008) Patent sharks. Harvard Business Review, pp 129–133

Rutz B (2014) Synthetic biology and patents. A European perspective. Presentation held at WWICS. Washington, DC http://www.synbioproject.org/process/assets/files/6384/_draft/rutz_slides1.pdf. Accesed 28 Feb 2014

Chapter 14
Stepping Stones: Extending the Open Source Idea to Synthetic Biology

Stephen M. Maurer

Abstract Open source methods offer a powerful and attractive model for organizing synthetic biology research. At the same time, the differences between biology and software are very deep. For this reason, attempts to design 'open parts collaborations' by naïve analogy to LINUX and other existing software institutions are likely to fail. Conversely, successful designs must be grounded in a careful understanding of (a) how current institutions manage the various social challenges of producing software, and (b) the extent to which synthetic biology research raises new and distinct challenges. I discuss these issues under four headings (appropriability, cartel effects, stability, and agency problems) and explain how existing open source institutions can be extended to accommodate synthetic biology research. I also identify particularly simple test cases where organizers can experiment with these ideas. These modest projects provide useful 'stepping stones' to demonstrating a full-scale parts collaboration.

Keywords Open source • Open biology • Synthetic biology • Standard biological parts • Drug development

14.1 Introduction

Open source biology – and especially open source synthetic biology – is beginning to look like Arthur Conan-Doyle's "dog that didn't bark" (Conan Doyle 1894). Ten years ago, most scholars seemed to think that open source methods would

S.M. Maurer
Goldman School of Public Policy and Berkeley Law School,
University of California, Berkeley, CA, USA
e-mail: smaurer@law.berkeley.edu

I. de Miguel Beriain and C.M. Romeo Casabona (eds.), *Synbio and Human Health: A Challenge to the Current IP Framework?*, DOI 10.1007/978-94-017-9196-0_14,

automatically spread to biology. After all, drugs – like software – have relatively small manufacturing costs and consist mostly of information. The case seemed particularly strong for synthetic biology, whose practitioners like to stress their intellectual debt to electronics and software engineering.

Clearly, that hasn't happened.[1] But why? The idea that open source models could spread automatically, with little or no outside help, worked well in software. Looking back, the reason was evolution. Open source began in the late 1980s as a niche activity among students and hobbyists. At that point, collaborations depended on non-commercial incentives like reputation and altruism. Over time, however, IT freelancers changed the model to make it more commercial. At this point, projects like Apache began using open source to share development costs. Still later, freelance communities gave way to big corporate sponsors like IBM and Oracle. This led to billion-dollar projects like Eclipse.[2] Crucially, hardly any of the original open source pioneers planned for – or even liked – these new models. Instead, they were replaced by new players who modified the original paradigm to pursue new goals. Time and evolution did the rest.

But evolution only works where improvement can be implemented through small, incremental changes. The economic and legal challenges facing synthetic biology, on the other hand, look very different from software. Coping with them will require large, simultaneous changes. Instead of evolving naturally, therefore, the first demonstration projects will require careful analysis and design. This article argues that the best path forward is to focus on one change at a time. This can be done by finding special cases ("stepping stones") that bridge the gap between existing open source software institutions and their hoped-for synthetic biology descendants.

This article presents a strategy for moving existing open source software methods into synthetic biology. Part B ("Why Open Parts?") argues that extending open source methods to synthetic biology would help to ensure that synthetic biology actually benefits society. The rest of the article then presents a roadmap for making open parts a reality. Part C ("The Starting Point") sets the stage by looking at the dynamics that have made modern commercial open source software collaborations possible. In the process, it identifies four key challenges (stability, appropriability, cartel effects, agency problems) that commercial open source collaborations must overcome. Part D ("The First Stepping Stone") argues that synthetic biology's first open source experiments should focus on shared biosecurity data, i.e. lists of potentially dangerous DNA sequences. This promises to be an especially simple case

[1] For an arguable exception, *see* Biobricks Foundation, "Biobrick Contributor Agreement" (2010) available at http://biobricks.org/wp-content/themes/bbf/bpa-sample.php. A close reading shows that the document is primarily designed to clarify parts donations. Crucially, it imposes no reciprocal obligation on users to improve the parts they receive or contribute data of their own. *See,* "Biobrick User Agreement" (2010), available at http://biobricks.org/bpa/users/agreement/. This is fundamentally different from the usual open source scheme in which programmers contribute software in exchange for guarantees that they will be able to use any later improvements without charge.

[2] See Eclipse Foundation Home Page, available at http://www.eclipse.org/.

because appropriability and cartel issues are limited. Section E asks how the open source model can then be extended to demonstrate open source sharing for a single standard biological part. Section F ("Colonizing Synthetic Biology") argues that this pilot demonstration would be enough to attract imitators. At this point, open source methods would resume the kind of incremental evolution that has worked so well in software. Section G presents a brief conclusion.

14.2 Why Open Parts?: Ensuring That Synthetic Biology Delivers Affordable (and Widely Distributed) Benefits

Advocates often assume the desirability of open source without saying anything very specific about how it is supposed to benefit society. This is understandable for software, where many users plainly value free code. By comparison, the case for open parts data is obscure. Even assuming that such a collaboration is feasible, why bother?

The answer starts by taking synthetic biology's dominant "standard biological parts" agenda seriously. According to this view, we should expect scientific progress – and eventually new products – to come from using a relatively small number of parts over and over again.[3] Scientifically, this is a story about the power of accumulated experiments, i.e. knowing which constellations of parts do and do not work. But this implies a social issue. All else being equal, we expect large companies that perform many experiments to have larger databases than those that do not. And because of these databases, we expect them to develop products faster, cheaper, and more reliably than their rivals. This suggests that large companies will grow even larger over time producing an industry dominated by natural monopolies and needlessly expensive goods.

For now, it is still too early to say how strong this dynamic actually is. Still, the example of industry-leader Amyris is suggestive. Five years ago, the company used Gates Foundation support to create designer organisms that synthesized antimalarial compounds. Since then, Amyris has built on this experience to design other organisms that make various related organic compounds including kerosene.[4] This is no bad thing, especially if prices are low. But that will depend on how many companies offer competing products.

This, of course, is where open parts come in. Amyris's data advantage originates in specific institutional arrangements that reward companies for keeping their data

[3] For a full discussion of these arguments, *see* Henkel and Maurer (2009) and Henkel and Maurer (2007). It is possible, of course, that the parts agenda will turn out to be misguided. Indeed, many synthetic biologists believe that there is less benefit in using "standard" parts than was previously thought. If so, the case for open parts sharing will likely be weaker. Suffice to say, this scientific question has yet to be settled. In what follows, we will assume that the "standard biological parts" agenda is valid, particularly since it is not at all clear what would replace it.

[4] Amyris Corp., "About Amyris," available at http://www.amyris.com/en/about-amyris.

"closed" or proprietary. But are these institutions unique? The open source idea argues that (a) alternative institutions for sharing data can be developed, and (b) that many synthetic biology companies will find it in their economic interest to share. If so, society can expect three important benefits. First, parts data will be accessible to more researchers at more companies. This will automatically increase society's chances of developing useful products. Second, shared information will level the information playing field, so that more companies will race for specific goals, for example, by competing with Amrysis to make organisms that synthesize kerosene. This redundancy would offer an important hedge against failure. Finally, sharing will increase the chances that two or more companies deliver competing products to market. Since competition reduces prices and increases access, this is likely to be biggest payoff of all.

14.3 The Starting Point: Today's Commercial Open Source

Any "stepping stones" strategy must start with an existing prototype. This means identifying whichever software collaboration seems "closest" to the hoped-for goal of an open parts collaboration. We start from the observation that most R&D will probably require large investments by corporations. This suggests that we should adopt commercial software collaborations like Eclipse as our model. This section looks at the generic problems that such collaborations face and the strategies they have evolved to overcome them.

Commercial Incentives and Shared Research. Early open source collaborations routinely claimed that members acted from altruism, a post-modern "gift economy," and other similarly mysterious motives.[5] But today, most open source is plainly commercial.[6] Here, all available evidence suggests that the economic incentives are quite prosaic – mainly using pooled knowledge to share R&D costs. And this makes sense. Consider the math: Assuming perfect sharing, two companies can immediately cut R&D costs in half. Moreover, these savings continue to grow indefinitely with the number of contributors.

Of course, shared research is an old idea. Indeed, IBM was already helping its customers trade and re-use code in the 1950s (Schwartz and Takheteyev 2009). Similarly, many corporations experimented with joint ventures in the 1980s. But these sharing arrangements turned out to be highly inefficient (Majewski and Williamson 2005). The question is whether today's commercial open source collaborations – and by implication commercial open parts initiatives – can do a better job.

---

[5] For a review of the literature on early open source collaborations, *see* S. Maurer & S. Scotchmer, "Open Source Software: The New Intellectual Property Paradigm," in T. Hendershott (ed.), *Handbook on Information Systems* (Elsevier: 2006).

[6] Strikingly, Eclipse developers deposit most of their code during business hours instead of weekends. Severin Weingarten, Friedrich Schiller University, Jena (personal communication)

Limits on Sharing. Like all institutions, commercial open source collaborations are far from perfect. Still, experience with Eclipse and other large software collaborations gives us a good idea of what problems to expect. These can be conveniently summarized as follow:

Appropriability. Sharing has costs as well as benefits. Consider for concreteness a typical case in which companies jointly develop an operating system for, say, cell phones. On the one hand, the new shared software makes the phones more useful. In theory, this means that customers should be willing to pay more for them. On the other, it also make *competitors*' products more desirable. This means that open source members may not be able to "appropriate" enough value to repay their development cost. If so, open source is a bad investment. More generally, we expect the desirability of sharing to depend inversely on competition. This suggests that open source incentives will usually be strongest where companies (a) belong to concentrated industries and/or (b) make highly unique or dissimilar products.[7]

Cartel Effect. Companies that produce proprietary (closed) software have a powerful incentive to write code – If they don't, they will quickly lose business to those who do. Under open source, on the other hand, *every* company automatically receives the *same* code. And this implies that *no* company can offer consumers more code than its rivals. Economically, the results are similar to an (illegal) agreement to limit R&D spending. In general, this "cartel effect" reduces, but does not erase the social value of sharing.[8] Furthermore, the effect is smaller when the collaboration faces strong competition from proprietary software or, better yet, other open source projects.[9] This is in keeping with US competitions policy's "five effort" rule which holds that joint ventures that include less than 20 % of an industry are seldom worth worrying about.

Stability. Even assuming strong appropriability, open source collaborations can still collapse if each member tries to consume shared R&D while keeping his or her own work proprietary. Open source institutions have traditionally addressed this issue by adopting "viral" licenses that force users to contribute improvements and certain related programs back to the project. That said, it is not clear how strong such licenses need to be to ensure stability.[10] All else equal, we want to

---

[7] For a formal economic exploration of this logic, *see* Maurer and Von Engelhardt (2010), available at http://papers.ssrn.com/sol3/papers.cfm?abstract_id=1542180.

[8] Though suggestive, the term "cartel effect" is not strictly accurate. The reason is that real cartels let members make side deals that restore part of the suppressed R&D investment. Strangely, open source suppresses R&D investment *more* than a formal cartel would (Maurer and Von Engelhardt 2010), available at http://papers.ssrn.com/sol3/papers.cfm?abstract_id=1542180.

[9] *Id.*

[10] The "General Public" or "GPL" license is almost certainly stronger than stability requires. Most commercial open source collaborations use significantly narrower licenses like Mozilla or even BSD. S. Maurer, "The Penguin and the Cartel," Utah Law Review 269–318 (Summer 2012) available at http://epubs.utah.edu/index.php/ulr/article/view/689/529

restrict open source knowledge as little as possible. After all, fewer restrictions means more uses – and even a closed source use is better than no use at all.

Agency Problems. So far we have assumed that companies that decide to share can do so perfectly. In practice, however, sharing faces significant technical limits.[11] Worse, experience with joint ventures suggests that participants may deliberately try (a) to shirk work, and (b) to divert research in directions that disproportionately favor themselves (Majewski and Williamson 2005). Large commercial open source collaborations like Eclipse often try to alleviate these problems by giving volunteers a stake in the collaboration by, for example, awarding honorifics and leadership titles that follow the programmer even if she changes jobs. At least in theory, this should dilute volunteers' incentives to favor their current employer over the common good.

These challenges are generic to most forms of commercial open source. Nevertheless, their importance varies from project to project. Consider, for example, the Apache project. Because companies seldom compete directly on the quality of their web servers, the collaboration's appropriation and cartel issues are negligible. This, in turn, explains why Apache was one of the earliest commercial open source models to succeed. We argue below that similar stepping stones can simplify the introduction of open source methods into synthetic biology.

How Special is Software? So far, we have concentrated almost entirely on economic factors. However, some scholars have argued that open source production is uniquely suited to UNIX-based software (Maurer and Scotchmer 2006). This suggests that extending open source production methods to data could be problematic. Fortunately, large physics databases have long relied on volunteer editors – a very close analog (Maurer 2003). Even so, the further extension to biology data will likely to require significant learning.

14.4 The First Stepping Stone: Open Biosecurity

In general, we expect companies that generate parts data to be significant competitors. This is bound to raise significant appropriability and cartelization issues. Our first, "stepping stone" experiments should avoid these complications as much as possible.

Biosecurity data – i.e. lists of DNA sequences that could be used to make weapons – are on the short list of projects that meet this requirement. On the one hand, pooled threat judgments offer significant savings.[12] On the other, competition is

[11] For example, Joachim Henkel has argued that the teams which write individual open source modules tend to be drawn from a single company (Henkel 2004).

[12] Threat evaluation is expensive. Most companies that make gene-length synthetic DNA currently pay human experts to check customer orders by (a) finding the closest Genbank analogs, and (b) examining the literature to find out what is known about the functions they code for. This process sometimes takes up to 2 hours – a significant cost in an industry where the average order sells for

weak. This is because no company can hope to compete by promising customers "more" and "better" security than its rivals. This means that appropriability and cartel concerns can be deferred. In the meantime, an open biosecurity issue would still break plenty of new ground including (a) novel legal arrangements to address stability, (b) controlling agency problems among volunteers, and (c) developing new habits and institutions for the open curation of biology data.

Stability. We have seen that open source software collaborations have traditionally used viral licenses to suppress free-riding. However, all existing licenses depend on copyright protection. Synthetic biology data, on the other hand, cannot be copyrighted. This means that licenses will have to invoke other forms of intellectual property, most likely patents or trade secrets.[13]

But patents are problematic. In particular, they are (a) very expensive to implement,[14] (b) unavailable for many kinds of data,[15] and (c) legally inconsistent with the viral principle.[16] This suggests that viral licenses must instead be based on trade secrets, i.e. the legal right to preserve and license commercially useful information that is not generally known.[17] But that will force significant changes in how open source is done. Most obviously, collaborations will no longer be able to post information on the Web for anyone to use. If they did, the information would immediately become non-secret and hence unprotectable. Instead, trade secret law will force members to limit distribution to parties who expressly consent to a license. This is not necessarily a bad thing. Indeed, the legal enforceability of most implied consent ("adhesion") agreements is doubtful. Even so, it is possible that many small or casual users – for example academic scientists – would be excluded.[18]

$10,000. Here, the good news is that the work only has to be done once – and screeners routinely report that they have seen roughly 3–5 % of all orders before. These savings are likely to grow several-fold if companies agree to pool their data in a shared facility. *See,* Maurer (2012), available at http://papers.ssrn.com/sol3/papers.cfm?abstract_id=2183306.

[13] Unlike the US, European law also offers formal protection for databases. This could provide a natural basis for protecting shared parts information. That said, it is hard to see how a transatlantic consortium would work without legal rights in the US market.

[14] Patents usually about $10,000 per application.

[15] Patent law only applies to "non-obvious," inventions, i.e. those demonstrating a large inventive step over prior knowledge. Individual entries in synthetic biology databases rarely rise to this level.

[16] Unlike copyright, the law lets inventors obtain improvement patents whether or not they own the underlying invention. Viral terms are expressly designed to block this outcome. It is hard to see how private contracts can overrule the Congressional scheme.

[17] US trade secret law lets companies protect information "that (i) derives independent economic value, actual or potential, from not being generally known to ... other persons who can obtain intellectual benefit from its disclosure or use, and (ii) is the subject of efforts to maintain its secrecy." Uniform Trade Secrets Act §1 (1985). Similar protections are available in Europe and the developing world. *See,* e.g., Mark D. Powell, "Overview of European Trade Secret Law," available at http://law.wustl.edu/Library/cdroms/IBL/License/Powell.htm; James P. Flynn, "Bumps Along the Silk Road," available at http://tradesecretsblog.info/2009/01/bumps_along_the_silk_road_prot.html.

[18] The drawbacks of limited distribution are weaker for biosecurity than other kinds of data. Posting dangerous DNA sequences on the web would help terrorists make weapons.

These difficulties can easily be overstated. After all, today's corporations routinely keep, share, and license trade secrets to each other and trusted academic partners. Whether and how much dissemination would be restricted is mostly an empirical question. Without a working biosecurity collaboration, we may never find out.

Agency Problems. We have already emphasized that biosecurity raises few, if any, appropriability problems. This suggests that companies promising to share biosecurity data will almost certainly follow through.[19] However, they might also discourage workers from donating time to collaboration activities beyond the bare minimum required. This gap would have to be filled by non-financial incentives like screeners' ideological commitment to security and/or their desire to impress peers and potential employers. In principle, the collaboration could imitate Eclipse's methods by awarding volunteers leadership status and honorific titles. This would presumably encourage volunteers to protect the collaboration whether or not their employers approved.

Pioneering Open Biology Data. Finally, an open biosecurity collaboration would provide crucial experience in using open methods to construct large biology databases. Depending on how much effort was invested,[20] this could range from unavoidable tasks like negotiating an agreed data deposit scheme ("typologies") to elaborate quality control initiatives. The latter could include:

Finding Errors. The collaboration could audit quality by various methods including (a) randomly spot-checking submitted data for accuracy, (b) using "expert programs" to search for instances where submitted data might contain errors, and (c) looking for instances in which two or more companies evaluated the same Genbank entry. These studies would also provide information about error rates within and across companies.

Certification. Companies have an obvious financial incentive to ignore security threats and sell as much DNA as they can. This could quickly lead to mutual suspicions and erode standards over time. The best way to stop this dynamic is to let members monitor each others' compliance in real time. Open source sharing provides a natural platform for doing this. A more formal solution would be for the collaboration to certify compliance. Detailed quality control audits would automatically generate data for doing this.

More Accurate and Replicable Threat Judgments. An open collaboration would rapidly improve the science and practice of screening. First, it would make screening more uniform across companies. Experience in fields ranging from particle physics to astronomy suggests that humans can be trained to make remarkably replicable judgments.[21] This, however, requires a period of shared

[19] Indeed, company work-flow software would likely make the deposits automatically.

[20] We have argued that a shared threat database would generate substantial savings compared to the current system. It is reasonable to think that participating companies would reinvest at least some of these funds in better security. This could be done by providing financial support and/or encouraging employees to donate more time to the collaboration.

[21] Wikipedia, Bevatron http://en.wikipedia.org/wiki/Bevatron; Jeremy Hsu, "NASA Crowdsources Hi-Res Mapping as an On-Line Game for Kids," PopSci.com. Available at http://www.popsci.com/technology/article/2009-11/nasa-crowd-sources-mars-mapping-online-game.

"training" or "socialization" in which participants learn to score situations they encounter the same way. More fundamentally, it would demand repeated judgments about which DNA sequences should and should not count as "threats." This would make the current, largely theoretical discussion far more practical and concrete.

Prospects. Unlike most open biology discussions the idea of a shared biosecurity resource is not just theoretical. Indeed, members of Europe's "Industry Association Synthetic Biology" or "IASB" have several times discussed the idea since 2009. For now, the main practical objection seems to be confidentiality, i.e. the risk that shared Genbank sequences could give outsiders information about which gene sequences are worth pursuing. However, this information is fairly limited and would not be disseminated beyond the collaboration. Preliminary discussions suggest that most customers – who also have a stake in biosecurity – would not object.

14.5 The Second Stepping Stone: A Pilot-Scale Parts Collaboration

Open biosecurity would provide a particularly simple test bed for experimenting with trade secret licenses, managing agency problems, and exploring open methods for curating large biological databases. This, however, is like crossing the ocean "except for the wet part." Open parts information is certain to be highly competitive. Our second stepping stone project must demonstrate that the resulting appropriability, stability, and cartelization issues are manageable. Fortunately, this can be done using pilot scale projects. Sharing data about one or, at most, several parts should be enough to demonstrate the principle.

Appropriability. We have already seen that a company's willingness to join a commercial open source collaboration depends on (a) the costs of participating, and (b) the ability to earn back its investment the face of competition. The existence of large, well-funded collaborations like Eclipse shows that this trade-off is often favorable in the software industry. This, however, is essentially an accident and the economics of synthetic biology could different.[22] This suggests that open source institutions may need to be redesigned to increase appropriability by, for example, letting companies defer sharing for some well-defined period of time. Significantly, companies that write the "embedded LINUX" used in everything from airplanes to consumer appliances already follow this strategy. As Prof. Henkel has noted, embedded LINUX licenses usually give members the right to withhold sharing for 18 months or so. Remarkably, however, companies actually choose to disclose about half of all code sooner than this. This suggests that the benefits of

[22] The problem, if it exists, almost certainly involves appropriability. Synthetic biology competition will likely follow the pharmaceutical model in which the first company to patent and/or bring a product to market almost always secures the most benefits. The costs associated with giving a competitor data in this environment could be large.

sharing (e.g. receiving user suggestions and improvements) outweigh continued exclusivity (Henkel 2006). More generally, we can imagine at least three possible sharing rules.

Immediate Sharing. Probably the simplest implementation would be to imitate classical open source by requiring companies to deposit new parts information immediately. The danger, as already noted, is that companies might refuse to join the collaboration on these terms. At this point, organizers would have to choose between granting greater appropriability and giving up open source entirely.

Delayed Sharing. The most obvious way to increase appropriability is to let companies withhold new data for some well-defined period of time – for example Prof. Henkel's 18 months. Alternatively, sharing could be triggered by some well-defined, economically-relevant event. For example, parts information is mainly valuable to the extent that it lets companies develop and/or patent products sooner than their competitors. This suggests that relatively little appropriability would be lost by compelled sharing within, say, 60 days of (a) sale of a product incorporating the part, (b) the filing of a patent application incorporating the part, or (c) a final decision to terminate development.

Optional Sharing. The "embedded LINUX" experience suggests that companies might find it in their interest to share without any formal agreement at all. This would permit maximal appropriability since companies could then decide to release data on a case-by-case basis. Despite this, sharing might still occur in collaborations where members have repeated interactions and can build up trust over time. The problem with these mechanisms is that they are unlikely to scale well as the number of collaboration members grows. More fundamentally, the fact that most commercial open source software collaborations use viral licenses suggests that purely voluntary reciprocity is unstable.

For now, there is no good theoretical intuition to decide among these choices. As usual, organizers will have to fall back on experiment – in this case negotiation – to find out how much appropriability is actually necessary for companies to join the collaboration.

Stability. Extending trade secret law from biosecurity data to parts information would be legally straightforward. However, the limits on dissemination could be painful. Large commercial software collaborations, after all, often receive important input from students and hobbyists. A synthetic biology collaboration would have to make careful judgments about whether such people could be trusted to keep its secrets.

That said, the fact that trade secret offers much weaker protection than copyright has an upside. We have said that protection disappears as soon as a secret becomes public. This means that third parties who independently discover the invention can use and even patent it so that the original owners can no longer use the information. Fortunately, this does not make trade secret protection useless. Instead, today's corporations routinely manage the risk by patenting some secrets and making others public ("defensive publishing") so that they become unpatentable. There is no reason why a well-run parts collaboration could not do the same thing. Organizers would, however, need to implement detailed rules for (a) deciding when and under what circumstances collaboration data could be made public,[23] and (b) setting the terms under which members could continue to access collaboration discoveries once patents issued.

Cartelization. As with software, shared parts information raises difficult public policy problems. For small collaborations, the five efforts rule suggests that cartelization effects can be safely ignored. However, collaborations that embrace more than 20 % of the industry could be problematic. Whether they are or not would depend, *inter alia*, on the extent to which member companies compete with one another. From this perspective a collaboration composed of members who are all focused on a single goal (e.g. turning sugar into kerosene) would likely be more problematic than a collaboration in which each company was focused on non-overlapping markets (e.g. treating rheumatism vs. heart disease). Furthermore, the analysis would have to consider how open source is likely to influence the industry's evolution over time. For example, small companies and new entrants could easily use sharing as a "weapon of the weak" to overcome dominant firms' information advantage. In these circumstances, it would be reasonable to argue that open source's long-term pro-competitive impacts outweighed any cartel effect. Finally, very large collaborations that embraced substantially all of a given industry would always be problematic. Even here, however, the benefits of sharing might sometimes outweigh cartelization concerns.

To some extent, prudent open source organizers can plan for and minimize these issues. Possible measures include:

Open Membership. In principle, companies could form parts-sharing alliances as a way to drive non-members from the market. (Such an arrangement would not, of course, involve "open parts" in any sense of the word.) The best way to block this scenario is to keep membership open to any company that is willing to observe the collaboration's sharing rules.

Membership Dues. Many commercial software collaborations ask corporate members to contribute financial support. However, large, fixed fees could easily keep small companies from joining. Large commercial software collaborations often mitigate these problems by implementing tiered or sliding scale memberships in which small companies pay less than large ones.

Use Fees. The collaboration would also need to avoid fees based on, for example, how often a part is used in organisms or sold to consumers. In principle, such fees can be used to implement monopoly pricing.

---

[23] One natural solution is to let whoever contributes the data decide when and if it should be released to the public. Here, the main practical difficulty would involve deciding who controlled data in cases where multiple inventors had directly or indirectly helped to discover the information.

14.6 Colonizing Synthetic Biology

By itself, sharing data for one or even several standard biological parts will do little to advance synthetic biology. On the other hand, many synthetic biologists are ideologically committed to the open source idea. For this reason, a successful demonstration project would likely spawn imitators. How many imitators will depend on economics. Here the relevant factors will include:

Appropriability. Synthetic biology companies could deliberately organize their R&D so that each pursued a radically different project. In this case, we would expect the benefits of sharing to outweigh any appropriability problems so that open source models spread quickly. More probably, at least some head-to-head competition is likely. Studies suggest that pharmaceutical companies often race to develop closely similar products (Di Masi and Paquette 2004).

Industry Structure. We have suggested that open source is a weapon of the weak – i.e. a way for small firms to pool their experience so that they can compete with industry frontrunners. Naively, Amyris's early dominance of organisms that manufacture organic chemicals could provide such an inducement.

Sponsors. Shared data promises to make parts use more popular. This, in turn, would increase synthetic DNA sales. This gives synthetic gene makers a direct interest in sponsoring open parts collaborations. This incentive will become even stronger as the synthetic gene industry becomes more concentrated and profit-margins rise.

Technical Factors . Finally, we have noted that the scientific case for reusing standard parts seems shakier than it used to be. If this trend continues, the benefits of shared information will inevitably decline.

If open source does spread we should expect the basic model – like its software cousins – to continue evolving. Our trade secret architecture has various flaws, most obviously its tendency to exclude hobbyists and other small players. A pilot collaboration will show how serious these problems are. Evolutionary improvements should mitigate, if not eliminate these drawbacks over time.

14.7 Conclusion: Doing the Experiment

The case for open source parts collaboration is suggestive but not conclusive. As previously noted, many biologists believe that Nature's parts are already pretty standardized. If so, the benefits of using a handful of parts over and over again may be exaggerated[24] – along with the case for open source. Still, it is reasonable to try. Many academics possess the required skills and law schools, in particular, have a

[24] Markus Fischer (Entelchon GmbH) (personal communication).

long history of intervening in practical problems. Furthermore, the required investments are small. Indeed, none of the "stepping stone" collaborations described in this paper would be significantly more difficult to organize than, say, a conventional patent pool transaction. And of course, they would be much more novel and interesting.

The main thing is to get started. Plainly, waiting for evolution hasn't worked. If academics don't step in, who will? Open source sharing has revolutionized the software industry and could deliver similar benefits to synthetic biology. The challenge now is to organize enough demonstration projects to prove the point.

References

Amyris Corp. About Amyris. Available at http://www.amyris.com/en/about-amyris

Biobrick User Agreement (2010) Available at http://biobricks.org/bpa/users/agreement/

Biobricks Foundation, Biobrick Contributor Agreement (2010) Available at http://biobricks.org/wp-content/themes/bbf/bpa-sample.php

Conan Doyle A (1894) The adventure of silver blaze. In: The memoirs of Sherlock Holmes (Dover 2010, 1894), George Newnes, New York

Dimasi J, Paquette C (2004) The economics of follow-on drug research and development. Pharmacoeconomics 22(2 Suppl):1–14

Flynn JP Bumps along the silk road. Available at http://tradesecretsblog.info/2009/01/bumps_along_the_silk_road_prot.html

Henkel J (2004) The jukebox mode of innovation – a model of commercial open source development, CEPR. Discussion Papers 4507

Henkel J (2006) Selective revealing in open innovation processes: the case of embedded Linux. Res Policy 35:953–969

Henkel J, Maurer S (2007) The economics of synthetic biology. Mol Syst Biol 3:117

Henkel J, Maurer S (2009) Parts, property, and sharing. Nat Biotechnol 27:1095–1098

Hsu J, NASA Crowdsources Hi-Res mapping as an On-line game for kids. PopSci.com. Available at http://www.popsci.com/technology/article/2009-11/nasa-crowd-sources-mars-mapping-online-game

Majewski SE, Williamson DV (2005) Incomplete contracting and the structure of collaborative R&D agreements. In: Libecap GD (ed) Intellectual property and entrepreneurship. Elsevier, Berkeley

Maurer SM (2003) New institutions for doing science: from databases to open source biology, Conference Paper, University of Maastricht. Available at http://www.merit.unimaas.nl/epip/papers/maurer_paper.pdf

Maurer SM (2012) Taking self-governance seriously: synthetic biology's last, best chance to improve security GSPP working paper 12-003. Available at http://papers.ssrn.com/sol3/papers.cfm?abstract_id=2183306 (this conference)

Maurer S, Scotchmer S (2006) Open source software: the new intellectual property paradigm. In: Hendershott T (ed) Handbook on information systems. Elsevier, Amsterdam and Boston

Maurer S, Von Engelhardt S (2010) The new (commercial) open source: does it really improve social welfare? Goldman School of Public Policy Working Paper. Available at http://papers.ssrn.com/sol3/papers.cfm?abstract_id=1542180

Powell MD Overview of European trade secret law. Available at http://law.wustl.edu/library/cdroms/ibl/license/powell.htm

Schwarz M, Takhteyev Y (2009) Half a century of public software institutions: open source as a solution to the holdup problem. National Bureau of Economic Research Working Paper 14946

Index

A
Access-to-knowledge frame (A2K frame) *vs.* IP frame, 25, 29
  BioBricks approach, 29–31
  commodification, property and IP, 33–36
  Craig Venter's model, proprietary science, 31–33
Anglo-America, patenting synbio. *See* Patents
Anticommons, 16, 105
Antimalarial treatment. *See* Artemisinin project
Applications, synthetic biology. *See* Human health, applications to
Artemisinin project
  antimalarial treatment, 4
  artemisinic acid productions, yeast, 15
  creative capitalism, 21
  ETC group criticism, 22
  Gates Foundation grant, 21
  intellectual property, age of, 22, 23
  Keasling's team on, 20, 21, 23
  metabolic engineering, 20
  poster child application, 20
  synthetic production, 22–23
Article 52 EPC, 149
Article 53, 90, 96, 97, 108, 190, 193
Article 53(a), 150, 152
Article 53(c), 197

B
BioBricks approach, 29–31
Biohybrid materials, 8
Biomedicine convention, 63
Biosafety, 129–130
  global panel on, 133–134
Biosecurity
  accurate and replicable threat judgments, 218–219
  agency problems, 218
  appropriability, 219
  cartelization, 221
  certification, 218
  errors finding, 218
  fees, 221
  membership dues, 221
  open membership, 221
  pioneering open biology data, 218
  prospects, 219
  sharing
    delayed, 220
    immediate, 220
    optional, 220
  stability, 220–221
  synthetic biology, 130–131
Biosensors
  cancer therapy, 7–8
  environmental pollutants, 5–7
  infection control, 7
Biosimilar products, 46–49 *See also* Intellectual property
Biotechnology applications
  biotech patents
    Directive 98/44/CE and Legislation, 66–68
    patent protection, 68–69
    regulative conflicts and emerging limits, 69–70
  genome and human health, 55–58
  human genetic heritage protection
    European Union regulations, 64–65

I. de Miguel Beriain and C.M. Romeo Casabona (eds.), *Synbio and Human Health: A Challenge to the Current IP Framework?*, DOI 10.1007/978-94-017-9196-0,

Biotechnology applications (*cont.*)
freedom and pluralism in research, 72–74
intellectual property law reorganization, 70–72
international documents, 62–64
patent protection and SB particularities, 59–62
BRCA patents, 49, 104, 178, 193

C
Cartelization, 221
Codon bias, 2
Co-evolution, 27–29
Commodification, property and IP, 33–36
Constitutionalization, 153, 161
Craig Venter's model, proprietary science, 31–33
Creative capitalism, 21

D
Deadweight loss, 36
Directive 98/44/CE and Legislation, biotech patents, 66–68
Disability-adjusted-life-years (DALY), 12–13
Do-it-yourself-biology, 134, 138
Drug delivery and therapeutic therapy, 196–197
Drug production, 195 *See also* Pharmaceutical industry
traditional *vs.* new method, 2

E
Embedded LINUX experience, 219, 220
Engineered biological parts, 188
Environmental issues, 194
Ethical issues, 193–194
Ethical/moral reasons, patentable subject matter, 107–109
Europe, patenting synbio. *See* Patents
European Group on Ethics in Science and New Technologies (EGE), 137
European Patent Convention (EPC), 146, 152
Art 83, 192
Article 52, 149
Article 53, 193
Article 53(a), 150, 152
Article 53(c), 197
microorganism, synthetic
economic effect, patent, 192–193
environmental issues, 194
ethical issues, 193–194
patentability of, 190–192
European Union Regulations, human genetic heritage protection, 64–65
European Union's Biotechnology Patent Directive (98/44/EC), 146, 152

F
Freedom of research and publication, 131–133

G
Gene patents, 27, 28, 158, 197
Gene therapy, 5
Genetically modified organism (GMO), 127
Genetic circuits, synthetic, 3
German Genetic Engineering Law (GenTG), 127
Global panel on biosafety, 133–134

H
Healthcare, synthetic biology. *See* Pharmaceutical industry
Health Impact Fund, 38
Human DNA, patents and, 83–84
Human genetic heritage protection
European Union regulations, 64–65
freedom and pluralism in research, 72–74
intellectual property law reorganization, 70–72
international documents, 62–64
Human health, applications to
biohybrid materials, 8
biosensors, environmental pollutants, 5–7
cancer therapy, 7–8
drug, microbial production, 3–4
gene therapy, 5
health, defined, 12
infection detection, 7
pharmaceutical industry (*see* Pharmaceutical industry)
quorum sensing mechanisms, 4–5
Human rights agenda, 97–98

I
Intellectual property (IP)
vs. A2K frame
BioBricks approach, 29–31
commodification, property and IP, 33–36
Craig Venter's model, proprietary science, 31–33
discovery *vs.* invention, 51–52
exclusion phenomenon, 49–50

human dignity and Oliver Brüstle *vs.* Greenpeace case, 84–85 (*see also* Patents)
justice and invention, 52–53
law reorganization, human genetic heritage protection, 70–72
naturally-occurring products *vs.* man-made products, 46–49
products *vs.* processes, 49
protection, 135–136
rights
open source and business agreements, 207–208
patenting system, human health, 204–207
regulation of, 203–204
and SB
patents, problems with, 104–105
science and IP protection, 103–104
system and human dignity, 78

L
Legal protection, patent
fundamental regulatory principles, 176–177
human body parts, 177–178
patent/alternative solutions, aspects of, 183–184
public order and morality, limit of
exclusions concerning human beings, 179–182
exclusions relating to animals, 179
patent exclusion clauses, 182–183

M
Medical patents, 196–197
Metaphoric framing, discourse and actor coalitions, 165–169
Microbial biosynthesis, 3–4
Microorganism, synthetic
economic effect, patent, 192–193
environmental issues, 194
ethical issues, 193–194
patentability of, 190–192
Mo cell line, 82
Moral clause, 108, 178
Morality tension, 89–91
Mycoplasma laboratorium, 31

N
Nanotechnology, 47, 52, 147
National Advisory Board for Biosecurity (NSABB), U.S., 132
Natural products *vs.* man-made products, IP, 46–49

O
Open biology data, 218
Open membership, 221
Open source
agency problems, 216
appropriability, 215
biology, 211–212
biosecurity, 216–221
and business agreements, 207–208
cartel effect, 215
colonizing synthetic biology, 222
commercial incentives and shared research, 214–215
principles
intellectual property, 31
model, BioBricks, 70–72
sharing limits, 215
stability, 215–217
stepping stones strategy, 214–216
Ordre public, 151
Oviedo convention, 63

P
Patents *See also* Intellectual property
biotechnology
Directive 98/44/CE and Legislation, 66–68
patent protection, 68–69
regulative conflicts and emerging limits, 69–70
for BRCA genes, 49, 104, 178, 193
decision-making authority
administrative arena, 156–157
judicial arena, 160–162
legislative arena, 157–159
eligibility and exemptions from patentability
exception, 150–155
exclusion, 149–150
human dignity and Oliver Brüstle *vs.* Greenpeace case, 84–85
and human DNA, 83–84
institutional design, patent eligibility
synthetic biology in administrative arena, 162–164
synthetic biology in legislative and judicial arena, 164–165
legal protection (*see* Legal protection, patent)
and living matter

Patents (*cont.*)
intellectual property system adjustment, 78
Moore *vs.* Regents, 81–83
and non-human living matter, 78–81
opportunity
emerging technologies, patent stability requirement, 116–117
ethically controversial patents, 115
Europabio, 114
Greenpeace maintain, 114
moral uniqueness, 113–114
social welfare balance, 113
originating in human tissue and data, 91–93
patentable subject matter
ethical/moral reasons, exclusion, 107–109
patenting requirements, 105–107
pharmaceutical industry innovation challenges, 16
protection and SB particularities, 59–62
Patent sharks, 204–206
Patent trolls, 204
Pharmaceutical industry
applications
artemisinic acid productions, 15
DSM application, 14–15
in human health improvement, 12–13
innovation in, 13–14
sitagliptin, 14
cost per new drug, 12, 13, 15, 16
innovation challenges, 15–16
Pluralism and freedom of scientific research, 72–74
Poster child, 20 *See also* Artemisinin project
Presidential Commission for the Study of Bioethical Issues (PCSBI), 134
Proceduralization of the law, synthetic biology, 134–135
Property
in human body, 95–96
tension, 94–95
Prudent vigilance, 134

Q
Quorum sensing mechanisms, 4–5

R
Red biotechnology, 61
Redesigned biological systems, 188

S
SB. *See* Synthetic biology (SB)
Screening processes and biological models, 195
Sitagliptin, 14
Social consistency and property, in human body, 95–96
Standard biological parts, 213–214
Stem cells *vs.* synthetic biology
lessons, 111–112
Venter's Synthia, 110–111
SynBio. *See* Synthetic biology (SB)
Synthetic biology (SB)
A2K frame *vs.* IP frame
BioBricks approach, 29–31
commodification, property and IP, 33–36
Craig Venter's model, proprietary science, 31–33
applications (*see* Human health, applications to)
appropriability, 222
biosafety, 129–130
biosecurity, 130–131
colonizing, 222
definition, 124–128
diagnostic methods, 197
drug delivery and therapeutic therapy, 196–197
drug production, 2, 195
freedom of research and publication, 131–133
global panel on biosafety, 133–134
iGEM competition, 40
industry structure, 222
institutional design, patent eligibility
in administrative arena, 162–164
in legislative and judicial arena, 164–165
and intellectual property
open source and business agreements, 207–208
patenting system, human health, 204–207
patents, problems with, 104–105
regulation of, 203–204
science and IP protection, 103–104
justice/fairness, 135–136
legal questions
general points on, 136
in Germany, 136–140
medical applications, 36–39

metaphoric framing, discourse
and actor coalitions, 165–169
new life, 136
participation in culture, 40–41
patentable subject matter
ethical/moral reasons,
exclusion, 107–109
patenting requirements, 105–107
patent opportunity
emerging technologies,
patent stability requirement,
116–117
ethically controversial patents, 115
Europabio, 114
Greenpeace maintain, 114
moral uniqueness, 113–114
social welfare balance, 113
patents *vs.* co-construction,
technology-neutrality, 25–29
Pogge's scheme, 37–39
screening processes and biological
models, 195
sponsors, 222
vs. stem cells
lessons, 111–112
Venter's Synthia,
110–111
technical factors, 222
and therapeutic applications, 195
U.S.A position, 134–135

T
TRIPS agreement, 25–26, 151

W
WARF SC patents, 105, 111

MIX
Papier aus verantwortungsvollen Quellen
Paper from responsible sources
FSC® C105338

If you have any concerns about our products,
you can contact us on
ProductSafety@springernature.com

In case Publisher is established outside the EU,
the EU authorized representative is:
Springer Nature Customer Service Center GmbH
Europaplatz 3, 69115 Heidelberg, Germany

Printed by Libri Plureos GmbH
in Hamburg, Germany